# Conversation Analysis

# Conversation Analysis

## SECOND EDITION

## Ian Hutchby and Robin Wooffitt

polity

First published in 2008 by Polity Press

Polity Press
65 Bridge Street
Cambridge CB2 1UR, UK.

Polity Press
350 Main Street
Malden, MA 02148, USA

ISBN-13: 978-07456-3865-2
ISBN-13: 978-07456-3866-9 (pb)

A catalogue record for this book is available from the British Library.

Typeset in 10.5 on 12 pt Monotype Times
by Servis Filmsetting Ltd, Manchester
Printed and bound in Great Britain by MPG Books Ltd, Bodmin, Cornwall

For further information on Polity, visit our website: www.polity.co.uk

# Contents

Contents

# Preface to the Second Edition

We are delighted to be able to prepare this Second Edition of *Conversation Analysis*, which was first published in 1998. When we wrote the original edition of the book, CA (as it has come to be abbreviated) was a burgeoning field of research enterprise across many parts of the globe: particularly in the UK and USA (where the discipline had originated) but also in Scandinavia, Continental Europe, South East Asia and Australasia. When it appeared, *Conversation Analysis* was the first full-length, comprehensive and accessible synthesis of central issues in the theoretical and methodological principles, the practical research techniques, and the real world applications of CA. In the intervening decade, CA has grown significantly in popularity, not just in terms of those who proclaim themselves committed to it as a method but also those who wish to utilize elements of the method to bolster their own research endeavours that may begin from a different agenda. It has grown in influence, becoming increasingly recognized and legitimated both by researchers in a range of social science disciplines and by gatekeepers of those disciplines (such as funding bodies, professional associations and conference committees). And it has demonstrated its vitality by continuing to expand its body of published research output: the books, chapters, papers, conference proceedings and the rest that collectively embody the state of knowledge in conversation analytic studies.

For all these reasons, we came to the conclusion that a new, Second Edition of *Conversation Analysis* was now timely. For while the core questions remain the same, the expansion of CA's topics and findings and the extension of its interdisciplinary influence mean that there is now the opportunity for providing both a broader and a deeper account of the principles, practices, applications – and implications – of conversation analysis than was possible a decade ago.

The developments we have made to the text can be seen on a range of levels. Although the contents of Chapters 1–5 in the first two sections, 'Principles' and 'Practices', cover broadly the same ground, they have been updated to incorporate new knowledge and in some places reorganized and augmented to improve their coherence. The foundational issues that these chapters address are vital to an understanding of what CA is really about, how it developed, and how those who wish to practise it on their own data should go about beginning that task. There is no doubt therefore that in a book of this kind, they require the in-depth coverage that we give them.

The major change from the First Edition is that we have substantially altered the third part of the book, now called 'Implications' (rather than the original 'Applications'). This part was always intended to show how CA expands beyond the boundaries of ordinary conversation, and to suggest some of the ways in which its intellectual enterprise connects with the concerns of related disciplines. In the original edition, we included under this heading studies of 'institutional' and workplace interaction, a CA approach to the analysis of sociological interview data, an account of the relationships between language use and factual claims, discussions of political rhetoric and persuasion, the design of automated speech communication systems, and some then very new work in the application of CA to the concerns of speech therapists.

The new edition retains updated versions of the chapters on institutional interaction (Chapter 6) and on social science interview data (Chapter 7), but reorganizes and makes substantial additions to the remaining topics. A chapter which was originally called 'The Practical Relevance of Conversation Analysis' is now retitled and fully reworked as 'Extensions of Conversation Analysis' (Chapter 8). Finally, a new chapter called 'Critical Engagements' provides a detailed consideration of something that was always implicit in the First Edition, but not brought to the surface in any systematic way. That is the relationship between CA and the main social scientific disciplines with which it has close connections: sociology, psychology, and linguistics. The new Chapter 9 seeks to show in a more explicit way how CA has begun to engage with some of the traditional themes in these disciplines, offering readers a better sense of how CA links with, contributes to and offers challenges to central concerns, issues and topics in the social sciences.

*Ian Hutchby*
*University of Leicester*

*Robin Wooffitt*
*University of York*

# Transcription Glossary

The transcription symbols used here are common to conversation analytic research, and were developed by Gail Jefferson. A more detailed discussion of the use of these symbols and others is provided in Chapter 3 (see also Jefferson, 2005).

| | |
|---|---|
| (0.5) | The number in brackets indicates a time gap in tenths of a second. |
| (.) | A dot enclosed in a bracket indicates a pause in the talk of less than two-tenths of a second. |
| = | The 'equals' sign indicates 'latching' between utterances. For example: |

S1: yeah September seventy six it would be=
S2: =yeah that's right

It can also be used to transcribe the continuation of a turn across intervening lines of transcript, for instance when another speaker's turn overlaps:

S1: yeah September [seventy six=
S2:                   [September
S1: =it would be

| | |
|---|---|
| [  ] | Square brackets between adjacent lines of concurrent speech indicate the onset and end of a spate of overlapping talk. |
| .hh | A dot before an 'h' indicates speaker in-breath. The more h's, the longer the in-breath. |
| hh | An 'h' indicates an out-breath. The more h's the longer the breath. |
| (( )) | A description enclosed in a double bracket indicates a non-verbal activity. For example ((banging sound)). Alternatively double brackets may enclose the transcriber's comments on contextual or other features. |
| soun- | A dash indicates the sharp cut-off of the prior word or sound. |
| sou:::nd | Colons indicate that the speaker has stretched the preceding sound or letter. The more colons the greater the extent of the stretching. |
| ! | Exclamation marks are used to indicate an animated or emphatic tone. |
| ( ) | Empty parentheses indicate the presence of an unclear fragment on the tape. |
| (guess) | The words within a single bracket indicate the transcriber's best guess at an unclear utterance. |
| word. | A full stop indicates a stopping fall in tone. It does not necessarily indicate the grammatical end of a sentence. |
| word, | A comma indicates a 'continuing' intonation. |
| word? | A question mark indicates a rising inflection. It does not necessarily indicate a question. |
| * | An asterisk indicates a 'croaky' pronunciation of the immediately following section. |
| ↑↓ | Pointed arrows indicate a marked falling or rising intonational shift. They are placed immediately before the onset of the shift. |
| a: | Less marked falls in pitch can be indicated by using underlining immediately preceding a colon: |

S:    we (.) really didn't have a lot'v cha:nge

| | |
|---|---|
| a: | Less marked rises in pitch can be indicated using a colon which itself is underlined: |

J:    I have a red shi:rt

| | |
|---|---|
| <u>Under</u> | Underlined fragments indicate speaker emphasis. |
| CAPITALS | Words in capitals mark a section of speech noticeably louder than that surrounding it. |
| ° ° | Degree signs are used to indicate that the talk they encompass is spoken noticeably quieter than the surrounding talk. |
| Tha(gh)t | A 'gh' indicates that the word in which it is placed had a guttural pronunciation. |
| > < | Inward chevrons indicate that the talk they encompass was produced noticeably quicker than the surrounding talk. |
| < > | Outward chevrons indicate that the talk they encompass was produced noticeably slower than the surrounding talk. |
| → | Arrows in the left margin point to specific parts of an extract discussed in the text. |
| [H:21.3.89:2] | Extract headings refer to the transcript library source of the researcher who originally collected the data. |

# Introduction

What do we do when we talk? Talk is a central activity in social life; but how is ordinary talk organized, how do people coordinate their talk in interaction, and what is the role of talk in wider social processes? Conversation analysis (CA) aims to address these questions. The answers it provides, and more particularly the means by which it provides those answers (its assumptions, methods, and procedures, together with the findings these enable us to generate), are the subject matter of this book.

Conversation analysis is characterized by the view that how talk is produced, and how the meanings of talk are determined, are the practical, social and interactional accomplishments of members of a culture. Talk is not seen simply as the product of two 'speaker-hearers' who attempt to exchange information or convey messages to each other. Rather, participants in conversation are seen as mutually orienting to, and collaborating in order to achieve, orderly and meaningful communication. At least in part, the aim of CA is thus to reveal the organized reasoning procedures which inform the production of naturally occurring talk. The way in which utterances are designed is informed by procedures, methods and resources, which are tied to the contexts in which they are produced and are available to participants by virtue of their membership in a natural language community. The analytic objective of CA is to explicate these procedures, on which speakers rely to produce utterances and by which they make sense of other speakers' talk.

CA originates in the pathbreaking lectures given by Harvey Sacks in the sociology departments of the University of California at Los Angeles, and later, Irvine, between 1964 and 1972. Sacks, who was killed in a car crash in 1975 aged 40, was a highly original, often iconoclastic thinker whose ideas have, since his death, radically influenced researchers in fields as diverse as sociology, social psychology, linguistics (especially sociolinguistics and pragmatics), communication studies, human-computer interaction and speech therapy.

Although Sacks published a number of influential papers in his lifetime, the vast bulk of his ideas were expressed in his university lectures. Sacks recorded huge numbers of these lectures on tape and had them transcribed. He would then send copies of the transcripts to anyone who contacted him to request them. Inevitably, for many years, this meant that only a relatively small number of individuals actually got to read these original texts with their wealth of insights and new ideas. In 1992, this was finally changed when the lectures, edited by Gail Jefferson, were published in book form (Sacks, 1992).

Even in the more finished form of a book, the lectures still convey the frisson of excitement that emerged from those earlier, often scrappy A4 pages: a sense of the ongoing creation of a radically new form of social science. Like Saussure and Wittgenstein before him, two other revolutionary thinkers who had used the freer form of lectures in preference to the constraints of finished publications as the principal means for putting their ideas across, Sacks must have been well aware that the contents of his lectures constituted a break with the way things had been hitherto. In fact, Sacks' awareness of this was something that he did not try to hide. In many ways, this consciousness of his own originality is crystallized in the following remarkable exchange between Sacks and one of his students, which occurs late in the series of lectures. Sacks has been lecturing in his usual way, based around a fragment of recorded conversation. The student interrupts the lecture to ask a question:

Student   I was just wondering if we're ever going to get around to topics of conversation.

Sacks   That's an amazing question. I wouldn't know what you're- What do you have in mind?

Student   I just think that we should get some content. I feel very frustrated about it.

Sacks   . . . What would be some content?

Student   I don't know. I expected at least that you're going to analyse conversations . . .

Sacks   Often you can do that kind of thing and figure that it will work. But as weird as it may be, there's an area called the Analysis of

Conversation. It's done in various places around the world, and I invented it. So if I tell you that what we're doing is studying conversation, then there's no place to turn, as compared to experimental psychology where you can say 'I want to know what the mind is like' and then you can choose to study humanistic psychology or something like that. There is no other way that conversation is being studied systematically except my way. And this is what defines, in social science now, what 'talking about conversation' would mean. Now surely there are other ways to talk about conversation. But in social science there isn't. And people take it that they have to learn from listening to the sort of things I say, what it could possibly mean to talk about a particular conversation, how a conversation works, or how the details of conversation work. Nobody has ever heard a characterisation in that detail, with that abstractness, of a fragment like that. It's just never been done. It's been done here for the first time. (Sacks, 1992, Vol. 2: 549)

To some, this may come across as mere arrogance. But what is remarkable about these comments is the extraordinary awareness Sacks shows of the originality of his thinking. As we outline in Chapter 1, it was in fact quite accurate at that point for him to say that no one else in social science was studying conversation systematically. In sociology, Sacks' 'home' discipline (even though he had started off studying law), there was virtually no interest in any aspect of language, let alone the mundanities of everyday conversation. And though the focus on conversation may suggest that Sacks would have most in common with researchers in linguistics, we will also show that his particular approach – especially the alluded-to focus on detailed, abstract description of fragments of naturally occurring talk – distinguished him from the predominant methodologies in that field also.

In fact, CA lies at a unique interface between sociology and other major disciplines within the social sciences: principally, linguistics and social psychology. This interdisciplinarity has been a feature of CA from the beginning; it is reflected, for example, in the fact that the earliest major publications appeared not in sociology journals but in others such as the *American Anthropologist* (Schegloff, 1968) or the major linguistics journals *Language* (Sacks et al., 1974; Schegloff et al., 1977) and *Semiotica* (Jefferson, 1973; Schegloff and Sacks, 1973). Throughout this book, but especially in the final chapter, we will show that CA addresses a range of substantive issues, both theoretical and methodological, with which readers from backgrounds in a wide variety of social sciences will be able to identify.

For instance, CA's sociological lineage draws on affinities with Goffman's explorations of the interaction order and with Garfinkel's programme of ethnomethodology. One of the key sociological issues that CA, like these perspectives, addresses is that of intersubjectivity. How do we share a common understanding of the world and of one another's actions in the world? From Weber onwards, various responses have been given to this question. CA's distinctive contribution is to show that analytic access can be gained to the situated achievement of inter-subjectivity by focusing on the sequential organization of talk: in other words, on the management of turn-taking.

A further issue is addressed by conversation analytic research on talk in institutional settings. This work makes a distinctive contribution to the long standing 'agency-structure' debate, in which key contributions (Knorr-Cetina and Cicourel, 1981; Boden and Zimmerman, 1991) have sought to transcend the traditional sociological distinction between micro and macro levels of social order so as to reach a new under-standing of how social action is related to social structures. In a similar way to some of Giddens' (1984) theories on this subject, CA takes the view that 'structure' should not be viewed as an objective, external source of constraint on the individual. Rather, 'structure' is a feature of situated social interaction that participants actively orient to as relevant for the ways they design their actions. Thus, while analysts may want to assert that some feature of social structure, such as class or power, is relevant for the way in which particular interactions are managed, the more difficult task proposed by CA is to show that such features are relevant for the participants themselves, as displayed, for example, in the design of their talk (Schegloff, 1991).

In the field of linguistics, CA is relevant for three main areas: the ethnography of communication, which has aimed to analyse the patterns of language in use and the ways in which these relate to social and cultural patterns (Gumperz and Hymes, 1972); pragmatics, with its interest in how meaning is communicatively established (Levinson, 1983); and discourse analysis, with its concern for the structural and sequential properties of spoken language (Brown and Yule, 1982; Sinclair and Coulthard, 1975). With these perspectives CA shares the view that everyday talk is a phenomenon that is worthy of analysis in its own right, rather than the disorganized and flawed manifestation of linguistic competence that Chomsky (1965) believed it to be. One of the most important contributions made by CA here is in terms of method-ology. CA emphasizes that analysis should be based entirely on closely transcribed examples of actual talk recorded in naturally occurring settings, extracts from which are made available as part of published research. In this way, the claims of the analyst him or herself are open to test by the reader or other researchers on the basis of the data (or at least, a transcription of it: in Chapter 3 we discuss the distinction between data and transcription). This stance has had a major influence on research in what is now known broadly as interactional sociolinguistics, leading to a move away from the reliance on intuitively invented examples of talk as data which typified some earlier work, especially in speech act theory (Schegloff, 1988a).

A further contribution stems from the position conversation analysts take on the question of how talk is related to contextual and sociological variables. In line with its stance on the agency-structure debate in sociology, CA takes issue with the standard sociolinguistic notion that there is an intrinsic and causal relationship between language and the social contexts in which it is produced. Again, rather than assuming such a relationship exists, CA demands that the relevance of sociolinguistic variables for the participants themselves must be demonstrated on the basis of the data. This does not mean that variables such as gender, class or authority are irrelevant; but it does require the analyst to pay close attention to empirical phenomena and to begin from the assumption that participants are active, knowledgeable agents, rather than simply the bearers of extrinsic, constraining structures.

Within social psychology, CA's contribution relates to similar methodological and conceptual questions. For instance, a great deal of research on interpersonal communication has been based on data generated in experimental settings, in which the researcher seeks to control for certain variables, such as gender. Once more, such an approach is criticized for paying too little attention to the relevance of such variables among the participants themselves, effectively seeking to create a situation in which the phenomena the researcher has decided are important can be observed. Similarly, social psychological studies in which interactional phenomena such as interruption are encouraged to occur through experimental control, then quantified and correlated with variables like the gender of the participants, run the risk of generating invalid findings by categorizing certain events as 'interruptions' when closer examination reveals that the participants may in fact be engaging in legitimate turn-taking activities that are not really interruptive at all (Drummond, 1989).

Conversation analysis also plays a role in the area of social psychology known as discursive psychology (Potter and Wetherell, 1987; Edwards and Potter, 1992). Discursive psychologists have been critical of the ways in which the discipline of psychology has tended to treat language as a passive or neutral means of communication. Drawing not only from CA but also from ethnomethodology and semiotics, they stress instead that language is both functional and constructive; in other words it can only be fully understood as a medium which people use to accomplish specific communicative tasks, and it is a vehicle through which our sense of the world, and indeed psychological concepts themselves (such as memory, attitude, or cognition) are actively constructed. Consequently, one of the main concerns has been to develop a research programme in social psychology which takes full account of the dynamic properties of language use, both spoken and written.

A crucial factor in this wide-ranging impact and influence of CA is that Sacks' way of applying his vision did not result in an idiosyncratic, one-off body of work. Rather, Sacks invented a method by which others could take up and develop his findings, and, more importantly, generate new ideas and findings of their own. In short, conversation analysis is a generative method for the study of a wide range of aspects of the social world. Since Sacks' death, conversation analysis has continued to develop, and the number of practitioners has continued to grow, so that now the body of work within the field is truly diverse, both in terms of its substantive themes and of its global distribution.

Importantly, practitioners do not just analyse the social organization of 'ordinary' conversation, the casual interactions in which we routinely engage on a daily basis; but also, through studying how people use specialized forms of talk, the nature of institutions and organizations, the properties of mass communication, the structures of conflict in interaction, as well as issues such as the role of gender differences, power, the importance of ordinary talk in legal and educational decision-making processes, and more.

Yet on a methodological level, that diverse body of work is recognizably consistent. This is because conversation analysis is an approach which incorporates general procedures for data collection and transcription, as well as techniques for data analysis. Part of our aim in this book is to introduce those general techniques and basic procedures, in such a way as to provide the reader with some of the practical tools for doing conversation analysis.

However, this is not a 'recipe book' which will provide easy-to-follow rules for the production of a piece of conversation analysis. Although the procedures and techniques are quite general, they are not the same as the formulae which one might apply to data in statistical analysis. Conversation analysis, first and foremost, represents a distinctive sociological vision, a way of seeing the world and of approaching data, which derives ultimately from the exemplifications provided by Sacks in his original lectures.

In this book we emphasize both the methodological distinctiveness and social scientific applications of CA. We will focus not only on what CA is, and on how to do it, but also on what can be done with it. The book is designed to work on three interrelated levels:

- On the first level, we will present CA as methodologically distinctive. A major part of the significance of CA lies in its approach to the production of social scientific research, and in the practical research methods which are associated with that methodological perspective. The chapters of this book are intended both to explain and to exemplify that methodology.
- A second level of significance is found in what has been described as the conversation analytic mentality (Schenkein, 1978): the distinctive way of seeing and thinking about the social world to which CA introduces us and which is essential to the application of its methods. Our approach to this will be to exemplify the CA mentality by practically working through examples of conversation analytic work, since an essential feature of CA is that concepts are developed from, and securely rooted in, empirical observations of recorded, naturally occurring talk-in-interaction.
- On a third level, we will introduce the range of social scientific applications and implications which emerge out of CA research. A criticism that is often levelled against CA, as against other qualitative methods, is that it only deals with the 'small-scale' features of social life, the 'mere details' of interaction, and does not connect in any meaningful way with what are seen as the major questions of the social sciences. Linked with this is the view that CA has no practical relevance in the world beyond scholarly research. However, as is suggested by the first few sentences of this introduction, one of our aims is precisely to demonstrate the relevance of CA for social science more generally, and to illustrate some of its practical applications.

In line with these aims, the book is divided into three sections: Principles, Practices, and Implications. The first two sections provide accounts of the foundational issues in conducting conversation analytic research. In Chapter 1 we provide an introduction to the intellectual and disciplinary context in which CA came into being, focusing principally on the early development of the field in Harvey Sacks' lectures. We also provide a first empirical introduction to the conversation analytic mentality. Chapter 2 goes on to give an account of some of the early influential studies in CA, with the aim of introducing some basic analytic concepts and their application. In Chapter 3, we begin to introduce the reader to the analytic techniques of CA, by means of a detailed discussion of the key issue of transcription and its close relationship with analysis of data. Chapters 4 and 5 continue this practical thread, by demonstrating a number of analytic techniques used in CA, ranging from the analysis of large collections of data to the detailed study of single cases.

The third section concentrates on how these analytic techniques and perspectives can be applied to various issues and problems in the social sciences. Chapter 6 discusses the analysis of interaction in institutional or organizational settings. Here, we demonstrate the power of CA as a technique for analysing a whole range of forms of talk using a single method. Chapter 7 addresses the issue of how CA can contribute to the analysis of data produced in social scientific research interviews. Here, we discuss key methodological questions both for standard interview-based social science research, and for CA itself in the form of how to analyse extended monologues such as interviewee responses in unstructured interviews.

The final two chapters review the implications of conversation analysis at the interdisciplinary interface between sociology, psychology, linguistics, and related areas such as computer science, politics and childhood studies. Chapter 8 discusses some of the ways that CA's methods and findings have been extended into areas concerned with the practical application of research findings, while Chapter 9 examines aspects of CA's relationship to key issues and debates around power, cognition, and language. Our aim in these chapters is somewhat broader than in the rest of the book. It is to give the reader a sense of CA's relevance beyond what might be thought of as its 'core business' of the technical analysis of speech exchange in interaction. The discussion is therefore primarily programmatic, although illustrated, where possible, via discussion of data or key empirical studies.

# Part I  PRINCIPLES

# 1

# What is Conversation Analysis?

We begin this book with a question: 'What is conversation analysis?' In a sense, the book in its entirety represents our answer to that question, because conversation analysis is best defined in terms of what it does, how it enables us to view the social world and to analyse social interaction, and that is what our subsequent chapters focus upon. But it is useful to begin with a brief definition, an overview, of what CA is. We start out in this chapter with such a definition, which then leads us into a discussion of the fundamental assumptions informing CA. The most central of these assumptions is that ordinary talk is a highly organized, socially ordered phenomenon. We trace this claim as it emerged in the early researches of CA's founder, Harvey Sacks. We then discuss the distinctively sociological background to the conversation analytic approach, before providing an initial illustration of the specific interests and concerns that motivate conversation analytic observations on empirical data.

## A definition of conversation analysis

At the most basic level, conversation analysis is the study of talk. To put it in slightly more complex terms, it is the systematic analysis of the talk produced in everyday situations of human interaction: talk-in-interaction. Throughout this book, we will refer to talk-in-interaction, rather than conversation, as the object of study for conversation analysts. The reason for this is simple. Although the field has adopted the name 'conversation analysis', practitioners do not engage solely in the analysis of ordinary conversation. As we will demonstrate in later chapters, the range of forms of talk-in-interaction that have been subject to study within CA is far larger than the term 'conversation' alone would imply (Schegloff, 2007: xiii).

Perhaps the most suitable way of approaching the definition of CA is to look at what CA does. If CA is the study of talk-in-interaction, how do its practitioners go about that study? Perhaps the most distinctive methodological trait of CA, and certainly a policy that underpins all its analytic findings, is that research is based on transcribed tape-recordings of actual interactions. Moreover, what is recorded is 'naturally occurring' interaction; in other words, the activities which are recorded are situated as far as possible in the ordinary unfolding of people's lives, as opposed to being prearranged, set up in laboratories, or otherwise experimentally designed. Researchers make extensive use of transcripts of these naturally occurring events, both in generating analyses and in presenting those analyses in published form. The issue of transcription is the subject of Chapter 3.

Overall, then, CA is the study of recorded, naturally occurring talk-in-interaction. But what is the aim of studying these interactions? Principally, it is to discover how participants understand and respond to one another in their turns at talk, with a central focus on how sequences of actions are generated. To put it another way, the objective of CA is to uncover the often tacit reasoning procedures and sociolinguistic competencies underlying the production and interpretation of talk in organized sequences of interaction.

In relation to this, there is a further significance in saying that CA is the study not just of talk, but of talk-in-interaction. On one level, talk involves language. In fact, it might be said that talk is the verbal instantiation of language. But CA is only marginally interested in language as such; its actual object of study is the interactional organization of social activities. CA is a radical departure from other forms of linguistically oriented analysis in that the production of utterances, and more particularly the sense they obtain, is seen not in terms of the structure of language, but first and foremost as a practical social accomplishment. That is, words used in talk are not studied as semantic units, but as products or objects which are designed and used in terms of the activities being negotiated in the talk: as requests, proposals, accusations, complaints, and so on. Moreover, the accomplishment of order, and of sense, or coherence, in talk-in-interaction is seen as inextricably tied to the local circumstances in which utterances are produced.

The upshot of all this is that CA's aim is to focus on the production and interpretation of talk-in-interaction as an orderly accomplishment that is oriented to by the participants themselves. CA seeks to uncover the organization of talk not from any extraneous viewpoint, but from the perspective of how the participants display for one another their understanding of 'what is going on'. As Schegloff and Sacks put it in an early summary:

> We have proceeded under the assumption (an assumption borne out by our research) that in so far as the materials we worked with exhibited orderliness, they did so not only to us, indeed not in the first place for us, but for the co-participants who had produced them. If the materials . . . were orderly, they were so because they had been methodically produced by members of society for one another, and it was a feature of the conversations we treated as data that they were produced so as to allow the display by the co-participants to each other of their orderliness, and to allow the participants to display to one another their analysis, appreciation and use of that orderliness. (Schegloff and Sacks, 1973: 290)

This is what underlies the focus on sequences: throughout the course of a conversation or other bout of talk-in-interaction, speakers display in their sequentially 'next' turns an understanding of what the 'prior' turn was about. That understanding may turn out to be what the prior speaker intended, or it may not; whichever is the case, that itself is something which gets displayed in the next turn in the sequence. We describe this as a *next-turn proof procedure*, and it is the most basic tool used in CA to ensure that analyses explicate the orderly properties of talk as oriented to accomplishments of participants, rather than being based merely on the assumptions of the analyst.

As an illustration of this, consider the following utterance, which is from an exchange between a mother and her son about a forthcoming Parent-Teachers' Association meeting (Schegloff, 1988a: 57–8):

**(1) [KR:2]**
1    Mother:    Do you know who's going to that meeting?

Mother's question here can be interpreted as doing one of two types of action. It could represent a genuine request for information about who is attending the meeting; or she could be using it as a 'pre-announcement' (Terasaki, 2005), that is, as a preliminary to some information she wishes to announce about who is going. In the first case, the required response would be an answer to the question; whereas in the second case, the response would be something like, 'No, who?', which would provide the opportunity for the news to be announced.

Thus, taken in the abstract, Mother's utterance is ambiguous, and on a purely analytical level it would be problematic assigning a meaning to it. However, for CA, the issue is how the participants understand, or make sense of, any given utterance. Conversation analysts pay serious respect to the fact that their raw data were not produced in the first place for the purposes of social scientific analysis, or under the aegis of any special research project. Rather, they were produced for the specific people present at the time, whether face-to-face or on the other end of a telephone line. Therefore, what we have to do is look to see how the recipient(s) of such utterances interpreted them.

When we do that, this is what we find:

**[KR:2]**

| 1 | Mother: | Do you know who's going to that meeting? |
|---|---------|------------------------------------------|
| 2 | Russ:   | Who? |
| 3 | Mother: | I don't know! |
| 4 | Russ:   | Ouh:: prob'ly: Mr Murphy an' Dad said prob'ly |
| 5 |         | Mrs Timpte en some a' the teachers. |

Russ's first response, 'Who' (line 2), clearly shows that he initially interprets Mother's utterance as a pre-announcement. However, Mother's next turn, 'I don't know!', displays that Russ's inference was in fact incorrect: she was actually asking an information-seeking question. Following this turn, Russ backtracks and re-interprets the first turn as a genuine request for information, and produces (in lines 4–5) the small amount of information that he has available.

This sequence demonstrates a number of things. First, that people's understandings of one another's actions can actually unfold as sequences themselves unfold. This is what makes it possible to analyse the co-production of mutual understanding using the next turn proof procedure: any 'next' turn in a sequence displays its producer's understanding of the 'prior' turn, and if that understanding happens to be incorrect, that in itself can be displayed in the following turn in the sequence. The sequence above also demonstrates that people's utterances in conversation are not necessarily determined by their individual beliefs, preferences or mental states but can be determined instead by their orientations to the structural organization of conversation. The fact that Russ displays in his final turn that he does possess knowledge about who is going to the meeting shows that in initially responding with 'Who?', it was not that he did not know but that he was orienting (incorrectly as it turned out) to Mother's first turn as doing a particular kind of action (a pre-announcement) requiring a particular kind of response.

The very turn-by-turn unfolding of interaction therefore assists the process of analysis. As Sacks, Schegloff and Jefferson (1974: 729) put it:

> [W]hile understandings of other turns' talk are displayed to coparticipants, they are available as well to professional analysts who are thereby afforded a proof criterion (and a search procedure) for the analysis of what a turn's talk is occupied with. Since it is the parties' understandings of prior turns' talk that is relevant to their construction of next turns, it is their understandings that are wanted for analysis. The display of those understandings in the talk of subsequent turns affords . . . a proof procedure for professional analysis of prior turns – resources intrinsic to the data themselves.

As such, the next-turn proof procedure will be key to many of our discussions in subsequent chapters.

These, then, are the crucial features of a definition of conversation analysis. In the rest of this chapter, in order to begin unpacking this series of assertions, we move to a discussion of the intellectual origins of CA, and of the fundamental assumptions about talk and its analysis that conversation analysts work with.

## Harvey Sacks: order at all points

Conversation analysis emerged in pioneering research into the structural organization of everyday language use carried out by the sociologist Harvey Sacks at the University of California between 1964 and 1975, when Sacks, still comparatively young, was killed in a car crash. Although Sacks was the initiator of this research programme, his work quickly began to attract a growing number of adherents in various places; most significantly, during his lifetime, his principal collaborators Emanuel Schegloff and Gail Jefferson.

Sacks originated a radical research programme which was designed to investigate the levels of social order which could be revealed in the everyday practice of talking. The hypothesis with which this programme was begun was that ordinary conversation may be a deeply ordered, structurally organized phenomenon. This question could best be explored, in Sacks' view, by using recorded data of naturally-occurring talk, which could thus be observed repeatedly. This would get round a problem endemic to other naturalistic methods used to study interaction, such as participant observation in ethnography, which relies on after-the-event reconstructions of interactional occasions written by the researcher in his or her notebook. Thus, as Sacks put it:

> It was not from any large interest in language or from some theoretical formulation of what should be studied that I started with tape-recorded conversations, but simply because I could get my hands on it and I could study it again and again, and also, consequentially, because others could look at what I had studied and make of it what they could, if, for example, they wanted to be able to disagree with me. (Sacks, 1984a: 26)

With this in mind, Sacks worked on whatever data became available to him. At first, this was a corpus of telephone calls to a 'suicide prevention centre', to which Sacks had gained access through a research post in the Los Angeles Center for the Scientific Study of Suicide. It was during his observations of these calls that a question occurred to him which turned out to be the starting point for CA.

Sacks had observed that, in the majority of cases, if the person taking the call within the organization started off by giving their name, then the 'suicidal' person who was calling would be likely to give their name in reply. But in one particular call, Sacks noticed that the caller (B) seemed to be having trouble with the answerer (A)'s name:

**(2) [Sacks, 1992(1): 3]**
A:    This is Mr Smith, may I help you
B:    I can't hear you.
A:    This is Mr <u>Smith</u>
B:    Smith

And, Sacks observed, for the rest of this conversation, the agent taking the call had great difficulty in getting the caller to give a name.

Now, for the personnel of the suicide prevention centre, this unwillingness of some callers to give their names constituted a particular kind of problem. Part of the way they worked involved them wanting to establish some kind of personal identity for the caller. Therefore, they wanted to know whether anything could be done about this. For Sacks, however, a quite different question began to suggest itself: namely, 'where in the course of the conversation could you tell that somebody would not give their name?' (Sacks, 1992, Vol. 1: 3). It was this question, and this sequence, that led to Sacks' unique approach to the study of talk. In a later memoir, Schegloff recounts this period:

> It was during a long talking walk in the late winter of 1964 that Sacks mentioned to me a 'wild' possibility that had occurred to him. He had

previously told me about a recurrent and much discussed practical problem faced by those who answered phone calls to the Suicide Prevention Center by suicidal persons or about them – the problem of getting the callers to give their names . . . On the one hand, Sacks noted, it appears that if the name is not forthcoming at the start it may prove problematic to get. On the other hand, overt requests for it may be resisted. Then he remarked: Is it possible that the caller's declared problem in hearing is a methodical way of avoiding giving one's name in response to the other's having done so? Could talk be organised at that level of detail? And in so designed a manner? (Schegloff, 1992a: xvi–xvii)

Three key points result from this 'wild' possibility. The first is that utterances may be viewed as objects which speakers use to accomplish particular things in their interactions with others. That is, rather than taking an utterance such as 'I can't hear you' at its apparently straightforward face value, we might analyse it to reveal how such an innocuous statement is being strategically employed to achieve a specific task at that point in the conversation: namely, the task of 'avoiding giving one's name'. As Sacks' subsequent analysis shows, by 'not hearing', the caller is able to set up a sequential trajectory in which the agent finds less and less opportunity to establish the caller's name without explicitly asking for it. Thereby, the caller is able to begin the conversation by avoiding giving a name without actually refusing to do so.

The second idea is that talk can thus be seen as methodic. Sacks here, as elsewhere in his work, takes as his starting point one particular, situated episode of talk and asks: Is there a way in which we can see this event as an outcome of the use of methods? As Schegloff (1992a) remarks in his account of Sacks' early work, the kinds of issues to which Sacks recurrently addresses himself can be couched in terms of how conversational moves are methodic answers to given problems. For instance, describing some of the first set of lectures, given in 1964 (the lectures themselves can be found in Sacks, 1992, Vol. 1):

How to get someone's name without asking for it (give yours), lecture 1.

How to avoid giving your name without refusing to give it (initiate repair), lecture 1.

How to avoid giving help without refusing to give it (treat the circumstance as a joke), lecture 2. . . .

How to get help for suicidalness without requesting it (ask 'how does this organization work?'), lecture 10.

How to talk in a therapy session without revealing yourself (joke), lecture 12. (Schegloff, 1992a: xxvii–xxviii)

It is important to emphasize that Sacks' approach in this was not to establish 'recipes, or rules, or definitions of types of actions' (Schegloff, 1992a: xviii). He is not saying that 'I can't hear you' always and everywhere represents a way of avoiding giving one's name. Rather, his approach, and the approach which CA generally has adopted, is to view utterances as actions which are situated within specific contexts. Thus, the methodic character of talk is always addressed to the details of the interactional and sequential context in which it is produced. In this particular instance, the respective activities being engaged in by the caller and the agent are, broadly speaking, those of seeking help about a feeling of suicidalness and of finding a way of providing that help. As Sacks remarks elsewhere, the agent has good organizational reasons for seeking the caller's name, since the Suicide Prevention Center tries to keep records of all its contacts. But the caller may have equally good social reasons for wanting to avoid giving a name, since by that act, she becomes organizationally categorized as a 'potential suicide'. It is in this interactional context that the conversational move of doing 'not hearing', in the sequential context following the agent's announcement of his name, becomes analysable as a method for avoiding giving one's name.

This approach differentiates Sacks' perspective from another well-known perspective on the social uses of language, namely speech act theory. Speech act theory originated in the work of J. L. Austin (1962), who argued that all utterances performed actions, rather than simply describing the world in ways that were either true or false (as had been maintained by philosophers of language such as the logical positivists of the Vienna School). Around the time that Sacks was developing his ideas, John Searle, in a famous paper called 'What is a speech act?', (1965) had applied this approach by taking the act of 'promising' and attempting to define the rules and conditions (the 'felicity conditions') that would make an utterance recognizable as a promise. However, Searle's analysis set out to define the act of promising in a decontextualized way: for instance, he began by invoking 'a typical speech situation involving a speaker, a hearer, and an utterance by the speaker' (1965: 221). Also, the rules he described were grounded in intuition rather than in the observation of any empirical examples of talk.

But as we have already seen, Sacks began with *actual* utterances in actual contexts. This concern with real-world data, and with the situated, contexted nature of talk-in-interaction, characterizes all of Sacks' work and is a core feature of the conversation analytic method. Although, as we will see presently, there is also a concern in CA to establish how conversational devices and sequence types exhibit general features and function in essentially similar ways across varying contexts, that concern differentiates itself from the speech act approach by being consistently and carefully grounded in particularized accounts of naturally occurring data.

The third idea that we referred to is one that is equally key to the distinctiveness of CA as a social scientific method. This is that talk-in-interaction can be treated as an object of analysis in its own right, rather than simply as a window through which we can view other social processes or broader sociological variables. This represents a challenge to conventional sociological thinking which sees talk as essentially trivial, except in so far as it is a tool for finding out about larger-scale social phenomena such as class, gender or deviancy, through responses to interview questions, for example. It also challenges the standard perspective in sociolinguistics, which attempts to show a causal relationship in the ways in which linguistic variables are themselves affected by sociological variables (Labov, 1972). As we will show in later chapters, there has developed a significant wing in CA that focuses on demonstrating the key role of talk in institutional, political, media and legal settings. But even this work takes the essential CA starting point that talk-in-interaction is to be seen as its own social process, governed by its own regularities.

Underlying all this is perhaps Sacks' most original idea; namely, that there is 'order at all points' in talk-in-interaction. Sacks pointed out that for the most part, theories in the social sciences have been based on a distinction between 'what are in the first instance known to be "big issues", and . . . those which are terribly mundane, occasional, local, and the like' (Sacks, 1984a: 22), where only the former are considered to be proper subjects for social scientific research. More or less explicit here is the view that:

> The search for good problems by reference to known big issues will have large-scale, massive institutions as the apparatus by which order is generated and by a study of which order will be found. If, on the other hand, we figure or guess or decide that whatever humans do, they are just another animal after all, maybe more complicated than others but perhaps not noticeably so, then whatever humans do can be examined to discover some way they do it . . . That is, we may alternatively take it that there is order at all points. (Sacks, 1984a: 22)

The upshot of this is that wherever we choose to direct our analytic gaze at the activities of humans, we will find some orderly phenomena, and we will be able to describe the order which informs the production of those phenomena. After all, a commonsense assumption is that conversation itself is a mundane, local event that is more random than ordered. The findings of conversation analysis represent a persistent challenge to that assumption.

It is important to emphasize that although we are citing here from a 1984 (and therefore posthumous) publication of Sacks', these remarks were actually made in 1966 (to be exact, in Lecture 33 from Spring 1966 – see Sacks, 1992, Vol. 1: 483–8). At almost exactly the same time, the linguist Noam Chomsky was arguing for the opposite view, which has underpinned most subsequent research in structural linguistics, namely that ordinary talk could not be the object of study for linguistics since it is too disordered; it is an essentially degenerate realization of linguistic competence (Chomsky, 1965). While this makes some sense within Chomsky's perspective, which is that linguistic competence mostly consists of tacit knowledge of syntactic structures, it is nonetheless a prime example of the approach that Sacks was arguing against: that the place where order can be found is decided purely on the basis of prior analytic assumptions.

Sacks (1984) quotes other examples. For instance, the famous linguistic anthropologist Edward Sapir, in his book *Language* (1921), suggests that language is like a motor powerful enough to drive an elevator but for the most part only driving a doorbell. Sacks cites a comment by Uriel Weinreich (1963: 147): 'The more pressing task for linguistics, it seems to me, is to explain the elevator, not the doorbell; avoiding examples of excessively casual or ceremonial speech . . .'. Once again, there is the assumption that 'we know, right off, where language is deep and interesting, [and] that we can know that without an analysis of what it is that it might be doing' (Sacks, 1984a: 24). For CA, the notion of order at all points means that nothing in talk-in-interaction should be dismissed as trivial or uninteresting before we have subjected it to analysis.

This brief contextualizing discussion has pointed up the key insights which serve as the methodological basis for conversation analysis. We can summarize these now in the form of the following propositions:

- Talk-in-interaction is systematically organized and deeply ordered.
- The production of talk-in-interaction is methodic.
- The analysis of talk-in-interaction should be based on naturally occurring data.
- Analysis should not initially be constrained by prior theoretical assumptions.

So far we have hinted at some of the intellectual background against which these ideas can be understood, by mentioning perspectives such as speech act theory and sociolinguistics, to which CA offers specific challenges. But in order to appreciate more fully the originality of Sacks' thinking, we need to describe the broader disciplinary matrix out of which CA emerged. In the next section we discuss this in terms of the social sciences more generally, focusing especially on the relevance of sociology. This is because, while its analysis of language use in the form of talk gives CA an obvious relevance for branches of linguistics such as sociolinguistics, discourse analysis, or pragmatics (Levinson, 1983), the key questions that CA addresses arise more from a sociological than a linguistic basis. Martin Montgomery has put this point very well. Distinguishing between discourse analysis in linguistics (Brown and Yule, 1983) and conversation analysis, Montgomery (1986: 51) remarks that the former approach tends to be concerned with 'verbal interaction as a manifestation of the linguistic order', whereas 'conversation analysis is more concerned with verbal interaction as instances of the situated social order'. Accordingly, we now turn to this interest in the situated social order.

## The sociological background

Sacks worked in a sociology department, and the significance of sociology might be seen merely as an outcome of that locational fact. But Sacks clearly viewed himself as engaging in work which not only addressed fundamental sociological problems, but also, problems within sociology itself. This is evident from the titles of some of his earliest publications, such as 'Sociological description' (Sacks, 1963), or 'An initial investigation of the usability of conversational data for doing sociology' (Sacks, 1972a).

The kinds of sociological issues which Sacks addressed centred around a particular conception of the kind of enterprise sociology should be. Principally, he was concerned to find a way in which sociology could become a naturalistic, observational science. As we have already hinted, Sacks did not have much time for the standard methodologies in either linguistics or sociology. In linguistics at that time, the prevailing procedure was to study invented examples of language for their formal properties, without paying any attention to how language is actually used in interaction. And while this may be an acceptable procedure if one is interested in the structures of syntax (Chomsky, 1965), once one becomes interested in *sequences* of talk then intuition becomes much less reliable. As Sacks put it:

It happens to be perfectly reasonable for linguistics and philosophy to proceed by considering: 'Well, let's take a certain locution, a sentence.

Would anybody say that? If they said it would we figure it was grammatical? or a puzzle? or not?' And pretty much reasonably educated people feel comfortable with such a procedure . . . One can invent new sentences and feel comfortable with them. One cannot invent new sequences of conversation and feel comfortable about them. You may be able to take 'a question and an answer', but if we have to extend it very far, then the issue of whether somebody would really say that, after, say, the fifth utterance, is one which we could not confidently argue. One doesn't have a strong intuition for sequencing in conversation. (1992, Vol. 2: 5)

We have already outlined the resulting insistence in CA that the talk to be analysed should be recorded in naturally occurring settings.

For sociology, Sacks' criticism similarly focused on the question of observability. In one of his earliest lectures, he put forward a powerful argument against the prevailing notion in sociology that the phenomena most worthy of analysis were unobservable – for instance, attitudes, class mobility, or the causes of deviance. This view, which Sacks traced back to the influence of the psychologist G. H. Mead (1934) (though it could be traced back further, to Durkheim), underlies the use of such standard sociological methods as in-depth interviews and survey questionnaires, the aim of which is precisely to enable the analyst to get at the unobservables which, it is assumed, lie behind people's actions and can only be discerned in the aggregate, usually through the use of some form of statistical analysis. However, as Sacks noted, 'social activities are observable; you can see them all around you, and you can write them down . . . If you think you can see it, that means we can build an observational study, and we can build a natural study' (1992, Vol. 1: 28).

As this view suggests, Sacks had a much more positive attitude towards the alternative, ethnographic school of sociology which had its roots in the Chicago School (e.g., Whyte, 1943; Park, 1952; Becker, 1953; Hughes, 1970). For these sociologists, the prime concern was a close attention to observational detail in their studies of the everyday lives of social groups such as street corner gangs, hobos and marijuana users. Sacks admired this work, but was still critical of it:

Instead of pushing aside the older ethnographic work . . . I would treat it as the only work worth criticising in sociology, where criticising is giving some dignity to something. So, for example, the relevance of the works of the Chicago sociologists is that they contain a lot of information about this-and-that. And this-and-that is what the world is made up of. (1992, Vol. 1: 27)

Nevertheless, ethnographic work is problematic for three main reasons, all of which are closely interrelated. First, it tends to rely very heavily on information gained through interviews with certain trusted members of the group or setting being studied. As Sacks put it:

> [T]he trouble with their work is that they're using informants; that is, they're asking questions of their subjects. That means that they're studying the categories that Members use . . . they are not investigating the categories by attempting to find them in the activities in which they're employed. (1992, Vol. 1: 27)

This brings us to the second point, which is that for Sacks, both ethnography and survey research have a close reliance on the commonsense knowledge of members of society, but use that commonsense simply as a resource, whereas it should be turned into a topic of study. This is a view which he owed to Harold Garfinkel (1967), about whom we say more below. For Sacks, what we as members know is interesting not so much as a resource but as something which needs to be systematically explicated: '[W]hat I want to do is turn that around: to use what "we" know, what any Member knows, to pose us some problems. What activity is being done, for example' (1992, Vol. 1: 487).

Related to these problems is a third, which is that in ethnographic research, the details of actual events are not made available to the reader. What is presented is an account of the practices of a setting's members based on information gleaned by the ethnographer from observations and interviews with informants. Thus, the reader has to take it on trust that what the ethnographer says happened, actually happened, and happened in the way reported. Sacks, as we began this section by saying, wanted to make sociology into a naturalistic, observational science of social life:

> The difference between [ethnography] and what I'm trying to do is, I'm trying to develop a sociology where the reader has as much information as the author, and can reproduce the analysis. If you ever read a biological paper it will say, for example, 'I used such-and-such which I bought at Joe's drugstore.' And they tell you just what they do, and you can pick it up and see whether it holds. You can re-do the observations. Here, I'm showing my materials and others can analyse them as well, and it's much more concrete than the Chicago stuff tended to be. (1992, Vol. 1: 27)

Sacks, then, was basing his critique of existing approaches in some way on a particular conception of how natural sciences such as biology go about producing and reporting their findings. Whether or not this model was an accurate one (see, for example, Lynch and Bogen, 1994), it shows once again the radicalism and originality of Sacks' thinking.

What Sacks sought to show was that we can deal purely observationally with the natural facts of everyday social life, and analyse them in an interesting, non-intuitive and non-trivial manner.

On a more theoretical level, Sacks' view of sociology was anchored fundamentally in two contemporary perspectives with which he had a great deal of affinity. One was Goffman's sustained attempt to establish the deep sociological relevance of the 'interaction order' of face-to-face communication (e.g., Goffman, 1959; 1983). The other was the field of ethnomethodology, which had developed in Garfinkel's studies of practical reasoning and commonsense knowledge in everyday life (Garfinkel, 1967). We will look in slightly more detail at each of these influences.

### Goffman and the interaction order

In the 1950s, Erving Goffman developed a form of sociology which focused on the presentation of 'self' in the multifarious situations of everyday life (Goffman, 1959). At the core of this work was the ritual nature of face-to-face interaction. His argument was that we 'perform' our social selves, managing the ways we appear in everyday situations so as to affect, in either overt or tacit ways, how others orient to us. At the same time, a person's self becomes treated as a 'sacred' object, which is shown by the ways we establish boundaries around our physical bodies and possessions, 'territories of the self' (Goffman, 1971) which we expect others to respect. The originality in Goffman's thinking came from his view that this domain of everyday interpersonal interaction, which was seen as deeply trivial and arbitrary by mainstream sociology, was a site of social order and should be the subject of structural sociological investigation.

The influence of this approach can be traced in Sacks' thinking, for instance in his concern with how people accomplish many of their communicative actions indirectly, which we touched on earlier in discussing the suicide prevention calls. Indeed, Sacks had been a student of Goffman's, and one of his early papers, 'Notes on police assessment of moral character' (Sacks, 1972b), was worked up from a graduate essay written for one of Goffman's classes. However, although Sacks undoubtedly drew from Goffman in his interest in the orderly properties of face-to-face interaction, his approach was ultimately very different to Goffman's.

In his investigations, Goffman was primarily interested in what he called the 'interaction order' (Goffman, 1983). Having begun from a central concern with the strategies of self-presentation which individuals use in the various settings of everyday life, he came in his late work to focus more and more on the central importance of language in every-day social interaction. In particular, his last book, published in 1981, was titled *Forms of Talk*, and as the title suggests Goffman had by that stage become influenced not only by the work of ethnographers of communication (Gumperz and Hymes, 1972), but also by the growing field of conversation analysis itself (about which he was critical, though Schegloff [1988b] has argued that many of his criticisms were based on misreadings of the CA literature).

But while this slight shift in focus occurred as Goffman's work developed, his interests remained essentially the same: his main aim was to document the ritual procedures which inform the orderly conduct of everyday life. The upshot of this is that when he studied talk, he maintained a strict distinction between its 'system' properties and its 'ritual' properties. System properties had to do with features ensuring basic intelligibility, such as orderly turn-taking, whereas ritual properties had to do with such things as the protection of 'face' – the ways in which we tend to avoid giving offence to others – politeness, and the many other 'ceremonial' aspects of interaction. For Goffman, these were two theoretically distinct modes of the interaction order.

For Sacks, however, there is no meaningful difference between system and ritual aspects of talk-in-interaction. This is aptly demonstrated by a paper called 'Everyone has to lie' (Sacks, 1975) in which Sacks shows that the 'polite' answer to a 'How are you?' inquiry, that is, 'Fine', has as much to do with what Goffman called system requirements as it does with ritual requirements. This is because the question itself sets up a particular sequential trajectory. We do not expect someone to respond to 'How are you' with a literal account of their state of health. Indeed Garfinkel (1967) had shown the power of this expectation by asking his students purposely to break it, treating the inquiries of their unknowing acquaintances literally. Predictably, this rapidly led to problems in the relationship between the 'experimenters' and their unwitting 'subjects' (see our discussion of ethnomethodology below). Thus, if someone wanted to 'tell the truth' about how they were, they would need to indicate that special circumstances were being brought into play. Similarly, to respond with anything other than a neutral 'Fine' or 'Okay', such as 'Terrible' or 'Fantastic', would set up its own sequential trajectory, in which the onus would then be on the original inquirer to invite one to expand on the reasons for this. Thus, Sacks' interest in the ritual or ceremonial order differed fundamentally from Goffman's, in that it began from the sequential order of talk-in-interaction itself.

Sacks also went beyond Goffman in terms of methodology. Goffman tended to eschew systematic methods of data collection and analysis in favour of a magpie-like selection from whatever materials he could find that usefully illustrated his theoretical point (be they snippets of overheard conversation, extracts from novels or TV shows, or segments from his own fieldwork in settings such as a Shetland Isle community or a mental asylum). Thus, in his work data is used largely illustratively and the main thrust of the writing is in the direction of the development of his particular theory of interpersonal interaction.

Sacks could also be eclectic in his use of illustrative data (for instance, he often drew from sources such as the writings of philosophers, Freud, and the Old Testament). However, the whole thrust of his argument is that theory ought to be data-driven, rather than data being used to support theory. Rather than generating a research idea and then going out to find data which supported it, Sacks maintained that research should begin with a process of 'unmotivated looking':

> [P]eople often ask me why I choose the particular data I choose. Is it some problem that I have in mind that caused me to pick this corpus or this segment? And I am insistent that I just happened to have it, it became fascinating, and I spent some time at it. Furthermore, it is not that I attack any piece of data I happen to have according to some problems I bring to it. When we start out with a piece of data, the question of what we are going to end up with, what kind of findings it will give, should not be a consideration. We sit down with a piece of data, make a bunch of observations, and see where they will go. (Sacks, 1984a: 27)

Ultimately, then, the similarities between Goffman's and Sacks' approach to studying the orderliness of everyday interaction are less significant than the differences, both theoretically and methodologically.

### Ethnomethodology

Contemporaneously with Goffman, Garfinkel was developing the form of sociology which became known as ethnomethodology (Garfinkel, 1967). Ethnomethodology similarly proposes that everyday interaction constitutes a legitimate domain of sociological study, but with a somewhat different emphasis. Garfinkel's work stands in clear opposition to the predominant sociological paradigm of that time, functionalism, especially as associated with Talcott Parsons (Parsons, 1937; see Heritage, 1984a). Functionalism was interested in constructing explanations for how societies manifest order and stability over time, and how it is that individuals normally avoid blindly pursuing their own appetites and desires and show the kind of other-awareness that Goffman studied in the form of the ritual order. Its explanation was that we internalize societal norms and values through a process of social-ization: negative and positive reinforcement exercised through institu-tions such as the family and the education system. Having internalized these values, we then unconsciously reproduce them in our actions, thereby ensuring that society carries on in an orderly fashion. Beginning from this model, the main issue for functionalism became the explan-ation of deviance.

Garfinkel argued, first, that Parsons' focus on the internalization of societal norms and values effectively denied the knowledgeability of ordinary members of society. For Garfinkel, members are capable of rationally understanding and accounting for their own actions in society. Indeed, it is precisely in that rational accountability that members come to be treated, and to see themselves, as 'members of society'. This is quite different from the logic of Parsons' perspective, which treats members as 'cultural dopes', to use Garfinkel's phrase. At the same time, functionalism's principal concern with deviance and transgression simply trades on the commonsense knowledge of members of society: rather than looking at how deviant categories are constructed and used in accountable ways by members, functionalism takes the existence of deviance for granted and seeks to locate its 'causes'. Against this, Garfinkel proposed that members' commonsense knowledge should become a topic of study, rather than simply a resource (for a detailed discussion, see Heritage, 1984a).

Thus, the aim of sociology is not to understand how norms are inter-nalized, such that people end up either reproducing these norms or deviating from them; but rather to describe the methods that people use for accounting for their own actions and those of others. These are the 'ethno-methods' which are the subject of ethnomethodological inquiry.

Sacks had a close association with Garfinkel in the early stages of his career, and the two co-authored an important paper (Garfinkel and Sacks, 1970). That paper drew many key parallels between the methods of practical reasoning and sense-making within cultural settings and members' mastery of ordinary language resources as the medium for this sense-making. Indeed, Garfinkel had always recognized the import-ance of language for ethnomethodological study (see, for instance, the discussion by Heritage [1984a] of the originality of Garfinkel's think-ing on this). But a crucial contribution was made by Sacks when he developed a systematic method by which the natural use of language could be studied. In fact, it is true to say that Sacks' approach, in its focus on the analysis of naturally occurring talk-in-interaction, repre-sents the most fruitful means of doing ethnomethodological study.

To expand on this a little, one of the problems that ethnomethodology encounters is that of how to gain analytic access to the level of commonsense knowledge which it seeks to study. Since the accounting practices Garfinkel was interested in were, on his own admission, taken for granted by members, 'seen but unnoticed', it was difficult to think of a method by which they could be revealed. The earliest research consisted of 'breaching' experiments in which the taken for granted routines of ordinary life were intentionally disrupted in order to observe how people dealt with their sudden lack of certainty (Garfinkel, 1956; 1963; 1967). For instance, Garfinkel would instruct his student 'experimenters' to engage others (called 'subjects') in interaction and then to repeatedly request that the subject clarify whatever he or she said. Thus, on being asked, 'How are you?', the experimenter would ignore the routine and expected use of this question as what Goffman might have called a 'ritual' utterance, and respond instead in the following kind of way:

**(3) [Garfinkel, 1967: 44]**
S:    How are you?
E:    How am I in regard to what? My health, my finances, my
      school work, my peace of mind, my . . .
S:    ((Red in the face and suddenly out of control)) Look!
      I was just trying to be polite. Frankly, I don't give a damn how you are.

Garfinkel's aim in designing these experiments was:

[T]o start with familiar scenes and ask what can be done to make trouble. The operations that one would have to perform in order to multiply the senseless features of perceived environments; to produce and sustain bewilderment, consternation, and confusion; to produce the socially structured effects of anxiety, shame, guilt and indignation; and to produce disorganized interaction should tell us something about how the structures of everyday activities are ordinarily and routinely produced and maintained. (Garfinkel, 1967: 38)

The breaching experiments led to many significant theoretical insights into the nature of intersubjectivity. Although Garfinkel designed these experiments (of which we have mentioned only one example) explicitly in order to undermine participants' sense of mutual understanding and trust in a shared reality, in fact he found that it was very difficult to accomplish this. Basically, subjects would find some way of accounting for the 'strange' behaviour of the experimenters. They did this principally by treating the experimenters as rational agents who had actively chosen to behave in this way, and/or who had some underlying reason for so doing. Thus, Garfinkel found that members' accounting practices were so powerful that even when an attempt was made to destroy what was 'taken for granted', people still found rational ways of sustaining their belief in those taken for granted features of social reality (for a detailed discussion of this point, see Heritage, 1984a: 75–102). This served to confirm Garfinkel's central proposition that:

> [A] concern for the nature, production and recognition of reasonable, realistic and analysable actions is not the monopoly of philosophers and professional sociologists. Members of society are concerned as a matter of course and necessarily with these matters both as features and for the socially managed production of their everyday affairs. (Garfinkel, 1967: 75)

However, as Garfinkel himself realized, the possibilities of breaching experiments are essentially limited, since they necessarily only tell us about what participants do in the 'special' situation constructed by the breach: they do not show how mutual understandings are constructed and maintained in the unremarkable course of mundane interaction. At the same time, what is really to be sought in ethnomethodology are not so much the methods used to repair 'breakdowns' in the taken-for-granted, but the commonsense methods used in the very construction and maintenance of accountable actions in the first place.

Other early research used variants of ethnographic methods such as participant observation and interviewing (Wieder, 1974). However, as we outlined above, the main problem here is that the analysis is based on the researcher's own account, generated in fieldnotes after the event, rather than the natural, situated actions of the participants. Hence, the analytic account is not only post hoc, but also a reconstructed version of what actually happened in the setting.

By deciding to focus on recorded conversations, therefore, Sacks managed to avoid these methodological pitfalls. The use of recordings provided a means by which members' sense-making, the establishment and maintenance of mutual understanding in interaction, could be observed both in situ and as it were 'in flight'. This method enabled Sacks to pursue his interest in 'ethno-methods' far more successfully than the alternatives, since the methods by which people understand each other in talk are available to observation in the close details of turn-taking itself, for instance through the next-turn proof procedure.

The reasoning behind these methodological concerns stems from Garfinkel's critique of conventional research methods in sociology, a critique which Sacks shared (see Garfinkel and Sacks, 1970). Most of sociology, in Garfinkel and Sacks' view, is *ironic*: that is, it claims that members of society do not 'really' know what's going on around them, even though they may think they do, and that it is up to sociologists to find out how social processes 'actually' operate. In short, sociology ironicizes members' knowledge, seeing people as the puppets of social forces which are beyond their comprehension (though apparently not beyond the understanding of sociologists).

Garfinkel was extremely critical of this prevailing trend in sociology, and his critique extended to the research methods which such a view leads to: principally, survey research and quantitative analysis. For him, the way in which findings are generated by a social survey is not objective, but essentially and unavoidably an interpretive process in which researchers and coders rely on their ordinary members' knowledge in order to fit each unique questionnaire response into the pre-established categories that will form the matrix for the findings (Garfinkel, 1967: 18–24). Of course, survey researchers are aware of the role of interpretation; but they refer to this in terms of problems in validity or reliability of findings, and attempt to establish methodological solutions for these problems. For instance, explicit coding instructions may be drawn up in order to avoid ad hoc interpretations of individual cases. For Garfinkel, however, this is to miss the point, because interpretation and common-sense knowledge are necessary and unavoidable aspects of the production of social science. As he observed in a beautiful remark on coding procedures: 'To treat instructions as though ad hoc features in their use were a nuisance, or to treat their presence as grounds for complaint about the incompleteness of instructions, is very much like complaining that if the walls of a building were only gotten out of the way, one could see better what was keeping the roof up' (1967: 22).

In fact, Garfinkel's critique of such approaches expanded into a critique of all attempts to treat sociology as a science which is capable of producing objective findings about society. With this view, Garfinkel placed himself squarely in the hermeneutic or phenomenological camp of social theory, which from the outset of the discipline has challenged the alternative positivist camp's argument that social research can and should be based on a model of objectivity derived from the natural sciences (for an introduction to this debate, see Cuff and Payne, 1984).

Sacks diverged from Garfinkel on this latter point, quite openly admitting that what he was trying to do was to construct a natural observational science of social life. In his earliest publication, Sacks had begun by saying: 'I take it that at least some sociologists seek to make a science of the discipline; this is a concern I share, and it is only from the perspective of such a concern that the ensuing discussion seems appropriate' (Sacks, 1963: 2).

And in a later lecture, while discussing a particular fragment of data, he made an explicit statement of a form of 'objectivism' in his research aims:

> [O]ur aim is . . . to get into a position to transform, in what I figure is almost a literal, physical sense, our view of what happened here as some interaction that could be treated as the thing we're studying, to interactions being spewed out by a machinery, the machinery being what we're trying to find; where, in order to find it we've got to get a whole bunch of its products. We can come to know that they can really be thought of as products, and that we can really think of a machine spewing them out. . . . And this would be another way to be interested in the whole thing as some actual sequence, i.e., as an assembled set of parts that could be otherwise fitted together. (Sacks, 1992, Vol. 2: 169)

In an important sense, then, Sacks was interested in finding the organization of talk-in-interaction in its own right, as a 'machinery' independent of individual speakers, which provides the resources drawn on by speakers in constructing their participation in any given interaction. This essentially structuralist view informs the contemporary research aims of conversation analysis, and its implications for the analysis of data and the discussion of findings will be drawn out in the chapters that follow.

Yet while this perspective appears to pay little attention to participants as subjects, and hence to go against the ethnomethodological concern with explicating methods of sense-making from the members' perspective, this is not the case. As we outlined earlier, CA shares this concern. The reconciliation of Sacks' vision of talk-in-interaction as the product of a 'machine' and his aim to see the order of conversation as a members' concern is found in his central idea that the structural resources used in conversation are simultaneously *context-sensitive* and *context-free* (Sacks, Schegloff and Jefferson, 1974). The resources are context-free in the sense that the techniques any set of conversationalists may use to get some interactional work done are not tied to the local circumstances of that specific occasion. Rather, we find that conversational patterns are enormously recursive: the same kinds of techniques are used by different participants in different circumstances. Yet at the same time, the use of those resources is context-sensitive in the sense that, on each specific occasion, these participants in particular are designing their talk in the light of what has happened before in this conversation, and possibly also in their relationship as a whole, among other contextual specifics. The aim of conversation analysis, as it has developed out of Sacks' work, is to explicate the structural organization of talk-in-interaction at this interface between context-free resources and their context-sensitive applications.

We began this chapter with a preliminary definition of what conversation analysis is; how it views the world of talk-in-interaction and the particular perspective it takes in the analysis of that activity. That definition was rather densely packed, and in expanding on it we subsequently traced the key features of the intellectual history through which the conversation analytic mentality was shaped. That involved a discussion of the pathbreaking work of Harvey Sacks, which we contextualized in relation to prevailing assumptions and methodologies in sociology and, to a lesser extent, linguistics.

Let us conclude the chapter with a more practical demonstration of the conversation analytic mentality: a way of approaching the observation of interactional data that is informed by the propositions outlined above and that leads the conversation analyst to search for possibly orderly properties at all points in talk-in-interaction. The conversation analytic mentality centrally involves developing the skill to make the fundamental conversation analytic move from 'seeing the obvious' in what people say to 'seeing the orderly' in how they say it and what they are using utterances to do in interaction.

## From 'obvious' to 'orderly': some remarks on conversational description

We can illustrate this move from 'obvious' to 'orderly' by exploring the commonplace activity of describing or producing accounts of versions of reality. We say 'versions' of reality because, as will be seen shortly, one important feature of factual description is that the facts themselves do not constrain the ways we may describe or refer to them. When we describe or refer to an object or state of affairs, there is a potentially inexhaustible range of words and combinations of words which may legitimately be used. Even when we are describing something routine or mundane, therefore, we can potentially produce an endless list of legitimate or logically correct statements.

Schegloff (1972: 81) provides a nice example of this in a consideration of the ways in which people produce descriptions of 'place' or the location of objects and people. He writes:

> Were I now to formulate where my notes are, it would be correct to say that they are: right in front of me, next to the telephone, on the desk, in my

office, in Room 213, in Lewisohn Hall, on campus, at school, at Columbia, in Morningside Heights, on the Upper West Side, in Manhattan, in New York, in the Northeast, on the Eastern Seaboard, in the United States, etc.

As Schegloff goes on to say, each of these descriptions are correct in so far as they do refer to where his notes were at the time of writing. In this sense, the statement 'At the time of writing Schegloff's notes were in New York' and 'At the time of writing Schegloff's notes were next to the telephone' are both equally true factual statements.

The implication is that even when speakers are describing the most routine and commonplace events or states of affairs they have a wide range of alternative words and combinations of words from which to choose. This means that on each occasion when speakers produce a factual report they have to select which referential item or descriptive utterance they wish to use on any occasion. If any factual reference or statement involves a process of selection, we can ask: what are the tacit reasoning procedures which led to this specific formulation of a fact at this point in the interaction?

Let us illustrate this by examining the factual observation, 'Neil you've got shoes on', produced in the extract below (Potter, 1996). An initial reaction to this utterance might be that it is a simple report of what someone is wearing, and therefore, an unlikely vehicle for delicate interactional work. However, what is important to bear in mind is that this simple report comes in a specific context: in this case, a sequence in which some young people are discussing a noise they can hear outside their flat:

**(4) [Potter, 1996: 108]**
```
1    Becky:   oi (.) sh shh (.) it could have been that
2    Neil:    NO [that's not making a noise
3    Alan:        [no (.) something outside
4             (0.4)
5    Alan:    it was definitely outside
6→   Diane:   Neil you've got shoes on
```

What happens after this is that there is a discussion about who should go outside and investigate the cause of the noise. So what we find is that the placement of a simple observation about Neil's footwear in a sequence of turns concerned with a mysterious noise is deeply consequential, because it constitutes an implicit request or suggestion that he should be the one to go and investigate. An apparently neutral, 'factual' observation about the world has been used to do a specific kind of interactional work.

This suggests that participants' interpretations of the work done by factual utterances should be informed by their reasoning about the context in which they are used. In extract (4), the observation about Neil's footwear can be seen to constitute a request for him to do something by virtue of the topic of the surrounding talk. However, topic may not be the only relevant context: the kinds of social actions participants are engaged in may also establish a sequential context in which apparently neutral factual observations can perform delicate interactional work.

Consider the following data extracts, which come from the transcript of a rape trial (Drew, 1990). In these extracts the counsel for the defence (C) is cross-examining the prosecution's main witness (W), the victim of the alleged rape. These data have a special relevance in as much as a courtroom case is an environment in which versions of events may be routinely contested or undermined. Note that both parties produce what might be termed competing factual descriptions of ostensibly the same event. Each version has been designed, however, to do a different kind of work: the counsel's questions refer to events in such a way as to undermine the witness's claims that she was raped, and the defendant's answers refer to the same events so as to warrant her claim that she could not be accused of encouraging the man who was alleged to have attacked her.

**(5) [Drew, 1992: 489]**

| 1 | C: | ((referring to a club where the defendant and |
| 2 |    | the victim met)) it's where uh (.) uh gi:rls and fella:s |
| 3 |    | meet isn't it? |
| 4 |    | (0.9) |
| 5 | W: | People go: there. |

**(6) [Drew, 1992: 489]**

| 1 | C: | An during the eve:ning: (0.6) uh: didn't mistuh ((name)) |
| 2 |    | come over tuh sit with you |
| 3 |    | (0.8) |
| 4 | W: | Sat at our table. |

In extract (5), the counsel builds a question through a description of one specific feature of the club in which the defendant and the witness met on the night of the alleged attack. The counsel does not refer to the patrons of the club as 'men or women' or 'local people', but as 'fellas' and 'girls'. Furthermore, he describes the club as a place where males and females meet each other. This description invokes the sense of young people out in the evening to make contact with members of the opposite sex. This in turn establishes the basis for the inference that people go to the club with a view to meet others for sexual purposes. This simple description works to undermine aspects of the witness's account which are crucial if her version of events is to be believed; for example, that in no way could it be suggested that she was encouraging any sexual relations between herself and her alleged attacker. Her reply, 'People go there', reformulates the 'function' of the club to escape the inference that it is a place in which males and females come together for sexual purposes. This is achieved primarily through the way she refers to the patrons as 'people': whereas a sexual division is emphasized and exploited by the counsel, she provides a gender neutral classification.

Similar concerns inform the sequence in extract (6): the question 'didn't he come over to sit with you' portrays a friendship between the witness and the alleged attacker; but by replying that the defendant 'sat at our table' the witness is able to establish that his behaviour was not prompted by any special relationship with her in particular, but was due to a familiarity with that group of people of which she was only one member.

These extracts suggest that differently formulated factual descriptions can be designed and used not just to describe some event that happened in the world, but to perform a range of subtle interactional and inferential tasks. Sometimes, as in extracts (5) and (6), different versions can be aimed at establishing the validity of one version of events over another.

Another aspect of conversational description that Sacks was closely concerned with, especially in his earlier lectures, is the use of *membership categories* (Sacks, 1972a; 1972c; 1979). Consider the many kinds of categories we have for referring to and describing people: 'man', 'woman', 'husband', 'wife', 'son', 'daughter', 'punk', 'skinhead', 'catholic', 'conservative', 'liberal', 'Canadian', 'English', 'widower', 'student', 'employee', 'employer', and so on. All of these are membership categories: we are all members of an indefinitely large range of categories such as these. These categories are culturally available resources which allow us to describe, identify or make reference to other people or to ourselves. And the interesting thing is that they are not exclusive. For example, it is not hard to imagine a single individual who could be accurately described as: a mother, daughter, accountant, divorcee, Piscean, protestant, English, and so on. This means that when we come to describe other people or ourselves, there is once more an issue of selection: why did we characterize our social identity, or the social identity of someone else in that particular way at that particular time?

In thinking about this issue it is important to bear in mind that categories are not neutral descriptions. They are what Sacks (1992, Vol. 1:

40–9) calls 'inference rich': there are strong expectations and conventions associated with them. For example look at these two sentences, which come from a story told by a small child:

The baby cried. The mommy picked it up. (Sacks, 1972a: 330)

Sacks (1972a) suggests that most people will interpret 'the mommy' as being the mother of the baby; similarly, the baby crying will have been read as the reason why the mother picked it up. None of this information is stated in the sentences themselves; so how do we understand it? Sacks argues that we are all able to arrive at the same interpretation because of categories and the commonsense expectations associated with them. There are specific 'category-bound activities' associated with membership categories like mother (for example, that they will, or should, care for their children when they are distressed) and baby (for instance, that they cry in order to indicate when they need attention). Similarly, categories can be understood (or as Sacks shows, should be understood) in relation to 'membership categorization devices': cultural conventions in terms of which categories are grouped in relation to other categories (such as the collection 'family'). The fact that the two sentences above were taken by Sacks from a published collection of 'stories' told by children as young as two indicates that humans learn to interpret the world in terms of membership categorization devices from a very early age.

Categories, then, do not merely provide us with convenient labels which allow us to refer to persons; they also provide a set of inferential resources by which we can come to understand and interpret the behaviour of persons so designated. That is,

Membership categories may conventionally be seen as having category-bound predicates . . . they are loci for the imputation of conventional expectations, rights and obligations concerning activities (for instance) which it is expectable or proper for an incumbent of a given category to perform. (Watson and Weinberg, 1982: 60)

What this means is that the assignment of a person to a category ensures that conventional knowledge about the behaviour of people so categorized can be invoked or cited to interpret or explain the actions of that person. Furthermore, in everyday conversation it is common to find sequences in which speakers clearly display their sensitivity to the inferential implications of category ascription. There are numerous interesting examples in the following extract:

**(7) [Sacks, 1992 Vol. 1: 44]**

| | | |
|---|---|---|
| 1 | A: | Corliss, the g- this chick I'm hanging around with now |
| 2 | | she's real nice she's got a real good personality, |
| 3 | | she's not- y'know she's just a real cute kid |
| 4 | B: | mm hm |
| 5 | A: | And last night we went to the Mardi Gras together |
| 6 | | and we were both well we were both pooped because |
| 7 | | I I ran in the track meet yesterday. And she- |
| 8 | | she's in the girls' tumbling team. I mean she |
| 9 | | doesn't like it she's just on it for the credits. |

Notice that at the start the speaker says 'Corliss, the g- this chick I'm hanging around with.'. Although we cannot be certain, it seems reasonable to assume that the abandoned word beginning with 'g-' was 'girl'. So, the speaker begins to say 'Corliss this girl I'm hanging around with', stops himself right at the start of the word 'girl' and produces instead the word 'chick'. There are, then, (at least) two alternative ways of referring to that person, 'girl' and 'chick'. Why would he start with one form of reference and then reject it in favour of another? One account is based in the alternative but non-equivalent inferences made available by the membership categories *girl* and *chick*. 'Girl' is a largely neutral form of address: it may be taken to indicate an approximate age, but it doesn't reveal much more about the person so described. 'Chick', however, performs a very different kind of work: it is a primarily male description which points to sexual attractiveness, as well as invoking a sense of being 'cool' or 'hip'. So by referring to his girlfriend as a 'chick', rather than a 'girl', the speaker is able to establish that she has the kind of personal and perhaps physical characteristics which would be highly valued among his peers at that time. (And this in turn suggests something positive about himself: that he's the kind of 'cool', 'hip' person a 'chick' would go out with.)

Later, in line 8, speaker A again characterizes his girlfriend, this time in terms of her membership of the school tumbling team. Immediately after that, however, he explains her membership of the team by reference not to any interest in gymnastics, but because she needs school credits. By accounting for her membership of the tumbling team in this way the speaker appears to be sensitive to the kinds of inferences which may be drawn about his girlfriend by virtue of her membership of the category 'girls' tumbling team'. For people of a certain age (teenagers, for instance) being a member of a school tumbling team might not be seen as 'cool', but an indication of a straight-laced or 'square' personality. However, his account for her membership is a way of indicating that common knowledge about that category does not apply in this case. The speaker's account for his girlfriend's activity is evidence that, as he was telling this anecdote, he was monitoring its production to assess the kinds of conclusions about his girlfriend which may be drawn by the recipient.

Membership categorization can also impact upon a speaker's perceived ability to make a legitimate factual claim about the world in the first place. Consider the following data which comes from recorded calls to the 911 emergency service in the United States. This call to the emergency switchboard (SB) comes from a hospital. This is indicated in the caller's (C) first utterance, 'This is General', which is a shorthand term for the name of a city hospital. By virtue of this institutional identification that caller categorizes himself as an employee of the hospital. He then goes on to make a statement about an event that is relevant to the emergency services:

**(8) [Whalen and Zimmerman, 1990: 483]**

```
1    SB:    Mid-City emergency
2    C:     Hi .hh this iz General - there's been an over dose (.)
3           twenty six twenty six .hh Columbia: hh upstairs
4           apartment num:::ber two
5    SB:    O:kay thank you
6    C:     umhm bye
```

Potter (1996) argues the caller makes a specialized kind of claim: to be able to identify that someone has taken an overdose at least implies medical knowledge about the toxic properties of a drug when large quantities are ingested, what counts as 'a large dose', compared to the recommended dosage, possible effects of an overdose and so on. As soon as the switchboard says 'O:kay thank you' what has happened is that she has processed the call and emergency services are being dispatched at once. So this call gets an instantaneous response. Note that the switchboard operator does not question the caller's competence to declare that the medical problem is an overdose. This is because of the expectations associated with membership of the broad category of medical personnel: people who identify themselves professionally with a hospital are taken to be competent to evaluate medical problems and make appropriate diagnoses.

In the next extract, however, the caller makes a similar kind of specialized claim when he states that a certain kind of crime is being committed. What is different here, it turns out, is that the caller is a member of the public:

**(9) [Whalen and Zimmerman, 1990: 473]**

```
1    SB:    Mid City emergency
2    C:     Would you send the police to eleven six oh Arvin Avenue
```

| 3 | | North |
|---|---|---|
| 4 | SB: | Eleven six oh Arvin Avenue North? |
| 5 | C: | Yes there's been raping goin' on |
| 6 | SB: | WHERE |
| 7 | C: | Eleven six [oh |
| 8 | SB: | [Inside or outside? |
| 9 | C: | Inside the house |
| 10 | SB: | There's somebody being RAPED? |
| 11 | C: | Yup= |
| 12 | SB: | How do you know this? |
| 13 | C: | I live next door. Two ladies bein raped, eleven six oh= |
| 14 | SB: | =Di-How do you know they're being raped inside that |
| 15 | | house. |

Unlike the previous extract, in this call the appropriate emergency service is not dispatched immediately. Instead, the operator seeks further details and then explicitly queries the basis of the caller's authority to make a claim about a rape (Potter, 1996).

What seems to be crucial in determining how seriously the operator treats the claims is the caller's category membership. The claims of the caller who establishes membership of a category of people who would be expected to be able to make specialized knowledge are dealt with unquestioningly. So, one powerful resource in producing a factual or warranted report is to establish membership of a category, incumbency of which is associated with specific kinds of skill, knowledge or expertise.

Perhaps because they are mainly discussed in the earlier part of the collected *Lectures on Conversation* (Sacks, 1992), Sacks's ideas about membership categorization are sometimes treated as a less important or less interesting aspect of his work, or as one which he consciously moved away from in later years (see the discussion in Schegloff, 1992a). But as our discussion of the above extracts shows, categorization and the inferential practices associated with it can in fact be seen as central to the accomplishment of order in many domains of language use and talk-in-interaction (see also Jayyusi, 1984; Silverman, 1998).

We have spent the last few pages illustrating some of the ways in which conversation analysts seek to go beyond what is seemingly obvious in talk-in-interaction to find its orderly properties. This way of looking (the conversation analytic mentality) is fundamentally influenced by Sacks' brilliant lectures, which for the first time revealed the dimensions of order that could be found at all points in human conversation.

It is important to stress, however, that while Sacks was an important founding figure, and during his lifetime the intellectual core of the developing subdiscipline of CA, by its very nature CA transcends the achievements and ideas of one person. Although the inception and, to some extent, the widespread adoption of the conversation analytic perspective owed much to his individually brilliant cast of mind, Sacks' way of working resulted in the development of a distinctive method which could be employed by others. Indeed, our primary aim in writing this book is to introduce that method to a still wider audience. At the same time, that method allows the production of a cumulative body of findings, and therefore CA can be accurately described as a research programme, whose aim is to describe the methodic bases of orderly communication in talk-in-interaction.

That research programme is by its very nature interdisciplinary. As Schegloff (1991: 46) has remarked, 'If it is not a distinctive discipline of its own (which it may well turn out to be), CA is at a point where linguistics and sociology (and several other disciplines, anthropology and psychology among them) meet.' From linguistics CA takes the view that language is a structured system for the production of meaning. But in line with certain subfields of linguistics such as pragmatics, CA views language primarily as a vehicle for communicative interaction. And, in line with other developments in sociology (Knorr-Cetina and Cicourel, 1981; Giddens, 1984; Thompson, 1984), CA sees both communication and interaction as inherently social processes, which are deeply involved in the production and maintenance of social institutions of all kinds, from everyday intersubjectivity, to the family, to the nation state. As the chapters of this book proceed, those interdisciplinary relevancies and relationships will become clearer as they inform our discussions of methodological and applied aspects of CA, including discussions of its relationship with the key disciplines of sociology, linguistics and psychology.

# 2

# Conversational Structures: The Foundations of Conversation Analysis

At the heart of CA is a concern with the nature of turn-taking in talk-in-interaction: how is it organized, how do participants accomplish orderly (or even apparently disorderly) turn-taking, and what are the systematic resources which are used in this accomplishment? We will refer to this as a concern with the *sequential order* of talk. It is intuitively evident that conversation, and other forms of talk-in-interaction, centrally involve people taking turns at talking. But a key notion in CA is that those turns are not just serially ordered (that is, coming one after the other); they are sequentially ordered, which is to say that there are describable ways in which turns are linked together into definite sequences. One aim of CA therefore is to reveal this sequential order.

Conversation analysts treat the transitions between turns during talk-in-interaction as revealing two kinds of things. First of all, the 'next turn' is the place where speakers display their understanding of the prior turn's possible completion. That is, it displays the results of an analysis that the next speaker has performed on the type of utterance the prior speaker has produced. Recall our discussion in the previous chapter about the importance of the next-turn proof procedure as a means of gaining an analytic foothold in the order of talk from the participants' perspective. Another aspect of this is that the relationship between turns reveals how the participants themselves actively analyse the ongoing production of talk in order to negotiate their own, situated participation in it. Moreover, a second important dimension revealed in speakers' next turns is their analysis and understanding of the action the prior turn has been designed to do.

For this reason, there is an additional emphasis on what we will call the *inferential* order of talk: the kinds of cultural and interpretive resources participants rely on in order to understand one another in appropriate ways. It is here that the continuing influence of ethnomethodology, with its emphasis on methods of practical reasoning about social relations, can be located. However, a distinctive feature of CA is its position that the sequential and the inferential orders in talk-in-interaction are in fact two sides of the same coin. That is, participants can utilize the sequential ordering of a turn – its place in an unfolding sequence – as a key resource in determining what kind of action its producer is engaged in.

A third crucial dimension that emerges from CA's emphasis on turn-taking is that talk-in-interaction has a *temporal* order. That is, talk is produced in time, in a series of 'turn constructional units' out of which turns themselves are constructed. Meanwhile turns at talk act as the vehicles for actions – complaints, requests, offers, warnings, and so on. Conversational structures – the patterns and sequences that conversation analysts have revealed to be at work in the unfolding accomplishment and mutual recognition of actions in interaction – are the crux of this interplay between sequential, inferential and temporal orders in talk. Our aim in the present chapter is to illustrate that through a discussion of key analytic concepts and findings. We will focus on four areas that are of general relevance: adjacency and preference structures; the rules of turn-taking; the management of overlapping talk; and repair and correction in conversation.

## Conversational sequencing: adjacency pairs and 'preference'

One of the most noticeable things about conversation is that certain classes of utterances conventionally come in pairs. For instance, questions and answers; greetings and return-greetings; or invitations and acceptances/declinations. The properties of these 'paired action sequences' interested Sacks throughout his career. In the earliest lectures Sacks was beginning to examine the ways in which what he called 'tying rules' operate in order to link paired actions together. In the later lectures, especially those for Spring 1972 (Sacks, 1992, Vol. 2: 521–70), Sacks developed an extraordinarily detailed formal account of what, by that stage, he was calling adjacency pairs. Basically, these are pairs of utterances which are ordered, that is, there is a recognizable difference between first parts and second parts of the pair; and in which given first pair parts require particular second parts (or a particular range of seconds). In other words, an invitation is the first part of the 'invitation-response' adjacency pair, and we recognize that invitations should be followed by a specific range of responses: mainly, acceptances or declinations. An initial invitation should typically not be followed by an initial greeting, for instance.

These sequences are called adjacency pairs because, ideally, the two parts should be produced next to each other. The basic rule for adjacency pairs was formulated in this way in an early publication by Schegloff and Sacks (1973: 295):

> given the recognisable production of a first pair part, on its first possible completion its speaker should stop and a next speaker should start and produce a second pair part from the pair type the first is recognisably a member of.

But although the term 'adjacency' is used, there is no absolute requirement for the parts of adjacency pairs to be strictly adjacent in all cases. There are systematic insertions that can legitimately come between first and second pair parts (see below). The point, however, is that some classes of utterances are conventionally paired such that, on the production of a first pair part, the second part becomes relevant and remains so even if it is not produced in the next serial turn. This brings in the key point that there is a difference between the serial nature of talk-in-interaction and its sequential properties. The next turn in an adjacency pair *sequence* is a relevant second pair part. But that need not be the next turn in the *series* of turns making up some particular conversation.

For instance, the following is a simple example of an insertion sequence (Schegloff, 1968):

**(1) [Levinson, 1983: 304]**

| 1 | A: | Can I have a bottle of Mich? | **Q1** |
| 2 | B: | Are you over twenty-one? | **Ins 1** |
| 3 | A: | No. | **Ins 2** |
| 4 | B: | No. | **A1** |

Line 1 represents the first part of a question-answer adjacency pair. When it is complete, the speaker stops, and the next speaker starts in line 2. However, what he produces is not the second part of the pair but the first part of another pair: a question-answer pair produced as an insertion sequence. The reason it is an insertion is because the question in line 2 does not ignore or propose not to answer the question in line 1. Rather, it serves to defer the answer until further relevant information (in this case, whether speaker A is old enough to buy beer) has been obtained. As we see, speaker A orients to that deferral by answering the inserted question in line 3, rather than, for example, asking his initial question again or complaining that it has not been answered. Once the insertion sequence is completed, B shows that he is still orienting to the relevance of the original adjacency pair by moving on in line 4 to provide the relevant second part.

This example illustrates a further aspect of paired action sequences. Note that we referred to the participants 'orienting to' the relevance of adjacency pairs and insertion sequences. What this means is that they display to one another their understandings of what each utterance is aiming to accomplish. Thus, the adjacency pair concept is not simply to do with the bare fact that some utterances come in pairs. Rather, adjacency pairs have a fundamental significance for one of the most basic issues in CA: the question of how mutual understanding is accomplished and displayed in talk.

As Schegloff and Sacks (1973: 296) put it:

> What two utterances, produced by different speakers, can do that one utterance cannot do is: by an adjacently positioned second, a speaker can show that he understood what a prior aimed at, and that he is willing to go along with that. Also, by virtue of the occurrence of an adjacently produced second, the doer of a first can see that what he intended was indeed understood, and that it was or was not accepted. Also, of course, a second can assert his failure to understand, or disagreement, and, inspection of a second by a first can allow the first speaker to see that while the second thought he understood, indeed he misunderstood.

Participants, then, can use the adjacency pair mechanism to display to one another, and hence to the analyst also, their ongoing understanding and sense-making of one another's talk.

These observations throw up a complex set of issues around how conversation analysts approach the nature of turn-taking and intersubjectivity, and the importance of repair and correction in the management of talk-in-interaction. In later sections of this chapter, we discuss these issues at greater length. For the present, however, we will proceed to say some further things about adjacency pairs themselves and other kinds of inferential work that can be involved in their production.

It is important to emphasize that the adjacency pair concept is not intended to capture some empirical generalization, such as that in 85% of cases first parts are followed by second parts (Heritage, 1984a:

246–7). Rather, what is to be stressed is the normative character of adjacency pairs. That is to say, whatever utterance follows a first pair part will be monitored by the first speaker for whether, and how, it works as a relevant second part. Inferences can be drawn about the non-appearance of a second pair part: for instance, not returning a greeting may lead to the inference that the first greeter is being snubbed.

Thus, for sequences such as adjacency pairs, the robustness of the sequence can often be seen precisely in those cases where what is normatively expected to occur does not (for instance, a question does not get an answer). This is described under the heading of *conditional relevance* (Schegloff, 1968). What this means is that given the initial condition of a first pair part being uttered, the second part of that pair is then relevant; consequently, the absence of such a second part is a 'noticeable absence', and the speaker of the first part may infer a reason for that absence.

An example of noticeable absence in a question-answer sequence is the following:

**(2) [TW:M:38]**

```
1    Child:     Have to cut the:se Mummy.
2               (1.3)
3    Child:     Won't we Mummy.
4               (1.5)
5→   Child:     Won't we.
6    Mother:    Yes.
```

The child asks the mother to confirm her observation that they will 'Have to cut the:se' (line 3), then, getting no response in the 1.5-second pause in line 4, draws attention to that absence of an answer by repeating the question (line 5). After this repeat try, the mother answers.

Another example comes from an attempted greeting sequence:

**(3) [IH:FN]**

(Two colleagues pass in the corridor)

```
1    A:    [[Hello.
2    B:    [[°Hi° ((barely audible))
3          (Pause: B continues walking)
4→   A:    ((shouts)) HEllo!
```

A initiates a greeting in line 1; however, it turns out that B also produces a first greeting at exactly the same time (the simultaneity is represented by the double square brackets: see Chapter 3 for a detailed discussion of transcription conventions). As well as being produced simultaneously, however, B's greeting is enunciated so quietly as to be almost inaudible, and as a result that greeting was not heard by A. Hence, while B, having heard A's greeting and produced his own, believes that a greetings exchange has been accomplished and continues walking, A, who has not heard B's greeting, believes that her greeting has not been reciprocated. Thus we see that after a pause, and as B continues walking away down the corridor, A displays her perception of an absent second pair part by shouting out a second attempt to initiate greetings.

Adjacency pairs thus constitute a powerful normative framework for the assessment of interlocutors' actions and motives by producers of first parts. This shows that talk-in-interaction is not just a matter of taking turns but is a matter of accomplishing actions. Within this framework, failure (or perceived failure) to take a turn in the appropriate place can itself be interpreted as accomplishing some type of action. As Sacks (1992) remarked, one reason why talk-in-interaction is such a good place for observing members' methods of sense-making is because it systematically requires hearers to attend to what speakers are saying, and to come to some understanding of it. Close monitoring is needed to identify when an appropriate juncture to take a turn occurs; by the same token, failure to take a turn when one is 'required' to can be treated as an accountable action.

## 'Preference'

Another inferential aspect of adjacency pair sequences stems from the fact that certain first pair parts make alternative actions relevant in second position. Examples include offers, which can be accepted or refused; assessments, which can be agreed with or disagreed with; and requests, which can be granted or declined. Research has shown that these alternatives are non-equivalent. In other words, acceptances, agreements or grantings are produced in systematically different ways than their negative alternatives. These design differences are described in terms of a 'preference' organization. The format for agreements is labelled the 'preferred' action turn shape and the disagreement format is called the 'dispreferred' action turn shape (Pomerantz, 1984a: 64).

The concept of preference as it is used in CA is not primarily intended to refer to the psychological motives of individuals, but rather to structural features of the design of turns associated with particular activities, by which participants can draw conventionalized inferences about the kinds of action a turn is performing. One thing Sacks (1987) observed is that initial actions can be designed to invite a particular kind of response. For instance, the phrase 'isn't it?' might be appended to an assessment, thereby inviting the recipient's agreement. In such cases, as in the following two extracts, the default response gets produced straight away (without any gap) and without any mitigation:

**(4) [JS:II:28]**
```
1    Jo:    T's- it's a beautiful day out isn't it?
2→   Lee:   Yeh it's just gorgeous.
```

**(5) [VIYMC:1:2]**
```
1    Pat:   It's a really clear lake isn't it?
2→   Les:   It's wonderful.
```

By contrast, turns that in some way depart from what seems to be expected incorporate a variety of 'dispreference markers' (Pomerantz, 1984a). One of the most significant ways speakers have of indicating the dispreferred status of a turn is by starting the turn with markers such as 'Well,' or 'Um':

**(6) [Sacks, 1987: 58]**
```
1    A:    Yuh comin down early?
2→   B:    Well, I got a lot of things to do before gettin
3          cleared up tomorrow. I don't know. I w- probably
4          won't be too early.
```

As Sacks (1987) observes, A's first turn here appears to 'prefer' a 'Yes' answer. Note, for instance, that the opposite expectation would be conveyed by 'You're not coming down early are you?'. However, B evidently does not want to go along with the assumption implicit in A's turn. He constructs his response so that it exhibits two principal features of dispreferred turn-shapes. First, the response is 'formed up so that the disagreement is as weak as possible' (Sacks, 1987: 58). Notice in particular line 3, where 'I w-,' which looks like a start on 'I won't be too early,' is changed so that it takes the weaker form 'probably won't be too early.' Secondly, the disagreement is not produced early in the turn, like the agreements in extracts (4) and (5), but is held off until B has not only produced a 'Well,' but also has presented an account for why he won't be early (lines 2–3).

Thus, preferred actions are characteristically performed straightforwardly and without delay, while dispreferred actions are delayed, qualified and accounted for. As we mentioned above, the concept refers to these structural features of turn-design and not to individual motivations or psychological dispositions. The reasoning behind this is not to claim that such motivations play no part in adjacency pairs such as invitations and acceptances/declinations. Rather, it is to emphasize that the alternative designs of second-pair parts represent institutionalized ways of speaking by which specific actions get accomplished.

Research has additionally suggested that the design features of preferred and dispreferred responses can be used as a resource for the maintenance of social solidarity in talk-in-interaction. This is so not only in the way that dispreferred responses may be accompanied by accounts or explanations; but also in the way that hesitations and other means of marking a dispreferred response can provide a source for a first speaker to revise the original first pair-part in such a way as to try and avoid disagreement or rejection (Davidson, 1984). This happens in the following extract, where Edna, hearing that Nancy may be about to turn down her invitation to come over for lunch, issues a candidate reason for Nancy to decline the invitation (line 4):

**(7) [NB:II:2:4]**

```
1     Edna:       Wanna come down an' have a bite a' lunch with
2                 me:?=I got some bee:r en stu:ff,
3                 (0.2)
4     Nancy:      Well yer real sweet hon:, uh::m (.) [let- I hav-
5→    Edna:                                          [Or do yuh have
6                 sum'pn el[se t-
7     Nancy:               [No: I have to uh call Bob's mother.
8                 .h I told 'er I:'d ca:ll 'er this morning.
```

Nancy's response in line 4 to Edna's first pair part (an invitation) in lines 1–2 has the characteristic features of a dispreferred turn-shape. It is preceded by a small pause, then the turn is begun with 'Well', followed by an appreciation of the invitation, followed by 'uh::m' and another slight gap. In other words, the response itself is considerably delayed. As Nancy begins on the response itself ('let- I hav-' being hearable as a start on 'I have to uh call Bob's mother', which is produced in line 7), Edna herself starts on a turn which displays her orientation to the declination work that the dispreferred turn is doing. Her 'Or do yuh have sum'pn else' in line 5 offers Nancy a way out of the invitation even before Nancy has actually stated that she cannot accept.

These points bring out again the centrality, for CA, of the inferential properties associated with speakers' moves in interaction sequences. They also address the ways that those inferences have a distinctly moral, or evaluative, dimension. Speakers can be seen not only to be establishing and maintaining mutual understanding of one another's actions in sequences of talk, but also to be holding each other accountable for those actions. In this sense the adjacency pair framework, and the preference organization that operates for some types of adjacency pair, constitute an important site in which to observe the relationships between patterns of language use and structures of social action.

In the following sections we continue to explore the basic findings of CA, this time bringing in the concern with temporal properties of talk by means of a general account of the core issue of turn-taking.

## The organization of turn-taking

In 1974 Sacks, along with co-authors Emanuel Schegloff and Gail Jefferson, published 'A simplest systematics for the organization of turn-taking for conversation' (Sacks et al., 1974). Published in the highly regarded journal *Language*, this paper has become a foundational study in conversation analysis. In it, the authors outline a model for describing how speakers manage turn-taking in ordinary conversation. A central aim of the paper is to provide a technical description of the structural characteristics of ordinary conversation as a specific type of 'speech exchange system'; that is, as a system of conventions regulating the exchange of turns and management of speaker roles among participants. As we show in Chapter 6, this approach can also be used to describe speech exchange systems that are very different from ordinary conversation: specialized, formalized or ceremonial forms of talk ranging from loosely structured interviews between doctors and their patients, to high ceremonies such as speeches or even weddings.

The turn-taking model developed in Sacks et al. (1974) begins from the idea that turns in conversation are resources which, like goods in an economy, are distributed in systematic ways among speakers. The authors note three very basic facts about conversation: (1) turn-taking occurs, (2) one speaker tends to talk at a time, and (3) turns are taken with as little gap or overlap between them as possible. This is not to say that there is never more than one speaker talking at a time, or that gaps and overlaps do not occur. Clearly such things do take place. The point is that the ideal, in conversation, is for as much inter-speaker coordination as possible. But that is not just an abstract ideal. In empirical materials, we do find that overwhelmingly, speaker change occurs with minimal gap and overlap, indicating that participants themselves orient to the ideal for coordination.

The turn-taking model has two components: a 'turn-construction' component and a 'turn-distribution' component. Turns at talk can be seen as constructed out of units, called turn-construction units (TCUs), which broadly correspond to linguistic categories such as sentences, clauses, single words (for instance, 'Hey!' or 'What?') or phrases. It is important to realize that it is not part of the conversation analyst's aim to define, in some abstract way, what a turn-construction unit is, as a linguist for instance may want to define what a sentence is. Conversation analysts cannot take a prescriptive stance on this question, because what a turn-construction unit consists of in any situated stretch of talk is a members' problem. That is, such a unit is essentially anything out of which a legitimate turn has recognizably – for the participants – been built.

This suggests two key features of turn-construction units. First, they have the property of 'projectability'. That is, it is possible for participants to project, in the course of a turn-construction unit, what sort of unit it is and at what point it is likely to end. This leads to the second feature, which is that turn-construction units bring into play 'transition-relevance places' at their boundaries. In other words, at the end of each unit, there is the possibility for legitimate transition between speakers. These two properties can be illustrated with the following extract:

**(8) [SBL: 1:1:10:15]**

```
1    Rose:     Why don't you come and see me some[times
2    Bea:                                        [I would
3              like to
4    Rose:     I would like you to
```

The second speaker here is able to recognize Rose's utterance, 'Why don't you come and see me sometimes', as a form of invitation, and to respond to it with an acceptance before it has actually finished (line 2). This is indicated in the transcript by the square bracket which shows that Bea's turn 'I would like to' overlaps Rose's talk in the middle of 'sometimes'.

One point to note is that although Bea's projection of the first turn's transition-relevance place – that is, after 'sometimes' – turns out to be accurate (as shown in Rose's following turn, 'I would like you to'), the turn could have taken a different shape. For instance, Rose could have been about to say 'Why don't you come and see me sometime this week', which would have made the invitation much more specific, and Bea may then have had to give a different response. By starting to talk when she does, therefore, Bea not only projects the end of a particular turn-construction unit, but also displays an understanding of what kind of invitation that unit represents. Recall, on this point, our remarks in the previous chapter about the next turn proof procedure as a means of gaining analytic access to participants' understandings of each other's talk.

But what would have happened if Rose had in fact been about to append something further, such as 'this week', to her invitation? This leads us to the second part of the turn-taking model: the mechanism for distributing turns between participants. Sacks et al. (1974) propose a simple set of rules which describe how turns come to be allocated at transition-relevance places. There are two main rules, with the first one being subdivided into three:

At the initial transition-relevance place of a turn:

*Rule 1*     (a) If the current speaker has identified, or selected, a particular next speaker, then that speaker should take a turn at that place.

          (b) If no such selection has been made, then any next speaker may (but need not) self-select at that point. If self-selection occurs, then first speaker has the right to the turn.

          (c) If no next speaker has been selected, then alternatively the current speaker may, but need not, continue talking with another turn-constructional unit, unless another speaker has self-selected, in which case that speaker gains the right to the turn.

*Rule 2*     Whichever option has operated, then rules 1(a)–(c) come into play again for the next transition-relevance place.

This set of rules is simple, but deceptively so, since it is able to account for the vast range of turn-taking practices in conversations involving any number of participants, in any set of relationships, speaking in whatever context and with whatever topics in play. In a series of early papers, conversation analysts explored the robustness as well as the interactional implications of this rule-set (Jefferson, 1973; Schegloff and Sacks, 1973; Schegloff, Jefferson and Sacks, 1977; Schegloff, 1982; see also Schegloff, 1992b). The main point that these papers sought to demonstrate was that the rule-set operates as an oriented-to set of normative practices which members use to accomplish orderly turn-taking.

The fact that it is oriented to, and thus normative, is crucial here. It is not being proposed that these rules are in some sense external to any concrete occasion of talk, nor that they furnish law-like constraints on participants. Rather, the rules are intended as descriptions of the practices which participants display an orientation to in actual, local occasions of turn-taking. Although different from the rules of syntax, which linguists have described as underpinning meaningful sentences in any given language, one similarity is that, like syntactic rules, it is not necessary for speakers to 'know' the turn-taking rules in any discursive sense. It is more accurate to say that they are learned and tacitly known, instantiated and therefore reproduced on each concrete occasion of talk-in-interaction.

There are a number of types of evidence which demonstrate that participants actively orient to the rule-set described by Sacks et al. (1974), and we will come to these presently. First, let us return to our hypothetical question about extract (8): what if Rose had not actually been about to finish her turn at the point when Bea projected its completion? Would Bea's turn then have been a 'violation' of the rules?

On one level, it should be clear that the answer is no. Bea projected a transition-relevance place at the end of what was a possibly complete turn-construction unit by Rose: the question, 'Why don't you some and see me sometimes?' As we have said, neither the rule-set nor CA itself goes about prescribing and predicting what turn-construction units can legitimately consist of. This is an issue for the participants in conversation, not the conversation analyst. So Bea acted entirely within the rules – or, to be more accurate, her behaviour shows her orienting to the rules: in particular, rule 1(b) as outlined above.

Even if her projection of a transition-relevance place had turned out to be inaccurate, that would not matter in terms of the rules for turn-taking, since as Schegloff (1992b) points out, participants orient to *possible* transition-relevance places, not to 'actual' ones. There are good organizational reasons for this. Given that the ideal in conversation is for one speaker to talk at a time with as little gap and overlap as possible between turns, speakers need to coordinate their bid for a turn as closely as possible with the completion of a current speaker's turn-construction unit. If they were to wait for the speaker actually to stop speaking, that would mean they may lose the opportunity of a turn to someone else, or else the current speaker may carry on with another unit. For this reason it is the possibility of completion, rather than its actual occurrence, that is the most relevant factor in managing turn-taking. If this were not the case, as Schegloff remarks, then we would expect to see gaps of silence between turns as next speakers made sure that the current speaker had actually finished. This is not what we tend to find in empirical materials.

This brings us back to the key idea of the temporal unfolding of talk-in-interaction. Looking at how this simple extract unfolds in time as it occurs between the participants, we begin to see the close relationship between the temporal, sequential, and inferential orders outlined at the start of the chapter. By 'inferential order', it will be recalled we mean the sense in which turns are vehicles for doing social actions, actions whose nature and import have to be worked out in the real-time unfolding of a turn by its recipient. Thus, Bea makes a *judgement* as to the type

of action Rose's turn is accomplishing at the particular point she elects
to start a turn of her own. We have seen that that is a legitimate point
in terms of the turn-taking system (a transition-relevance place), but in
terms of the temporal unfolding of the turn it is slightly pre-emptive:
there has been no moment of silence in between which might serve as a
more certain indication that Rose's action (the invitation to 'come and
see me sometimes') is complete. As time unfolded, a different action
could in fact have emerged ('come and see me sometime this week',
'come and see me sometime this afternoon'), and this would have had
implications for the sequence.

An important thing to note here is that this means that the question
of whether Bea's turn would, in the latter set of circumstances, have
been considered a violation of turn-taking rules would be an issue that
was worked out by the participants themselves, on that occasion of talk.
In other words, it would have been up to Rose, as the continuing
speaker, to indicate to Bea that her turn was in some way 'interruptive'
of Rose's unfinished talk. Of course, this kind of thing frequently
happens, as illustrated by the following extract, which is taken from a
discussion on a talk radio show about the problem of dogs fouling
public walkways:

**(9) [H:2.2.89:4:1–2]**

```
1   Host:      Well did you- did you then explain that, you
2              understood that, you know dogs have the call of
3              nature just as er as people do, and they don't
4              have the same kind of control and so
5              the[refore, s- so
6   Caller:       [No, but dogs can be tr[ained
7   Host:                                 [I haven't finished,
8              so therefore the owner . . . being there has the
9              responsibility . . .
```

In line 7, the host treats the caller's utterance as an interruption, by
saying 'I haven't finished', and then carrying on with his point about
dog owners being responsible. Thus, he treats her as having vio-
lated turn-taking rules by not orienting to the completion of his turn.
Looking more closely, however, we see evidence that temporal unfolding of talk plays an important role in the development of this sequence.
The caller does, in fact, orient to a possible completion point in the
host's turn: i.e., after 'dogs have the call of nature just as er as people
do, and they don't have the same kind of control', at which point she
comes in with her argument: 'No but dogs can be trained'. However, the
host knows that before the caller actually starts talking he has begun on

a next turn-construction unit of his own: 'and so therefore . . .' (lines 4–5). So what we find in this extract is both speakers orienting to different aspects of the rule-set. The caller orients to rule 1(b): at a (possible) transition-relevance place a next speaker may self-select; while the host orients to 1(c): at a (possible) transition-relevance place the current speaker may continue talking, unless another has self-selected. Here, although the caller has self-selected, she does so too late in the temporal unfolding of the sequence; the host therefore treats himself as the first starter on the next unit, and hence as having rights to the turn.

Clearly, then, the issue of how the rules operate in the temporal unfolding of talk-in-interaction is a matter for the participants. It is in this sense that our preceding comments about the rules being oriented to by members rather than invisibly 'driving' members' actions is to be understood. In fact, a great deal of work on apparent violations of the rule-set demonstrates how those apparent violations are actually robust illustrations of how closely members do orient to the rules. We will discuss two areas of this work: overlap and repair.

## Orienting to turn-taking rules: overlapping talk

On the face of it, overlapping talk may be considered evidence of an incoming speaker's failure to take notice of whether the current speaker is or is not finished. However, conversation analysts have shown that most instances of overlap occur in the environment of possible transition-relevance places (Jefferson, 1983, 1986; Schegloff, 2000). While it may seem that overlapping talk is disorderly, Jefferson's work in particular has emphasized that both the onset and the termination of overlap are indeed extremely orderly. In fact, the occurrence of overlap is one prime way in which we can observe participants orienting to the rules of turn-taking that Sacks, Schegloff and Jefferson (1974) outlined.

Consider the following extract, which comes from the beginning of a telephone conversation.

**(10) [NB:II:2:1–2]**

```
1    N:    Hello:,
2    E:    .hh HI::.
3          (.)
4    N:    Oh hi:::='Ow are you Edna,
5    E:    FI:NE yer LINE'S BEEN BUSY.
6    N:    Yeah (.) my u-fuhh! h- .hhhh my fa:ther's wife
7          ca:lled me,h .hhh So when she calls me::, h I
8          always talk for a lo:ng ti:me cuz she can afford it
```

```
9          an' I ca:n't.hhh[hhhhh[huh]
10   E:             [↑OH::[ ::: ]: my [go:sh=Ah↑th]aght=
11   N:                         [ ↑AOO::::hh! ]((falsetto))
12   E:    =my phone was outta order:
13         (0.2)
14   N:    n[:No::?
15   E:     [I called my sister an' I get this busy en then I'd
16         hang up en I'd lift it up again it'd be: busy.
17         (0.9)
18   E:    .hh How you doin'.
19   N:    .t hhh Pretty good I gutta rai:se.h .hh[hh
20   E:                                          [Goo:[ud.
21   N:                                               [Yeh
22         two dollars a week.h
23         (.)
24   E:    Oh wo:w.
```

There are a number of overlaps here; they are indicated using the standard convention of a left-hand square bracket (for other conventions
used here see the Transcription Glossary, and Chapter 3). We can
describe each of them as orderly, and as displaying the participants' orientation to possible transition-relevance places as the points where they
may start a turn. For instance, in line 9, what Edna's extended 'OH::::'
overlaps is a quiet laugh, 'hhh hhh huh', which Nancy fits onto the end
of her turn: 'So when she calls me::, h I always talk fer a lo:ng ti:me cuz
she c'n afford it en I ca:n't'. Thus 'OH' starts at a legitimate transition-
relevance place, even though that start up results in overlap. Another
example is at line 21. Here, what Nancy's talk overlaps is the last
phoneme of a recognizable turn-construction unit: 'Goo:ud', which
Edna has produced in response to Nancy's announcement, 'I gutta
rai:se'.

Other instances appear more complex, but can still be accounted for
as orderly. In line 11, what we have transcribed as 'AOO:::::hh!
((falsetto))' by Nancy is in fact a high-pitched laugh, or hoot, which
seems to be produced in overlap with – but before the recognizable
completion of – Edna's remark that she thought her phone was out of
order (since she had tried numerous times to get through and failed).
However, looking more closely at the sequential context, we find that
Nancy begins to laugh at a possible transition-relevance place. In the
prior turn, Nancy had made a joke about talking on the phone for a
long time when her father's wife calls, 'cuz she c'n afford it en I ca:n't'.
She then begins quietly to laugh (indicated by the rows of 'h's). Edna's
turn is begun with a loud, and high-pitched 'OH::::: my go:sh', to

which Nancy almost immediately responds with her similarly high-
pitched 'AOO:::::hh!' It is quite possible that Nancy at this point treats
Edna as responding to her joke, and starts to laugh by reference to
'OH::::: my go:sh' as a recognizable, and potentially complete, joke-
response.

Now it turns out, as we see, that Edna carries on with her turn:
'OH::::: my go:sh=Ah thaght my phone was outta order'. Yet the
overlap caused by Nancy can be seen as the product of her orienting to
the first possible completion point in that turn. In this way, even apparently 'disorderly' talk can be seen as the product of participants' orientations to the rule-set.

In a large-scale study of overlap in conversation, Jefferson (1986)
found that enormous amounts of overlapping talk could be accounted
for in this sort of way. She identified three major categories of overlap
onset: (1) Transitional onset (when a next speaker orients to a possible
transition-relevance place); (2) Recognitional onset (when the next
speaker feels they recognize what current speaker is saying and can
project its completion, even if that is before the end of a turn-construction unit); and (3) Progressional onset (when there is some dis-
fluency in the current turn and a next speaker suggests a completion in
order to move the conversation forward). These categories can be used
to account for the orderly production of overlapping talk, even when
it is apparently interruptive.

For instance, to return to extract (9):

**(9) [H:2.2.89:4:1–2]**

```
1    Host:      Well did you- did you then explain that, you
2               understood that, you know dogs have the call of
3               nature just as er as people do, and they don't
4               have the same kind of control and so
5               the[refore, s- so
6    Caller:       [No, but dogs can be tr[ained
7    Host:                                 [I haven't finished,
8               so therefore the owner . . . being there has the
9               responsibility . . .
```

The caller's overlapping turn in line 6 can be described as an instance
of the first category, transitional onset. As we remarked earlier, although
the host treats this as an interruption, it is equally possible that the caller
has identified and oriented to a possible completion point, a transition-
relevance place, in the current turn.

Jefferson (1983: 6) comments as follows about transitional overlap
onset:

[A]t the point of overlap onset the recipient/now-starting next speaker is doing something perfectly proper, perfectly within his rights and obligations as a recipient/next speaker. He is not doing what we commonly understand to be 'interrupting' – roughly, starting up 'in the midst of' another's turn at talk, not letting the other finish. On the other hand, the current speaker is also doing something perfectly proper. He is producing a single turn at talk which happens to have multiple components in it.

Our extract shows something further: namely that while transitional onset may be a perfectly orderly place for overlap to occur, it may also systematically be open to being treated as 'interruptive' by the current speaker. We return to the issue of interruption as part of our discussion in Chapter 4. For now, the point is that overlapping and apparently interruptive talk, far from being a violation of the rules for turn-taking, actually displays how closely participants orient to the rules; indeed, it can be an outcome of such close orientation.

## Repair

Related to this discussion of overlap is the broader area of 'repair'. This is a generic term which is used in CA to cover a wide range of phenomena, from seeming errors in turn-taking such as those involved in much overlapping talk, to any of the forms of what we commonly would call 'correction' – i.e., substantive faults in the contents of what someone has said. The term repair is used in the first sense because one way of seeing what is going on is in terms of a 'repair of the turn-taking system'. In the second sense, the term repair is used in preference to alternatives such as correction, because as Schegloff, Jefferson and Sacks (1977) point out, not all conversational repair actually involves any factual error on the speaker's part. In this second sense, repair involves the suspension of ongoing turns or sequences in order to attend to some trouble that has become apparent. We return to this aspect of repair in the following section.

The area of repair has generated a large amount of work in CA (to take a few examples, Jefferson, 1972, 1987; Schegloff, 1979a, 1987a, 1992c; Schegloff et al., 1977). As with overlap, one of the thrusts of this work has been to show how repair illustrates participants' orientations to the basic turn-taking rules. There are two main ways in which this is done. First, as Sacks et al. (1974) noted, the turn-taking system itself incorporates its own means of repairing faults. That is, in cases of overlapping talk there is a violation of the 'one speaker at a time' ideal. But this is repaired by a practice that is itself 'a transformation of a central feature of the turn-taking system' (Sacks et al., 1974: 724): namely, one speaker tends to stop speaking before the completion of a first turn-construction unit. Following are some examples of this.

**(11) [SBL:2:2:3:38]**

| 1 | Zoe: | an' he sorta scares me |
|---|------|---|
| 2 | Amy: | Have you seen 'im? |
| 3 | Zoe: | .hhh We:ll I(m) I've met 'im, |
| 4→ | Amy: | .hhhhh Well uh actually: [when she's- |
| 5→ | Zoe: |                            [An' the way the:y |
| 6 |  | pla:y. Oh:- |
| 7 |  | (.) |
| 8 | Amy: | Serious huh? |
| 9 | Zoe: | .h Yah, |

**(12) [TRIO:2:III:1]**

| 1 | Marjorie: | We:ll? She doesn't kno:w. .uhhh: |
| 2 |  | huhh [huh-huhh-huh-huh-heh-heh] |
| 3 | Loretta: |       [O h h   m h y   G h o : d, ] |
| 4→ | Marjorie: | hhhhh Well it [was an- |
| 5→ | Loretta: |                      [Are you watching Daktari:? |
| 6 |  | (0.2) |
| 7 | Marjorie: | nNo:, |
| 8 |  | (.) |
| 9 | Loretta: | Oh my go:sh Officer Henry is (.) ul-locked in |
| 10 |  | the ca:ge wi- (0.3) with a lion. |

**(13) [SBL:2:2:3:42–3]**

| 1 | Amy: | So: uh:::::: she said [don't worry about i:t= |
| 2 | Zoe: |                        [Mm hm. |
| 3 | Amy: | =an:d so an' I jus' thought .hh the nex' ti::me |
| 4→ |  | uh that [I have- |
| 5→ | Zoe: |           [No:w uh see Pat anno:ys my Frank. hh |
| 6 |  | (0.3) |
| 7 | Amy: | Ye:ah. |
| 8 |  | (0.2) |
| 9 | Zoe: | Uh he:'s told me that. |

In each of these three extracts, as seems generally to be the case, the current speaker abandons their turn very shortly after the onset of overlap (line 4 in each of the extracts). In the first two cases, there are different aspects of the turn-taking system that are being oriented to by these speakers as they drop out. In extract (11), Zoe and Amy are talking about a couple they know who play recreational bridge in a particularly aggressive manner. Zoe's turn in line 5 seems to be a continuation of her previous utterance (line 3), marked here by the use of 'And';

i.e., 'I've met 'im . . . An' the <u>way</u> they pla:y . . .'. In between these components, Amy has taken the opportunity to start a turn of her own (line 4), which she abandons two words into the overlap, without having come to the end of a recognizable turn-construction unit.

Extract (12) is taken from a return telephone call in which the caller, Marjorie, is calling back to report on a conversation she has just had with a mutual acquaintance. Apparently, as she answers the phone, Loretta is watching *Daktari* (a popular 1960s show) on TV. So while Marjorie takes Loretta's '<u>O</u>hh my <u>Gho</u>:d' (line 3) to be a response to her own initial announcement that the third party 'doesn't know', and continues to talk by reference to that, in fact this is Loretta's reaction to a dramatic event that is happening in the TV show ('Officer <u>H</u>enry is (.) ul- l<u>o</u>cked in the ca:ge wi- (0.3) with a l<u>i</u>on' – line 9–10). Again, although the two speakers' talk here is disjunctive, Marjorie repairs that disjunction by abandoning her turn two words into the overlap (line 4), giving the floor to Loretta.

Extract (13), however, seems to be much more clearly 'interruptive'. Taken from later in the same call as extract (11), here Amy and Zoe are talking about another couple they play bridge with. At the point Zoe overlaps Amy with her remark that '<u>Pat</u> an<u>no</u>:ys <u>my</u> Frank' (line 5), it is not at all clear what Amy is going on to say about 'the nex' ti::me u-that I have . . .'. So this is not a case of recognitional or transitional overlap, to go back to Jefferson's (1983) categories. Neither has there been any immediately prior disjunction in the speakers' topics, as in extract (12); nor is Zoe's utterance a continuation of a previous turn, as in (11). Rather, what it seems she is doing is 'interrupting' in order to empathize with Amy's complaints about 'Pat', who, as she says, also annoys her husband Frank. (For more on various different types of interruption, see Goldberg, 1990.)

One form of repair, then, is a procedural type in which participants orient to various aspects of their ongoing talk in order to manage turn-taking problems. The point Sacks et al. (1974) stress is that in their management of these problems, participants display their continuing orientation to the turn-taking rule set.

## The sequential organization of repair

The bulk of the literature on conversational repair has actually been directed towards the second sense of repair we introduced above: repair which involves the temporary suspension of a turn or sequence in progress in order to attend to an emergent trouble of some kind. As we will see, the kinds of trouble that are oriented to vary widely and are not restricted simply to errors of fact, logic, or correctness.

Schegloff, Jefferson and Sacks (1977) foreground an important distinction between the initiation of repair (marking something as a source of trouble), and the actual repair itself. There is also a distinction between repair initiated by self (the speaker who produced the trouble source), and repair initiated by other. Consequently, as they outline, there are four varieties of repair sequences:

- Self-initiated self-repair: Repair is both initiated and carried out by the speaker of the trouble source.
- Other-initiated self-repair: Repair is carried out by speaker of the trouble source but initiated by the recipient.
- Self-initiated other-repair: The speaker of a trouble source may try and get the recipient to repair the trouble – for instance if a name is proving troublesome to remember.
- Other-initiated other-repair: The recipient of a trouble-source turn both initiates and carries out the repair. This is closest to what is conventionally understood as 'correction'.

Let us briefly illustrate each of these types by reference to empirical data. First, self-initiated self-repair.

**(14) [Heritage I:II:1]**
1    I:      Is it flu: you've got?
2→  N:     No I don't think- I refuse to have all the:se things

Here speaker N starts to produce an answer to a question ('No I don't think-') and then terminates that in mid-production to make a claim about her general attitude to minor illnesses ('I refuse to have all the:se things'). Extract (15), from a call to a flight information service, provides an example of self-initiated self-repair on an incorrect word selection (C's cut-off 'ga(t)-'):

**(15) [T1:SA:F:F]**
1    A:      er heathrow or gatwi[:ck,
2→  C:                            [oh sorry er: from ga(t)-
3            er heathrow.

Extract (16) is an example of other-initiated self-repair:

**(16) [GTS:5:3]**
1    Ken:         Is Al here today?
2    Dan:         Yeah.

```
3              (2.0)
4→   Roger:    he is? hh eh heh
5    Dan:      Well he was.
```

Roger's turn 'he is? hh eh heh' is an example of what is called a Next Turn Repair Initiator (NTRI). Other NTRIs may be words like 'what?' or 'huh?', or even non-verbal gestures, such as a quizzical look. NTRIs perform several tasks in interaction. Consider the following extracts, in which NTRIs take the form of partial repeats of the prior turn.

**(17) [GTS:III42(r)ST]**
```
1    A:    Hey (.) the first ti:me they stopped me from selling
2          cigarettes was this morning.
3          (1.0)
4→   B:    From selling cigarettes?
5    A:    Or buying cigarettes.
```

**(18) [GTS:II:2:54]**
```
1    K:    'E likes that waider over there,
2→   A:    Wait-er?
3    K:    Waitress, sorry,
4    A:    'Ats bedder,
```

In both cases, it transpires that the first speaker has made the kind of error which, in lay terms, would be characterized as a 'slip of the tongue'. However, the co-participants do not simply produce the correct name or noun. Nor do they explicitly announce that a mistake has been made. They provide a partial repeat of the prior turn and thereby recycle the trouble source. On an inspection of this turn the first speaker can infer that there was a problem connected to their earlier utterance, and the partial repeat of that earlier turn identifies the precise source of the trouble. Furthermore, as a trouble source has been identified but not repaired, speakers can analyse the NTRI as establishing the relevance of self-repair.

Extract (19) illustrates self-initiated other-repair: the first speaker's reference to his trouble remembering someone's name initiates the second speaker's repair.

**(19) [BC:Green:88]**
```
1→   B:    He had dis uh Mistuh W-m whatever k- I can't
2→         think of his first name, Watts on, the one that
3          wrote [that piece
4    A:          [Dan Watts.
```

Finally, we may consider other-initiated other-repair. In both the following extracts there is an explicit correction which is then acknowledged and accepted in the subsequent turn.

**(20) [GJ:FN]**

```
1    Milly:     . . . and then they said something about Kruschev has
2               leukemia so I thought oh it's all a big put on.
3→   Jean:      Breshnev.
4    Milly:     Breshnev has leukemia. So I don't know what to
5               think.
```

**(21) [T2:SA:F:M]**

```
1    C:     erm I'm just checking is that (.)
2           right you know (0.5) I d- I don't know
3           his flight number and [I'm not sure
4    A:                            [(whi-)
5    C:     whether he's coming in to channel four
6           eh:
7           (.)
8→   A:     terminal four
9    C:     yeah
```

Other-initiated other-repair does three tasks: it assigns the trouble source to the prior turn, thereby exposing it; it locates the source of trouble, and it locates and resolves trouble in one turn. It is the repair type which most explicitly raises the speaker's 'error'.

## Repair positions

Repair is bound up with the temporal organization of talk-in-interaction. That is, in the unfolding production of a turn by means of its turn-construction units, there are a number of different structural positions in which a repair initiation may occur in relation to the trouble source or repairable item. The first two places in which repair can occur are within, or immediately after, the turn construction unit containing the trouble source.

**(22) [T1:SA:F:F]**

```
1→   A:     .h >Well< >yu've< actually wro(t)-
2           rung the wrong number
```

In this extract the trouble source is an incorrect word which is abandoned mid-way through its production and replaced with the correct item ('wro(t)' to 'rung'). Here, therefore, self-repair is initiated before the end of the turn's first turn-construction unit.

The second place in which repair can be done occurs immediately at the next transition relevance place after the trouble source. In the following extract the trouble source (line 8) is 'another address', and this is repaired with 'another telephone number' precisely at the start of the next turn-construction unit following that containing the error.

```
(23) [Heritage I:Call 6:1]
1    Mrs. H.  Uh:m I: wanted to know if it were at all
2             possible to make an appointment,h .hh uh:::
3             with Mister Andrews.=
4    E:       =.t Oh dear uh::m .hhh yes ih-it's his father
5             talki:ng?
6    Mrs. H:  Ah ha:h?=
7    E:       =Uh::m:, (.) .t in fact he now has his clinic
8→            at another addr:ess. Another, another telephone
9             number I'm sorry:,
```

This kind of 'second position' repair can also be initiated and executed in the turn following the turn containing the trouble source, that is, in a next speaker's subsequent turn:

```
(24) [Heritage:II:I:call 3:1]
1    S:   Mister Samson's house? c'n [ I help you?]
2    I:                              [ H e l l o: ]
3    I:   Mister Samson?
4→   S:   It's not M'st Samson it's his assist'n can I help you.
```

The trouble source here is I's apparent belief that he is talking to 'Mister Samson' (line 3) when in fact, as S indicates by initiating and carrying out repair in his next turn (line 4), 'it's his assist'n'.

Schegloff (1992c) has argued that the majority of troubles are identified and dealt with within these structural repair positions: that is, during the TCU containing the trouble source, in the next TCU immediately following that containing the trouble source, and in the next turn following the turn containing the trouble source. Moreover, each of these types of repair can be initiated either by self or by other; though in the first type of position, other-initiated repair would involve the other speaker potentially being held to account for interrupting the current speaker.

In other circumstances, however, there are problems which require a repair 'after the next turn'. This situation arises when one person has not understood what their co-interactant has said, yet that misunderstanding does not become immediately clear. Schegloff (1992c) cites the following case involving two office colleagues as an instance.

**(25) [From Schegloff, 1992c: 1321]**

| 1 | M: | Loes, do you have a calendar, |
|---|----|---|
| 2 | L: | Yeah ((reaches for her desk calendar)) |
| 3 | M: | Do you have one that hangs on the wall? |
| 4→ | L: | Oh you <u>want</u> one. |
| 5 | M: | Yeah |

In this case the utterance 'Loes, do you have a calendar,' turns out to be problematic because of its ambiguity: it could be interpreted as a request for a calendar to keep, or a request to see a calendar to check some specific information. The recipient makes the latter interpretation, displayed by her movement towards a desk calendar. M's subsequent turn 'Do you have one that hangs on the wall?' establishes that he wants a calendar to keep. The trouble source (L's misunderstanding of 'do you have a calendar?') is acknowledged and resolved in the fourth turn. The repair itself is marked, as are many of these 'repairs after next turn', by the use of 'Oh': a change-of-state marker (Heritage, 1984b) that displays L's re-interpretation at this point in time of an utterance that, previously, she had interpreted and acted upon otherwise. You might recall that we saw an example of something similar early in Chapter 1, with Russ' misunderstanding of the Mom's turn 'Do you know who's going to that meeting?'

Schegloff (1992c) makes the point that conversational repair can thus be seen as central to the management of intersubjectivity as an ongoing process in interaction. In other words, it is not just about 'getting things right', it is about establishing that participants are working with similar understandings of what one another is saying and meaning as their talk unfolds. It is noticeable in this respect that all of the positions in which repair tends to occur are in close proximity to the trouble source. There is a simple reason for this: a system that required speakers to 'back track' or recall a trouble source from several turns before would be at best cumbersome, at worst unworkable. Moreover, trouble sources which are not addressed in one of the repair spaces can quickly can lead to significant problems in an exchange. Schegloff (1992c) provides an example of a call to a radio talk show in which the host and caller fail to identify and deal with a misunderstanding about the reference of each other's talk. Without realizing, they both continue to talk about different events. The resulting confusion soon leads to disagreement, which then escalates to hostility, and Schegloff observes that by the end of the call both parties are practically shouting at each other. In this sense, one important function of the repair system as we have outlined it here is the maintenance of mutual orientation to common topics and fields of reference in talk-in-interaction.

We could discuss many other aspects of repair and how it is organized and used in the course of talk-in-interaction. However, our aim has not been to provide an exhaustive review: rather, we have sought in this section to outline the way in which repair procedures are implicated in the management of turn-taking, and how they impinge upon the shape and subsequent trajectory of utterances (for further discussion, see Schegloff, 1979a). Neither have we done more than sketch the extent to which interpersonal alignment may be an outcome of repair work (for further discussion, see especially Schegloff, 1992c). The emphasis of this chapter has been on providing a general flavour of the kinds of findings which the conversation analytic method enables us to make about the structures of talk-in-interaction.

Yet CA is not to be viewed as a textual museum but as a dynamic and progressive research programme. Consequently, this book is not intended to be merely an account of the collected findings of previous work, but is also an introduction to, and illustration of, the craft of empirical research. With this in mind, it is now time to turn away from the description of existing studies to some of the more practical aspects of data transcription and analysis.

# Part II PRACTICES

# 3

# Data and Transcription

Conversation analysis places a great deal of emphasis on the use of extracts from transcriptions of tape-recorded, naturally occurring interactions in its research. This chapter is designed to be both a theoretical and a practical introduction to the style of transcription employed in CA. The focus is on the practice or craft of transcription as well as on the methodological and theoretical bases of the transcription system. This is because, as we emphasize, not only the analytic use, but also the actual practice of transcription is a fundamental part of doing CA.

The transcription of data is a procedure at the core of analysis, in two important respects. First, transcription is a necessary initial step in enabling the analysis of recorded interaction in the way that CA requires. Secondly, the practice of transcription and production of a transcript represent a distinctive stage in the process of data analysis itself.

It is important to stress that, for CA, transcripts are not thought of as 'data'. The data consist of tape-recordings of naturally occurring interactions. These may be audio or video tapes – although clearly, when the people who are being recorded have visual access to one another, an audio-only tape will necessarily miss out what could be very salient features involved in the management of interaction, such as gaze direction (Goodwin, 1981) and hand gestures (Schegloff, 1984). In the early years of CA researchers tended to restrict their attention to recordings of telephone conversations, precisely because this allowed them to focus purely on the organization of talk in the absence of such factors (Hopper, 1992). Since then, video-recordings have become more widely used, but CA's explicit focus on the organization of *talk*-in-interaction means that gesture, body movement and facial expression are not studied in their own right, as may be the case in the field of interactional kinesics (Kendon, 1990), but rather in exploring the relationships *between* speech and body movement. However, it is possible, within CA, to analyse audio-only recordings even when the participants have visual access to one another. For instance, Marjorie Goodwin's (1990) detailed study of the management of disputes among children at play on the street offers a compelling analysis of the role of talk in the social organization of the children's groups using as its data only an audio record supplemented by ethnographic fieldnotes.

Given this conception of the data, the aim in CA is not simply to transcribe the talk and then discard the tape in favour of the transcript. As Hopper (1989a) observes, the latter is often the practice in social psychology where it is transcripts alone that are analysed in terms of the categories of action which interest the researcher. Conversation analysts, by contrast, do not analyse transcripts alone: rather, they aim to analyse the data (i.e. the recorded interaction) using the transcript as a convenient referential tool. The transcript is seen as a 'representation' of the data; while the tape itself is viewed as a 'reproduction' of a determinate social event.

Of course, the tape is only one form of reproduction; and whether it is an audiotape or a videotape, it does not reproduce everything that went on in the vicinity of the recording device during the time it was switched on. (Indeed, we find it difficult to conceive of any way in which such an abstract 'everything' could possibly be recorded.) But conversation analysts take a pragmatic view on this issue. As Sacks once put it, describing why he initially became interested in working with tape-recorded conversations:

> Such materials had a single virtue, that I could replay them. I could transcribe them somewhat and study them extendedly – however long it might take. The tape-recorded materials constituted a 'good enough' record of what had happened. Other things, to be sure, happened, but at least what was on the tape had happened. (Sacks, 1984a: 26)

Wherever possible, then, the transcript is used in conjunction with the tape during analysis. As both Hopper (1989a) and Psathas and Anderson (1990) point out, in their descriptions of CA transcription procedures, repeated listening to the original recording is central to the

CA technique. This allows the analyst to gain an intimate acquaintance with the recording at the necessary level of detail. For this reason, and because analysis is not performed on the transcript alone, it is not standard practice in CA to have transcription done by secretaries or professional transcribers. Rather, transcription is done by the analyst him or herself. Transcription thereby becomes an integral part of analysis, since in repeatedly listening to the tape one begins to hear and to focus on phenomena that may subsequently form part of an analytic account.

The process of transcribing a data tape is not simply one of writing down the words that people exchanged. Rather, it is a process of writing down in as close detail as possible such features of the recorded interaction as the precise beginning and end-points of turns, the duration of pauses, audible sounds which are not words (such as breathiness and laughter), or which are 'ambiguous' vocalizations, and marking the stresses, extensions and truncations that are found in individual words and syllables. Because CA is concerned with how people manage and accomplish the sequential ordering of talk-in-interaction, transcription is, first of all, an attempt to capture talk as it actually occurs, in all its apparent messiness. As a result, CA transcripts can often appear formidably complex to the untrained eye.

It is possible, however, to learn relatively quickly how to read transcripts of conversation. This is because CA, unlike many other approaches which use recorded talk as their data, has developed a distinctive style of transcription, involving a comprehensive range of standardized conventions (see Hopper, 1989a; Ochs, 1979). This system, developed initially by Gail Jefferson (see Jefferson, 2005), is in general use by conversation analysts working in many different countries on widely varying forms of recorded interaction. One of the aims of this chapter is to provide the resources by which it is possible to become familiar with conversation analytic transcription conventions.

## Approaching transcription: some preliminary issues

Clearly, there are innumerable phenomena in any given stretch of talk which could be transcribed to varying levels of detail. No transcription system exists which is able, or even lays claim to being able, to capture all the possible features of talk that may be observable. As Kendon (1982: 478) puts it:

> It is a mistake to think that there can be a truly neutral transcription system, which, if only we had it, we could then use to produce

transcriptions suitable for any kind of investigation . . . Transcriptions, thus, embody hypotheses.

Similarly, Ochs (1979: 44) describes transcription as 'a selective process reflecting theoretical goals and definitions'.

This is no less true of CA transcriptions. A CA transcript embodies in its format and in the phenomena it marks out the analytic concerns which conversation analysts bring to the data. These concerns are of two types:

- Dynamics of turn-taking. On this level, transcripts seek to capture the details of the beginnings and endings of turns taken in talk-in-interaction, including precise details of overlap, gaps and pauses, and audible breathing.
- Characteristics of speech delivery. Here, transcripts mark noticeable features of stress, enunciation, intonation and pitch.

At the most basic level, the central concern with turn-taking is embodied in the very layout of CA transcripts, in which talk is represented in the form of utterances following one another down the page. Conversation analysts are also concerned to transcribe as precisely as possible all of the sounds that are uttered by participants, whether or not these are conventionally recognizable words. This is because CA assumes that any sound may have interactional import and communicative meaning. Hence there are conventions for transcribing such things as audible breathing, because an audible in-breath is often a signal that its producer is about to speak, and so that sound can be consequential for the management of turn-transition.

Two particular aspects of speech delivery that are of great importance for doing conversation analytic work are: (a) when spoken syllables are stretched; and (b) basic features of intonation. Both aspects can be closely related to issues of turn-taking. For instance, stretching a sound at the possible boundary of a turn, or possible transition-relevance place, can be a way of 'holding the floor' or preventing another speaker from starting a turn at that point. And different intonation contours used at the boundaries of turn-construction units such as clauses can indicate whether the speaker may be intending to continue, or, if the intonation is markedly falling, possibly coming to the end of a full turn.

The way these characteristics of speech delivery are marked tends to be relatively gross when compared, say, to transcripts produced by professional phoneticians who have their own sets of technical symbols for representing such phenomena. Indeed, phoneticians such as Kelly and

Local (1989), who are basically sympathetic to CA, have questioned the utility of these aspects of CA transcription. They remark that for the details of turn-taking, for example gaps and pauses, overlaps, and audible breathing activity, CA transcription is 'consistent and systematic. At other places, however – in reflecting features of tempo, pitch, loudness, vowel quality and voice quality, for example – the transcriptions [seem] inconsistent and arbitrary' (Kelly and Local, 1989: 204).

Kelly and Local suggest that there is much to be gained analytically from paying more serious attention to phonetic phenomena. However, their approach requires of both the analyst and the reader some degree of knowledge of phonetic techniques; whereas in general, the noting of prosodic characteristics in CA transcription is linked to a different aim: 'to get as much of the actual sound as possible into our transcripts, while still making them accessible to linguistically unsophisticated readers' (Sacks, Schegloff and Jefferson, 1974: 734).

Before going further into these kinds of issues, we need to introduce the set of transcription conventions used by conversation analysts. We will begin, in the next section, by describing the basic conventions and the rationale underlying their use; then we will illustrate their main strengths with a transcript of a recorded telephone conversation.

## Transcription conventions

The first necessary step in doing transcription is to understand the transcription conventions that CA uses, and to have a sense of which features of talk to concentrate on when listening to tape-recordings. It is often said that CA transcription procedures are designed to make for more and more 'accurate' transcripts of naturally occurring talk (Graddol et al., 1994: 181). However, this is only partly true. The principal features of talk represented in CA transcripts are almost all involved with particular analytic issues: issues to do with analysing the local production of order in naturally occurring talk-in-interaction. The features that should be listened for during transcription, as we have already noted, fall into two broad categories: those to do with turn-taking and those to do with what we loosely call 'speech delivery'. In this section, we introduce the principal conventions used to transcribe these features.

### Turn-taking and overlap

Most research in CA is based on the 'Simplest Systematics' model outlined in Sacks et al. (1974). That account of conversational turn-taking stressed the exchange of turns with minimal gap and overlap between them. Of course, in actual conversations, both gaps and overlaps are frequent; and so they must be marked even if only for representational adequacy. However, overlaps in particular are bound up with the management of turn-taking and the observable achievement of mutual understanding in talk-in-interaction. As we saw in the previous chapter, Jefferson (1986) has shown that, on close inspection, much overlapping talk which appears interruptive is in fact closely coordinated with the occurrence of transition-relevance places.

Overlap onset is marked in transcripts by the use of left hand square brackets:

**(1) [SBL:1:1:11:5]**

```
1     B:     Uh huh and I'm so:rry I didn' get Mar:gret I
2            really['ve been wanning to.
3→   D:            [W'll I think she mu:st've stayed out'v
4            to:wn
5            (0.2)
6     B:     I thi[nk so too.
7→   D:            [in Fre:sno sh- see she'n Pe::g (0.7)
8            dro:ve over to 'er sister's 'oo lives in Fresno::.
```

As we see with this extract, the aim is to be as precise as possible about marking the point at which overlap begins: even when, as in lines 6 and 7, that is in the middle of a word. By marking the precise points of onset in overlapping talk, very close calibrations in the understandings that speakers display of each other's talk become available for analysis.

Other forms of overlap may also be marked. For instance, speakers may start a turn simultaneously. This is marked by the use of a double left-hand bracket:

**(2) [Heritage:I:II:3]**

```
1     I:     Well .h I a-always feel it's best to get it
2            all over at [the same time y]ou know.
3     N:                 [ Well ye::s. ]
4     N:     Ye:s.
5→   I:     [[It's uh:
6→   N:     [[And and who did you go to.
```

While it is not always strictly necessary to mark the end of a stretch of overlapping talk, studies such as Schegloff's (1987a) account of 'recycled turn-beginnings' show how, by focusing on the point at which overlap ends, important aspects of the ongoing management of conversation can thereby be revealed. When the end of overlap is marked, that is done by a single right-hand square bracket:

**(3) [Schegloff, 1987a:75]**
```
1    R:      in fact they must have grown a culture, you
2            know, they must've- I mean how long- he's
3            been in hospital for a few days right?
4            Takes a[bout a week to grow a culture]
5→   K:             [ I  don't  think  they  grow  a ] I don't
6            think they grow a culture to do a biopsy.
```

It is noticeable here that K, finding himself beginning to speak in overlap with R's continuation of his turn about growing a culture for a biopsy, does not drop out of the competition for the floor but keeps going until R comes to a next recognizable completion point. At that stage, however, rather than simply carrying on talking, K, with remarkable precision, restarts his turn, thereby displaying how speakers can coordinate turn transitions with transition-relevance places even when a first attempt to do so has failed.

Utterances also may sound 'latched' together: they may occur right next to each other with absolutely no gap, but also no overlap, between them. This is marked by equals signs, thus:

**(4) [NB:IV:10]**
```
1    E:      Is the swimming pool enclosed with the
2            gla:ss bit?=
3    N:      =No::, it's uh: ou:ts- (.) eh no outside
```

Equals signs are also used to deal with a problem inherent in the attempt to represent naturally occurring talk on the page: the fact that page lines are physically limited in length, whereas conversational turns are not. This means that a single utterance may need to be broken up, if, for instance, another speaker says something during its course. In such a case, the two parts of the longer turn are connected by equals signs, with the embedded utterance transcribed on a line between:

**(5) [NB:IV:14]**
```
1    N:      But eh- it's- it's terrible to keep people
2            ali:ve and [you know and just let them=
3    E:                 [Right.
4    N:      =suffer day in and day out,
```

In a similar sense, a protracted spate of simultaneous talk may require a combination of left and right brackets and equals signs, if the spate extends across a number of lines on the page:

**(6) [NB:IV:14]**

```
1    E:    Well, we don't know what it's all about
2          I g-I- ((sniff)) Don't get yourself=
3    N:    =[[ Oh I'm not. I just- you know I wish ]
4    E:       [[Honey you've got to get a hold of your- I know]=
5    N:    =I'd- I'd kind of liked to gone out there but
6          I was afraid of the fog
```

It is also worth noting that an early device for transcribing the onset of overlap was the double slash (//). This is no longer widely used in transcription. Occasionally, though, it will be used to mark the point of overlap onset when a single line from a longer data extract is being discussed in the text. Thus, in the following extract:

**(7) [SBL:2:1]**

```
1    B:    I still haven't my dishes done, I'm
2          right in the middle of doing them, but
3          I stopped [to call you.
4    J:              [Well I worked on my- medicine
5          cabinet again, I'm so mad at that painter,
```

B's turn might be cited in this way: 'I still haven't my dishes done, I'm right in the middle of doing them, but I stopped//to call you.'

## Gaps and pauses

From the beginning, conversation analysts have timed intervals in the stream of talk relatively precisely, in tenths of a second. Again, this is not just a matter of accuracy. Work on dispreferred responses (Davidson, 1984; Pomerantz, 1984a) has demonstrated that pauses even as short as two or three tenths of a second can have some interactional, and therefore analytic, significance. Slightly later, Jefferson (1989) produced an extensive exploration of the interactional significance that is attached to silences of one second in length during conversation. It is clear that using a catch-all device such as writing 'pause' in transcripts would not have enabled many of the finer analytic points contained in these papers to be made.

Timings of pauses, then, are important features of transcripts. The timings, which are usually done with a stopwatch, are inserted in the transcript at the precise point of their occurrence in the recording. They may occur within a turn:

**(8) [SBL:2:7:20]**
1     A:       I- if you want to uh(b) (1.1) maybe get up a game . . .

Or they may occur between turns:

**(9) [SBL:2:7:20]**
1     A:       I- if you w ant to uh(b) (1.1) maybe get up a game
2              some morning while you're out the:re,=why that's
3              always fu:n,
4     B:       Mm <u>h</u>m.
5→             (0.5)
6     A:       So let me kn<u>o</u>:w.

Pauses that are detectable, but run for less that 0.2 of a second, are indicated by a period within parentheses:

**(10) [SBL:2:7:20] (Continuation of [9].)**
6     A:       So let me kn<u>o</u>:w.
7→             (.)
8     B:       Yah w<u>i</u>ll do:.

### Breathiness

Breathiness which is audible to the transcriptionist is marked by 'h' for exhalation and '.h' for inhalation. As we have already remarked, this feature of recordings is transcribed because (among other reasons) audible in-breaths may be involved with the management of turn-taking, in as much as an open-mouthed in-breath may mark a participant's attempt to start a turn. Notice how in the following extract, speaker E draws in a long breath at line 3, which overlaps substantially with P's invitation. This inbreath signals her attempt to take the floor and respond to the invitation; although the reasons for it may be analytically complex. One relevant factor is that P's invitation has multiple possible completion points ('you wanna go to the store/ er anything/ over at the Market Basket/ er anything?'), so that E's inbreath may be connected to her having decided on her response, but waiting for the invitation to come to an end (see Davidson, 1984). As soon as the final 'er anything?' has been produced, she stops her inbreath and begins to speak:

**(11) [NB:52:2:66]**
```
1    P:    Oh I mean uh: you wanna go to the store er anything
2          over at the Market [ Basket  er  anything? ]
3    E:                       [.hhhhhhhhhhhhhhhhhhh]h Well honey . . .
```

In transcripts, the longer the breath, roughly, the longer the line of 'h' or '.h' provided in the transcript:

**(12) [HG:28]**
```
1→   N:    .hhh
2          (0.5)
3    N:    A::nywa::y,
4          (.)
5→   H:    eh-eh .hhhhhhh Uh::m,
```

The lengths of these breaths are not timed in any strict sense. Rather, the length of a breath is assessed impressionistically, relative to the general tempo of the surrounding talk (although more precise measurement is possible, of course, when the entire breath takes place within overlap, as happens in line 3 of extract [11] above).

Transcripts also mark plosive aspiration within a word: this happens, for instance, when someone speaks 'through' laughter (that is, laughs while enunciating a word or phrase). This is indicated by placing the 'h' in parentheses. However, due to the nature of the phenomenon, this can be very hard to do, and the transcriptionist may need to listen to the same word or group of words many times before he or she can achieve a satisfactory textual rendering of the sounds that occur on the tape:

**(13) [EB:1]**
```
1    S:    I hope by next semester it'll be a bi(h)t
2          b(h)edd(h)er heh heh heh heh .hh (('a bit better'))
```

**(14) [H:2.2.89:4:3]**
```
1    H:    Yes but you ca:n't actually:, take anybody to
2          la::w, .h jus:t on:, an accusation.
3          (1.1)
4    C:    .p .hhh (.) No I kno:w I'm not just making
5          accusations I've got proof of my own
6→         ey(h)(huh huh hih)es! .hhhh (('my own eyes'))
```

## Laughter

In a series of papers on laughter, Jefferson (1979, 1985; Jefferson, Sacks and Schegloff, 1987) showed that laughter, as it occurs in talk-in-interaction, is a finely coordinated interactional phenomenon. This in turn meant that laughter, which may previously have been represented descriptively by the transcriber simply writing '(laughs)', now should be transcribed as literally as possible in the form of onomatopaeic renditions of laugh particles: 'ha ha', 'heh heh', 'hih hih', and so on. The particles are designed to represent as closely as possible the sounds emitted by the participants:

**(15) [Goodwin:GR:40]**

```
1    J:      So I said look Gurney, yer just a big ass
2            kisser, (0.4) en [ yer  getting  yer  wa:y, ]
3→   B:                      [AAHh hah-uh hah-uh huh]=
4    J:      =[ I(h)  ju(h)st ] lai[d it a:]ll on,
5→   B:      [.hhhhhhhhhhhh ]    [ hhah ]
6            (.)
7→   B:      ehh huh uh-huh uh-huh
```

One of the difficulties with transcribing laughter is that participants frequently laugh *together*. This can make for a highly complex transcribing job, especially when the recorded talk involves more than two people. In the following fragment, there are only three participants; but their extended stretch of laughing together (even though it only last for a few seconds) leads to a rather daunting-looking section of transcript:

**(16) [Goodwin:AD:56:r]**

```
1    B:      he:uh[he[ uh-ha]
2    C:          [he[ ha: : ]ah ha-ha-ha-ha-ha-ha-a-ha]
3    L:            [ah!ah!] ah!ah!ah!ah!ah!ah!ah!ah! ]=
4    C:      =[.hhh [he]he ]:h=
5    L:      [ah!a![a!]
6    B:            [ah hh]
7    C:      =he[:h he-ehh-e]he- [he- [.e[.hhee[hh!]
8    B:         [ Oo:::::ps, ]  n[he [u [huh [
9    L:                                      [eh!]=
10   C:      =[ e::::a::yee: ]°ee::°
11   L:      [uh!ah!ah!ah!]
```

We have used these features of speech production to illustrate some of the reasons why conversation analysts have developed the transcription system currently in use. However, this is not an exhaustive description; other symbols are explained in the glossary of transcription conventions found at the front of the book.

One final thing to mention is that the transcriber may sometimes be in doubt as to what actually occurs on the tape. For instance, it may be that a speaker evidently says something, but it may not be clear precisely what it is he or she has said. (One place in which this is likely to occur is during stretches of overlapping talk.) In such cases, the standard convention is to enclose one's best hearing of what was said in brackets (if no actual words are discernible, the brackets may enclose empty space, signifying at least that some sound occurred at that point). On other occasions, the transcriber may want to record some descriptive properties of the speaker's voice, such as that it is 'gravelly', or 'smiley'. This is usually done as an aid to the memory for those occasions when the transcript is being observed without the accompanying tape. Such descriptions are enclosed within double brackets: e.g., ((smile voice)).

To summarize this section, then, the transcription system used in CA goes to produce transcripts that are accurate at the relevant levels of detail (levels of turn-taking and actual speech delivery), while avoiding being technically inaccessible to the majority of readers. The purpose of the transcription conventions, however, is not merely to produce accurate representations of talk, but to focus attention on those features of talk-in-interaction that are analytically significant from the standpoint of CA. We have illustrated that point in brief outline in this section. How the transcription system is used to bring out the finer analytic points in a stretch of talk can be illustrated in more detail by means of the following exercise.

## A comparative exercise

A good way of showing up the features of talk that are highlighted by a CA transcript is to compare such a transcript with one produced in a different way. Below, we reproduce two transcriptions of the same stretch of talk, in which two middle-aged, middle-class English women are talking on the telephone. Transcript (A) aims to present the words that were spoken, and some non-verbal activities such as laughter, in a standard orthography which makes the text look like a script for a play. Transcript (B) shows how the CA conventions introduced above are used to transcribe the same stretch of talk.

# A comparison between two treatments of the same conversation

## Transcript (A)

**[Holt:Xmas 85]**

| | | |
|---|---|---|
| 1 | L: | Are you not feeling very well? |
| 2 | J: | No I'm all right. |
| 3 | L: | Yes. |
| 4 | J: | Yes I'm all right. |
| 5 | L: | Oh. You know I. . .I'm broiling about something. |
| 6 | | (Laughs) |
| 7 | J: | What. |
| 8 | L: | Well that sale. At the vicarage. |
| 9 | J: | Oh yes. |
| 10 | L: | Your friend and mine was there. Mister 'R'. |
| 11 | J: | Oh yes. |
| 12 | L: | And um, we really didn't have a lot of change that |
| 13 | | day because we'd been to Bath and we'd been |
| 14 | | Christmas shopping, but we thought we'd better go |
| 15 | | along to the sale and do what we could. We hadn't |
| 16 | | got a lot of ready cash to spend. |
| 17 | J: | Mm. |
| 18 | L: | In any case we thought things were very expensive. |
| 19 | J: | Oh did you? |
| 20 | | (Pause) |
| 21 | L: | And we were looking round the stalls and poking about, |
| 22 | | and he came up to me and he said, 'Oh hello Lesley, |
| 23 | | still trying to buy something for nothing!' |
| 24 | Both: | (Sharp intake of breath) |
| 25 | J: | Ooo Lesley! |
| 26 | L: | Ooo! (Laughs) |
| 27 | J: | Isn't he. . . |
| 28 | L: | What do you say? |
| 29 | J: | Oh isn't he dreadful. |
| 30 | L: | Yes. |
| 31 | J: | What an awful man. |

**Transcript (B)**

**[Holt:Xmas 85]**

```
1    L:    Are you not feeling very [we:ll,
2    J:                            [°(  )°
3          (.)
4    J:    No I'm all ri:ght
5          (.)
6    L:    Yes.
7          (0.6)
8    J:    °Ye:s I'm all right,°
9    L:    °Oh:.° .hh Yi-m- You know I- I- I'm broiling about
10         something hhhheh[heh .hhhh
11   J:                    [Wha::t.
12   L:    Well that sa:le. (0.2) At- at (.) the vicarage.
13         (0.6)
14   J:    Oh ye[:s,
15   L:         [.t
16         (0.6)
17   L:    u (.) ihYour friend 'n mi:ne was the:re
18         (0.2)
19   J:    (h[h hh)
20   L:      [mMister:, R:,
21   J:    Oh y(h)es, °(hm hm)°
22         (0.4)
23   L:    And em: .p we (.) really didn't have a lot'v cha:nge
24         that (.) day becuz we'd been to Bath 'n we'd been:
25         Christmas shoppin:g, (0.5) but we thought we'd better
26         go along t'th' sale 'n do what we could, (0.2) we
27         hadn't got a lot (.) of s:e- ready cash t'spe:nd.
28         (0.6)
29   L:    In any case we thought th' things were very
30         expensive.
31   J:    Oh did you.
32         (0.9)
33   L:    AND uh we were looking round the sta:lls 'n poking
34         about 'n he came up t' me 'n he said Oh: h:hello
35         Lesley, (.) still trying to buy something f'nothing,
36         .tch! .hh[hahhhhhhh!
37   J:    .        [.hhoohhhh!
38         (0.8)
39   J:    Oo[: : :[: L e s l e y ]
40   L:      [OO:. [ ehh heh heh ]
41         (0.2)
42   J:    I:s[ n 't ]    [he
43   L:       [What] do y[ou sa:y.
44         (0.3)
45   J:    Oh isn't he drea:dful.
46   L:    °eYe::s.°
47         (0.6)
48   J:    What'n aw::ful ma:::n
```

The first thing that will be noticed about these two renditions is the sheer amount of detail that Transcript (B), the CA transcript, shows up which is absent from Transcript (A). For instance, the CA transcript includes a large number of pauses, overlaps, word stresses and other production features which the first transcript has edited out or 'cleaned up'. However, we have emphasized that the transcription system is not just aimed at accuracy of detail. Like all transcription systems, it is designed to highlight analytically relevant features of talk-in-interaction. We can illustrate this point by focusing on a particular section of the interchange transcribed in these two extracts.

It will be clear that what happens during this interchange is that L tells a story to J about having been insulted by someone referred to as 'Mister R' (this pseudonym is used on the tape itself, not just in transcription) at the local vicarage sale. The story is introduced at the beginning of the extract as something that L is 'broiling about'; just what she is broiling about, it turns out, is Mister R's comment that L, by rummaging about in the stalls at this charity sale, is 'trying to buy something for nothing' (that is, pick up a bargain).

What we are interested in is what happens immediately after L has delivered the punchline of her story: that is, the sequence which begins in line 24 of Transcript (A), and line 36 of Transcript (B). In each of these transcripts, what happens here is represented radically differently. In Transcript (A), we find the following:

**Transcript (A)**

```
22   L:      and he came up to me and he said, 'Oh hello Lesley,
23           still trying to buy something for nothing!'
24   Both:   (Sharp intake of breath)
25   J:      Ooo Lesley!
26   L:      Ooo! (Laughs)
27   J:      Isn't he. . .
28   L:      What do you say?
29   J:      Oh isn't he dreadful.
```

While Transcript (B) gives us the following:

**Transcript (B)**

```
34           about 'n he came up t' me 'n he said Oh: h:hello
35           Lesley, (.) still trying to buy something f'nothing,
36           .tch! .hh[hahhhhhhh!
37   J:              [.hhoohhhh!
38           (0.8)
39   J:      Oo[: : : [: L e s l e y ]
40   L:         [OO:. [ ehh heh heh ]
```

```
41          (0.2)
42    J:    I:s[ n 't ]      [he
43    L:       [What] do y[ou sa:y.
44          (0.3)
45    J:    Oh isn't he drea:dful.
```

There are two immediately noticeable differences. The first is that what is discursively represented in Transcript (A) (line 24) as: 'Both: (Sharp intake of breath)' is represented typographically in Transcript (B):

```
36    L:    .tch! .hh[hahhhhhhh!
37    J:          [.hhoohhhh!
```

The second difference is that Transcript (B) shows up how the reactions to the story do not occur simply as a series of utterances following one after another, as suggested by Transcript (A). Rather, they occur in three couples, separated by short pauses. Moreover, each of the coupled reactions occurs in overlap with its partner.

What is the relevance of this? First of all, we have mentioned that CA transcripts have moved from representing laughter (and other non-lexical phenomena) discursively, to developing distinctive typographic representations. What occurs immediately after L's story in this interchange is not laughter, but something similarly non-lexical: emphasized, open-mouthed inbreaths which are conventionalized expressions of moral indignation (and so are quite well-fitted to the character of the punchline).

However, it is not clear that, on reading Transcript (B) alone (that is, without the tape) we would be able to interpret these vocalizations in the way they were produced. This appears to be one advantage that Transcript (A) has over the CA transcript. In describing what happens as a 'sharp intake of breath', it informs us in a way that Transcript (B)'s line of 'h's does not. But this only serves to emphasize the importance, for CA, of the original data tape, as we stressed earlier on in this chapter. Without the tape, it is difficult to 'hear' what is going on at this point in Transcript (B). With the tape, however, that problem disappears. So Transcript (A) only has an advantage over Transcript (B) on the assumption that the analyst does not have access to the tape, which is not the case in CA research.

More importantly, Transcript (B) allows us to analyse the interactional production of this stretch of talk in ways which are not possible with Transcript (A). The fact that we can see the set of coupled reactions each being done in overlap brings out the collaborative nature of these expressions of indignation. That is, it is not just that both speakers react with sharp intakes of breath, followed by indignant 'Ooo!'s, but they do so almost simultaneously. By this means, the story recipient, J, displays for the story teller the fact that she understands and empathizes with L's sense of being insulted by Mister R. She does this by vocalizing, on two closely timed occasions, precisely the indignant reaction which L's punchline requires.

The fact that their reactions are not exactly simultaneous is itself important in this respect. Looking closer still, we find that on the first occasion, L, as the story teller, is momentarily the first to embark on a response:

```
36→  L:     .tch! .hh[hahhhhhhh!
37   J:            [.hhoohhhh!
```

On the next occasion, however, J takes over the first starter role:

```
38           (0.8)
39→  J:     Oo[:  :  :[:  L e s l e y  ]
40   L:        [OO:! [ ehh heh heh ]
```

The point is that not only are these reactions closely coordinated; there is even more delicate interactional work going on which is revealed in the timing. Remember that L had set the story up as something she is 'broiling about'. One question that J faces as the story recipient is what form of response would be appropriate to Mister R's comment. This issue is resolved when L herself embarks on a response by manifesting the feeling she had at the time. Having heard the beginning of this sharp intake of breath, J is able to join in (line 37), in a way treating L's response as a 'cue' to show how the story should be treated. After the pause in line 38, J is able to take over the leading response role without waiting for a further cue from the teller. This in turn can then be treated as a cue by L, with which she can coordinate a matched response.

By these means the two women display for one another that they are 'with' each other on this tale. But there is evidence to suggest that this does not just happen by accident. They are, it seems, actively coordinating their actions by cueing each other, so that their talk is brought off as closely matched both in timing and in content. This sort of matching is likely to continue only for a short time without becoming a joke (interestingly, notice that L breaks into laughter as early as the second 'round': line 40). Consequently, after the next short pause in line 41, they both go off on separate paths:

```
41              (0.2)
42→  J:         I:s[ n 't ]      [he
43→  L:            [What] do y[ou sa:y.
44              (0.3)
45    J:        Oh isn't he drea:dful.
```

These fine-grained observations about the interactional production of this sequence are only made possible because of the CA transcript's focus on features of detail such as overlap. At the same time, we only notice the overlapping production of the inbreaths following the punchline because the CA transcript favours the typographic representation of sounds over their discursive representation. In short, it is clear that the more complex CA transcript gives us access to the interactional management of talk at a much deeper analytic level than the 'cleaned up' version.

In the way that transcripts are laid out on the page, as well as in the kinds of phenomena that are represented, we find a reflection of CA's distinctive perspective on talk-in-interaction. It has not been our aim in this chapter to discuss the relative merits of the wide range of various transcription systems that currently exist, nor to compare their different theoretical underpinnings. But we have emphasized that different research interests will require different selections from the vast range of features of talk-in-interaction that can possibly be transcribed. CA has a specific set of research interests, and the transcription system is extremely well-fitted to the associated requirements.

We have also stressed the intrinsic relationship between the processes of transcription and analysis of data. The development of the transcription conventions themselves testifies to that relationship. The system was not just invented in the abstract, but evolved as analysts sought to understand new features of interactions recorded on tape, leading to the development of new means of transcribing these features.

Overall, this suggests that the CA transcription system is not a finished object, but one that may develop and evolve as new analytic themes themselves emerge. Transcripts too develop and evolve. They are not intended as 'objective' representations of social reality, as Graddol et al (1994: 181) somewhat critically propose. Transcripts are necessarily impressionistic: they represent the analyst/transcriber's hearing of what is on the tape. And of course, that hearing may alter. Repeated listening to tapes almost always throws up phenomena which were simply missed first time round. So as a piece of data is subjected to closer and closer analysis, the transcript itself evolves as part of that analytic process. This again illustrates the close connection between data, transcription, and analysis.

A final point is that transcripts play a key role in the claim of CA to be a rigorous empirical discipline. An important aspect of this is that analyses produced by one researcher do not amount merely to idiosyncratic and untestable assertions about what is going on in a stretch of talk. Rather, the analysis is projected into a public arena in which it can, if necessary, be challenged and even altered. This is made possible not only by the fact that publications in CA routinely contain examples of data transcripts (as, indeed, we do throughout this book); but also by the fact that conversation analysts' transcripts (and, ideally, the data they are transcriptions of) are made publicly available to anyone who requests them in order to test the accuracy of the analysis, or to re-analyse the data. By this means, transcripts are central to guaranteeing the cumulative and publicly verifiable nature of conversation analytic research.

# 4

# Analysing Data I: Building Collections and Identifying Phenomena

Having introduced the transcription procedures of conversation analysis, we begin in this chapter to look at some of the basic techniques with which researchers approach the analysis of their data. Conversation analysts place great emphasis on building 'collections' of instances of a particular conversational phenomenon. The aim is to produce analyses of patterns in the sequential organization of talk-in-interaction. Analysing patterns in this way enables the analyst to make robust claims about the ways in which culturally available resources may be methodically used to accomplish mutually recognizable interactional tasks.

In this chapter we look in detail at the principal analytic techniques which are used in building collections and analysing the phenomena that such collections exemplify. Using case studies of three pieces of CA research, ranging in time between a study first published in 1968 and one appearing in 1992, we focus on techniques for the identification, description and analysis of singular conversational devices, which can be shown to function in robustly patterned ways across large numbers of sequences. In different ways, these case studies allow us to illustrate the steps by which analysis in the CA mode is approached and developed.

However, it is important to emphasize that while CA has adopted a relatively strict and systematic style of data transcription, the techniques with which researchers approach the actual analysis of data rely as much on what Schenkein (1978) called the 'conversation analytic mentality' as on any formal rules of research method. Like most forms of qualitative research in the social sciences, CA cannot readily be reduced to a formula which can be applied to data in order to generate appropriate findings. In fact, conversation analysts employ a wide range of essentially interpretive skills in their research. The conversation analytic mentality involves more a cast of mind, or a way of seeing, than a static and prescriptive set of instructions which analysts bring to bear on the data. The best way of describing this and the following chapter, therefore, is as an illustration of the practical application of the conversation analytic mentality.

## Collections and patterns

The main research procedure in CA progresses through three stages. The first is to locate a potentially interesting phenomenon in the data. This might be a particular type of turn, for example, one in which the item 'Oh' is used (Heritage, 1984b). Or it might be a noticeable kind of sequence, such as opening sequences in telephone conversations (Schegloff, 1968), or sequences in which an invitation is made and responded to (Drew, 1984). One thing that is important to stress here is that data are not necessarily approached with a particular question in mind. Indeed, conversation analysts try to avoid letting preconceptions about what may be found in some set of transcribed recordings direct their mind when first encountering the data. The preferred policy is one of 'unmotivated' looking. As Sacks once put it:

> When we start out with a piece of data, the question of what we are going to end up with, what kind of findings it will give, should not be a consideration. We sit down with a piece of data, make a bunch of observations, and see where they will go . . . I mean not merely that if we pick any data we will find something, but that if we pick any data, without bringing any problems to it, we will find something. And how interesting what we may come up with will be is something we cannot in the first instance say. (Sacks, 1984a: 27)

Thus, in each of the cases to be discussed in this chapter, the analysis grew out of the researchers' noticing of a potentially interesting, possibly orderly phenomenon: Schegloff's (1968) study of a particular 'deviant' opening in a large collection of telephone conversations; Drew's (1987) analysis of serious or 'po-faced' reactions to teases; and Hutchby's (1992a) account of a device for accomplishing scepticism in arguments.

First, then, identify a possibly interesting phenomenon. The second step, having collected a number of instances, is to describe one particular occurrence formally, concentrating on its sequential context: the types of turn which precede and follow it. If patterns can be located in the sequential contexts in which the potential phenomenon occurs in the data, then there begins to be the basis for a robust description. The third step is to return to the data to see if other instances of the phenomenon can be described in terms of this account. In the process, the description will need to be refined and, gradually, a formal account of a sequential pattern can be developed.

The aim in this type of work is to produce formal descriptions of large collections of data which can account for the whole set of examples which the researcher has collected. But this is not the only analytic technique that is used. As we show in Chapter 5, a no less significant aspect of CA is the description and analysis of singular sequences of talk-in-interaction. But particular methodological lessons can be learned by looking at how large collections of data are used in conversation analysis. Consequently we begin by discussing one classic early study using this technique: Schegloff's (1968) analysis of opening sequences in telephone calls.

There is a particular reason why this is a significant case. It illustrates especially clearly CA's insistence on building analytic accounts which are both particularized and generalized. In other words, conversation analysts aim to be able to describe the specific features of individual cases, and at the same time bring those specifics under the umbrella of a generalized account of some sequential pattern or interactional device.

Schegloff's (1968) interest was in how participants coordinate their entry into interaction at the very beginnings of telephone calls. Starting with a collection of 500 examples of telephone openings, he described a pattern which turned out to account for all but one of his cases. But rather than simply accepting that this one was a 'deviant' case which proved the rule, Schegloff wondered whether there might be a better alternative which would account for even the deviant case. In other words, was there a description of the organization of telephone openings which would describe this activity generically, even in cases which seemed out of the ordinary?

Schegloff's initial attempt at describing the management of telephone openings took the form of a rule that 'answerer speaks first' in telephone conversation. He described this as a 'distribution rule', because turns with which telephone calls were opened in his corpus were distributed in a certain way between participants in the respective roles of 'caller' and 'answerer'. This rule accounted for 499 of his cases, in which the first turn of the call was indeed an answerer's 'Hello', or equivalent.

The one case in his collection of 500 which did not fit this pattern was one in which the caller spoke first:

**(1) [Schegloff, 1968]**
(Police make the call. Receiver is lifted and there is a one second pause)
| 1 | POLICE: | Hello. |
| 2 | ANSWERER: | American Red Cross. |
| 3 | POLICE: | Hello, this is Police Headquarters . . . er, |
| 4 | | Officer Stratton ((etc.)) |

Since it is the caller, rather than the answerer, who speaks first in this case, the distribution rule does not apply. Schegloff (1968) suggests that there are two analytic strategies for dealing with this. The first is to treat this as a 'deviant case', and develop an analysis focusing on its particular features: describing how it might be that this case came to differ from the rule. This would represent what Schegloff calls an 'ad hoc' attempt to save the distribution rule.

The second alternative is to go back to the corpus as a whole and see if the original analysis can be reformulated in such a way that this case could be accounted for in the same way as all the others. This was the strategy that Schegloff adopted. His solution was to describe the openings of telephone conversations not in terms of the 'answerer speaks first' rule, but as a form of adjacency pair called summons–answer sequences. Thus, whereas we might think of the answerer's first 'Hello' as an intial greeting, Schegloff suggests that whatever the answerer says in their first turn is an answer to the summons issued by the telephone's ring. As Schegloff pointed out in a later analysis, it is therefore the caller's first turn (i.e. the second utterance of the call) that, typically, represents a first greeting (Schegloff, 1986). Consider the following typical telephone conversation opening:

**(2) [HG:1]**
(Hyla and Nancy are teenage friends)
| 1 | | ((Ring)) |
| 2 | Nancy: | H'll<u>o</u>? |
| 3 | Hyla: | <u>Hi</u>:, |
| 4 | Nancy: | <u>Hi</u>::. |
| 5 | Hyla: | How <u>are</u> yuhh= |
| 6 | Nancy: | =F<u>i</u>:ne how er you, |
| 7 | Hyla: | Oka:[y, |
| 8 | Nancy: | [G<u>oo</u>:d, |

```
9                    (0.4)
10   Hyla:          .mkhhh[hh
11   Nancy:              [What's doin',
```

Note that here we have included the telephone ring as part of the transcript. Thus, lines 1 and 2 represent the summons–answer sequence, in which Nancy issues an answer to the phone's ring. Only after that, in lines 3 and 4, do the two speakers engage in an exchange of greetings, in which the first greeting comes from Hyla (the caller). Schegloff (1986) shows that this kind of structure is extraordinarily robust in a large collection of telephone conversations involving different participants in different social relationships across varying contexts.

Thus, the new summons–answer description enabled Schegloff in his earlier analysis to account for the one case where the answerer did not speak first. This was done by treating the caller's 'Hello' as a *repeat summons*. That is, having made an initial summons via the telephone ring but received no answer, the caller issues another summons (line 1 of extract [1]) which, this time, receives an answer: 'American Red Cross' (i.e., the organization that was called). More than that, however, the new version also accounts for all the other cases in the corpus, since in those 499 cases, the initial summons issued by the telephone's ring gets answered in the next move in the sequence, immediately after the answerer picks up the telephone.

Schegloff's analysis of this single 'deviant case' thus resulted in a revision of the analysis and a new, more adequate formal description. By this means he was able to explicate the organizational basis which was common to all the cases in his data. We have used this example to begin with because it is a particularly clear cut one. Not many studies in the CA literature start off with such a well-defined problem and come to such an elegant answer. And, more importantly, not all patterns or phenomena in talk-in-interaction are so economically describable, as we will show in the following sections. But the case illustrates three very important principles of the conversation analytic method:

• The insistence on rigorous, formal description;
• The attempt to maximize the generalizability of analytic accounts;
• The serious attention given to 'deviant' cases.

With regard to the last point, this study also nicely illustrates a further important analytic notion in CA. There is another major importance given to deviant cases, which is connected to what we introduced in chapter 2 as conditional relevance. As we explained previously, given the initial condition of a first pair part being uttered, the second part of that pair is then relevant; consequently, the absence of such a second part is a 'noticeable absence', and the speaker of the first part may search for a reason for that absence. Adjacency pairs such as question–answer, or greeting-greeting, display the property of conditional relevance. The summons–answer sequence also has this property, and Schegloff (1968) lists a number of examples of how speakers may pursue an answer following no response to a summons (e.g., repeat the summons), and of the kinds of inferences that may be drawn upon in order to account for the absence of an answer (e.g., the target did not hear/is asleep/is being intentionally rude).

As we have said, with certain kinds of sequences, conditional relevance can assist the analyst in defining the sequence as a robust interactional phenomenon, precisely because of this accountability feature. If someone displays in their conduct that they are 'noticing' the absence of a certain type of turn from a coparticipant, then that demonstrates their own orientation to the relevance of the sequence that the analyst is aiming to describe. It is important to stress, however, that not all patterned sequences will exhibit conditional relevance. In other cases, alternative techniques will have to be used in order to produce an analysis which is generalized and which attends to the participants' orientations to the phenomena being described. In the following sections, we use two further case studies to illustrate in closer detail the ways in which such rigorous analyses may be built.

### Conversational devices

It is important to stress at this stage that the aim in CA is not simply to build descriptions of patterns in large collections. Underlying the research is a sociological interest in the social and interactional functions of identifiable conversational phenomena. In other words, what interactional work is the phenomenon, or device, being used to do? When we add this to the emphasis introduced in the previous section on how the participants themselves can be said to recognize and use (to orient to) the device being described, we have the two core analytic questions in CA:

- What interactional business is being mediated or accomplished through the use of a sequential pattern?
- How do participants demonstrate their active orientation to this business?

We will illustrate the first question through a discussion of Drew's (1987) analysis of 'po-faced' responses to teases.

Drew begins by observing a recurrent phenomenon in his data: people who are the object of a tease will frequently react with a serious, or 'po-faced', response. Why might this be so? First of all, Drew describes the features of the po-faced responses themselves. This shows that it is not the case that people respond seriously because they do not realize they are being teased. Rather, indications that they recognize the humour of the prior turn are visible even as they produce the response. Consider the following example from Drew's paper:

**(3) [Goodwin: Family Dinner]**
```
1     Dot:       Do we have two forks cos we're on television?
2→   Mother:     [[No we-
3     Father:    [[Huh hh [huh  hh [h (    )
4     Angie:              [Yeahah [h hah .hh
5→   Mother:                      [Uh huh [huh huh
6     Angie:                              [heh heh heh
7     Father:                             [Right yeh
8                pro[bably the answer right the[re
9     Angie:        [Eh hah hah              [
10    Mother:                                [.hhh You have
11               pie you have pie:: tonight.
```

Here Dot's tease in line 1 refers to the fact that this family dinner is being videotaped (hence, 'on television'). Mother starts to respond by saying 'No we-', which appears to be the beginning of a serious account for the presence of two forks. At this point, however, laughter starts among the other participants, and Mother herself joins in (line 5). Yet at the end of the extract, Mother completes the serious response she began earlier: 'You have pie you have pie:: tonight'. Thus, although she has laughed at the joke, her immediate response is a serious or literal one, and that response is completed following the laughter with which she joins in.

The same pattern of a recognition of the joke produced within the immediate environment of a serious response can also be seen in the following extracts.

**(4) [AL:83 002]**
(B has just come into the house with A's mother.)
```
1     A:     Hell[o:
2     B:         [He:llo:: how are you:[:.
3     A:                               [All right thank you?
```

```
4    B:     I saw your mum at the bu:s stop so
5           I [ (give her a li(h)ft ]
6    A:         [And you started ya]cking
7→   B:     N(hh)o I gave her a lift back
```

A's tease in line 6, that B 'started yacking' to her mother at the bus stop, is responded to in a 'serious' way with a negation in line 7. Notice, however, that the 'N(hh)o' actually has a small laugh particle embedded within it, thus exhibiting B's recognition of the playful nature of the tease.

In the next extract, Nancy extols the virtues of a man she has met, and responds to Edna's tease, in which she playfully suggests that the man is the type who pays attention to a woman only prior to his sexual conquest of her (line 9) by first laughing (line 11), then producing a serious answer (line 13):

**(5) [NB:II:4:R:14]**
```
1    Nancy:  VERY personable VERY SWEET. .hhh VE:RY: (.)
2            CONSIDERATE MY GOD ALL I HAD TO DO WAS LOOK AT
3            A CIGARETTE AND HE WAS OUT OF THE CHAIR LIGHTING
4            (h)IT Y(hhh)OU KNO(h)W [.hehh .hh One of those=
5    Edna:                          [I: KNO:W IT
6    Nancy:  =kind .hhhh
7    Edna:   [[Yes.
8    Nancy:  [[A:nd so[: but we were
9    Edna:            [THEY DO THAT BEFORE AND A:FTER THEY
10           DO:n't
11→  Nancy:  HAH HAH .hhh
12   Edna:   (Or he's-)
13→  Nancy:  NO:? e-MARTHA HAS known Cli:ff . . . ((a good thirty
             years and he's an absolute boy scout))
```

In developing his account of the production of po-faced responses to teases, Drew next describes some features of the sequential environments in which the teases occur. Focusing first on the types of responses found in the data, he notes that not all teases are reacted to seriously. Occasionally, a recipient will go along with the tease, as in the next example in which Bill describes symptoms of a current illness.

**(6) [Campbell: 4:5]**
```
1    Bill:   ee I think it was food poisoning (last night)
2            cos I was . . . I'm still gettin:g you know,hh
3            .hh stomach pains I spewed last ni:ght,. . .
4            chronic diarrhea as we-e-ell, just before I
```

```
5                    went to bed and. . .this morning (well) I've had
6                    this bad stomach. So I guess the same thing's
7                    gonna happen tonight. . . I've been getting funny
8                    things in front of my eye:s actually. .hh
9                    A bi:t, just slightly, Li:ght flashes. ((. . .))
10    Bill:          But uh, (0.3) .tsk (sti:ll.)
11    Arthur:        Well you probably got at least a week.
12                   (0.4)
13    Bill:          What of thi:s.
14                   (0.3)
15    Arthur:        No a week before you die:,
16                   (0.7)
17    Bill:          Ohh yhhe heh heh uh- [.hhhhh
18    Arthur:                            [It's a rare disea:se
19                   see,
20    Bill:          Yeh yeh yeh.
```

At first Bill does not seem to recognize the tease about having a week left
to live (line 13). But once Arthur explains it to him (line 15), he responds
by laughing, thereby both recognizing and going along with the tease.
Noticeably, unlike the speakers in the previous two extracts, he does not
make any attempt to attach a serious response to his laughter.

Drew (1987: 225) describes a 'continuum' of responses in which there
are four main types: '(i) initial serious response . . . prompted to laugh
by others, [but] returning to po-faced rejection; (ii) simultaneously
laughing at tease and rejecting its proposal; (iii) laughing acceptance,
followed by serious rejection of the proposal in the tease; (iv) going
along with the tease'. But he notes that overwhelmingly, there is some
component of po-faced rejection of the tease. In order to address why
this might be the case, Drew next looks at the prior turns or actions
which have occasioned the tease.

Here, we find that a feature common to many (but not all) of the cases
is that the tease follows a stretch of talk which is recognizably over-done
or exaggerated. For instance, in extract (6) above Bill describes the
symptoms of his illness in quite graphic terms. Arthur's tease in line 11
pokes fun at the over-elaborate nature of the description by suggesting
that Bill is in fact close to death. Similarly, in the conversation from
which extract (5) was taken, Nancy's glowing appreciation of her new
male friend has been going on for an extended period of time prior to
Edna's tease, and the 'nice guy' virtues of the man have been described
in elaborate, if not exaggerated terms. For instance, in prior talk Nancy
has referred to him as 'a real, dear, nice guy, just a real nice guy . . . real
easy going . . . he was a captain in the marines . . . he's got a real good

job . . . he's intelligent . . . not handsome but he's nice looking . . . just a real nice, personable . . .' and so on.

In both these cases, the teases produce a non-serious gloss or upshot of the exaggerated talk by the prior speaker. In (5), Edna's tease undermines the elaborate recommendation of Nancy's potential boyfriend by suggesting that these qualities will evaporate once he has succeeded in winning her over. And in (6), Arthur's tease undermines the overplayed severity of Bill's illness by sarcastically suggesting that Bill is about to die. Although Bill does not in fact offer a po-faced rejection, this nonetheless suggests one account for the production of po-faced responses to teases: the respondent is attempting to reassert the seriousness or warrantability of the stretch of talk which the teaser has targeted.

However, not all the cases in Drew's data fall into this pattern. He next looks at other instances which suggest a more general account. This focuses on the way that the design of the tease subtly ascribes a 'deviant identity' to the recipient. For instance, consider the following example of an entirely po-faced response to a tease.

**(7) [Northridge:2:JP/DP:1]**
(A telephone conversation in which Del is the caller.)

| | | |
|---|---|---|
| 1 | Del: | What are you doing at ho:me. |
| 2 | | (1.7) |
| 3 | Paul: | Sitting down watching the tu:[be, |
| 4 | Del: |                                   [khnhhh:: ih-huh |
| 5 | | .hhh Wa:tching n-hghn .h you nghn (0.4) |
| 6 | | watching dayti:me stories uh? |
| 7 | | (.) |
| 8 | Paul: | No I was just watching this: uh:m: (0.7) .h |
| 9 | | .khh you know one of them ga:me shows, |

Here, the tease in lines 5–6, 'you . . . watching dayti:me stories uh?' focuses on the fact that Del has called Paul in the daytime and found him at home 'watching the tu:be', as against, say, being at work, college, or whatever. So the tease trades on the negative or 'deviant' identity which can be attributed to Del of being slobby or lazy. This is found in Del's 'teasing characterization of infantile, pulp, noninformative, noneducational television, "dayti:me stories"' (Drew, 1987: 234).

We find a similar pattern of the suggestion of negative identities on the part of the tease target in other examples. To return to extract (3), Dot's tease, 'Do we have two forks cos we're on television' implies that Mother is being pretentious by laying out two forks just because of the presence of the video camera. In extract (4), 'And you started yacking' proposes the frivolous or gossipy nature of the encounter at the bus stop (in contrast, for instance, to 'started talking' which could suggest greater portent in the words or topics involved than 'yacking' could possibly imply). While in extract (5), Edna's 'THEY <u>DO</u> THAT BE<u>FORE</u> AND <u>A</u>:FTER THEY <u>DO</u>n't' implies naivety on Nancy's part about the wiles of men.

Thus, a common pattern has been discovered in this collection of teases. The pattern is not so much that they follow recognizably exaggerated stretches of talk, but that they implicate negative or 'deviant' identities for their recipients. And although recipients often exhibit that they can see the joke, the po-faced response is designed to counter that implication of a negative identity.

Drew finally draws out some of the sociological implications of this account. Beginning with the question of why teases may be responded to in a po-faced manner, the analysis has ended up suggesting that a recursive pattern in conversational teasing is that the tease ascribes a mildly deviant identity to its recipient. The implication of scepticism and the suggestion of negative qualities about the teased person serve to act as a subtle form of social control for these minor forms of deviant behaviour. And as Drew points out, like any form of social control, it can be resisted. In these cases, the resistance takes the form of a po-faced response.

## Participants' orientations to a conversational device

We mentioned the two core questions with which to approach data: what interactional business is being mediated or accomplished through the use of a sequential pattern or device; and how do participants demonstrate their active orientation to this business? Addressing the first question, we showed how po-faced receipts of teases are a way for teased parties to resist the attribution of tease-implicated deviant identities. We now want to look at a device used in arguments, in order to show more clearly how participants can display their orientations to the interactional work that is being accomplished with a sequence.

Why is this important? So far, we have stressed how analysts bring interpretive resources to bear on data in order to develop a general account of the interactional business being negotiated in collections of data extracts. As in all CA, the essential way in which these accounts are grounded is by looking at how an utterance is responded to in the next turn. But as we suggested with the earlier discussion of conditional relevance, an account of the ways in which a particular conversational device is used to accomplish specific interactional business will be strengthened if we can show that recipients display an orientation to those properties of the device which the analytic account emphasizes. By this means, we can get a deeper sense of the robustness of interactional devices.

We will illustrate this by way of the analysis of a device for exhibiting scepticism which Hutchby (1992a) found to be recurrent in arguments on radio phone-in shows (though the device is one that is generic to argument, rather than being restricted to talk in this particular setting). The device takes the form of a contrast between what the prior speaker has just said ('You say [X]') and what the current speaker suggests is the case ('What about [Y]'). By this means, speakers subtly undermine their opponent's claims by using the (Y) component to suggest that the (X) claim could not be true – or at least, is at fault – as opposed, say, to actively negating the prior claim.

Following is an example, from Hutchby's paper, of how the device appears in arguments on talk radio.

**(8) [H:30.11.88:2:1]**

```
 1   Caller:  I think we should (.) er reform the la:w on
 2            Sundays here, (0.3) w- I think people should have
 3            the choice if they want to do shopping on a
 4            Sunday, (0.4) also, that (.) i-if shops want to
 5            open on a Sunday th- th- they should be given the
 6            choice to do so.
 7   Host:    Well as I understand it thee: (.) the la:w a:s
 8            they're discussing it at the moment would allow
 9            shops to open .h for six hou:rs, .hh [ e:r ] on a=
10   Caller:                                       [Yes.]
11   Host:    =Sunday,
12   Caller:  That's righ[t.
13   Host:               [From:, midda:y.
14   Caller:  Y[es,
15   Host:     [They wouldn't be allowed to open befo:re that.
16            .hh Erm and you talk about erm, (.) the rights of
17            people to: make a choice as to whether they
18            shop or not, [o:n] a Sunday,=what about .hh the=
19   Caller:               [Yes,]
20   Host:    =people who may not have a choice a:s to whether
21            they would work on a Sunday.
```

Here, the caller begins by putting forward a position on the issue of whether British laws forbidding general trading on Sundays should be repealed, so that shops could legitimately open for business seven days a week. The host responds to this initially by clarifying a point of detail (lines 7–15). The 'You say X' device appears in lines 16–21, where we find that the host first attributes a position to the caller: 'you talk about . . . the rights of people to make a choice as to whether they shop or not, on a Sunday' (lines 16–18), followed by a challenge in which he seeks to undermine the caller's view: 'what about the people who may not have a choice a:s to whether they would work on a Sunday' (lines 18–21). Thus, the host uses a contrast structure which juxtaposes an attributed position ('You say X') with a competing version ('What about Y').

One of the principal ways in which we can ground the claim that 'You say X but what about Y' is an argumentative device for exhibiting scepticism is by showing that recipients actively orient, in the design of their talk, to the two principal properties of the device: first, the fact that it is a contrast, or at least, that it consists of two main parts; and second, the fact that it is used to undermine and exhibit scepticism about the recipient's prior assertions.

First of all, it can be shown that recipients (who are mainly callers, since it is almost always the host who makes use of this device) recognize the 'compound' nature of the device. This means that the device takes more than one turn-constructional unit to produce. For instance, in the previous extract, the host's quotation in lines 16–18, 'you talk about . . . the rights of people to make a choice as to whether they shop or not, on a Sunday', could constitute a possibly complete turn, since it is a technically complete sentence. However, notice the caller's action just before the completion of this sentence, in line 19:

```
16   Host:    . . . you talk about erm, (.) the rights of
17            people to: make a choice as to whether they
18            shop or not, [o:n ] a Sunday,=what about the=
19→ Caller:              [Yes,]
20   Host:    =people who may not have a choice a:s to whether
21            they would work on a Sunday.
```

The 'Yes' here may be seen as a continuer (Schegloff, 1982: 80). Continuers are tokens such as 'mm hm', 'uh huh', 'yes' or 'right', which display a recipient's understanding that a turn-in-progress is not complete, even though a possible transition-relevance place may have been reached. Goodwin (1986) shows that continuers are frequently placed at a particular point in the course of an ongoing turn: namely, at or near the end of one phrase or sentence and extending into the beginning of another. In this way, continuers act to 'bridge' turn-constructional units, and show their producers passing on what is a possible opportunity to take the floor. Using this analysis, we can see the continuer in line 19 above as a bridge between the first part of the contrastive device, 'You say X', and its second part, 'What about Y'.

Extract (9) shows up the same features.

**(9) [H:21.11.88:11:3]**

```
1    Host:    You sa:y that you would not force people to do
2             it. You do however accept that there is prejudice
3             against .hh er certain kinds of, homes and
4             er, [.hh] hospitals in communities [.hh] so .h=
5    Caller:  [Yeh]                          [Yeh]
6    Host:    =if: that prejudice exists people aren't going
7             to gi:ve ti:me. Or money for that matter.
```

In this extract, the caller's first continuer (line 5) comes after the host has projected the continuation of the turn with 'and er. . .'. But the second once more occurs precisely at the bridge between the two types of unit: sentences and contrast parts. Both continuers, like the 'Yes' in the previous extract, signal the caller's acceptance of the host's attributed version of his position. But what they also exhibit is the caller's recognition that, having produced this attribution, the host has not yet completed his turn, and is going on to produce a further component: in other words, the host is doing something more than simply quoting their assertions back at them.

The second type of evidence for callers' orientation to the use of this device is found when callers attempt to resist the sceptical potential involved in an attribution. This can operate at very subtle levels of detail in the talk. For instance, in the following extract host and caller are arguing about the problems caused by dogs fouling public walkways:

**(10) [H:2.2.89:12:1–2]**

```
1    Caller:  U:sually when a dog fouls:, .hh e::r it, it
2             lea:ves-=the scent that is left behind even if
3             you, clean up with boiling water an'
4             disinfectant,.hhh is a marker. .h An' when 'e
5             comes on 'is e::r, w:-wa:lk the next da:y, when
6             'e gets to that ma:rk, he does the same thing again.
((. . .))
7    Host:    er you s-seem to be suggesting that they go to
8             the same place every ti:me. Because they've been
9             there before.
10   Caller:  Ooh yes,=quite often ye:s.=
11   Host:    =Yeah but er(h)n(h) then:, .h e:r=
```

```
12      Caller:  =An[d other dogs will °also°.]
13      Host:        [ this- this mea:ns that ] they never go in
14               a different pla:ce,=doesn't it.
```

The host attributes to the caller the claim that dogs 'go' in 'the same place every ti:me' (line 8). In the second part of his contrast he casts doubt on this position by pointing out that 'this mea:ns that they never go in a different pla:ce' (lines 13–14). Thus, the host uses the 'You say (X)' device to imply that the caller's claim is erroneous because common sense tells us this could not be so.

Notice, however, that the host is actually reformulating the caller's claim. The caller began in a qualified manner by using the word 'usually' (line 1); and his argument remains qualified in the sense that what he is saying amounts to something like 'if the dog passes his own mark on another walk, he'll do the same thing again'. This is somewhat different from the host's version: 'they go to the same place every ti:me'. It thus becomes interesting that the caller, in line 10, not only agrees (apparently) with the host ('Ooh yes') but modifies the attribution by adding, 'quite often'. Thus, while appearing to go along with the host, the caller is actually sustaining the more cautious version of his position. Clearly, if the caller's more cautious version were to be allowed to stand as a modification of the host's version, then the host could no longer complete the sceptical contrast he has begun. That is, 'quite often' could not be effectively contrasted by 'never go in a different pla:ce'.

The host deals with this by utterly ignoring the 'quite often' component, and treating the prior turn simply as an affirmation. In line 11, the host displays his intention to go on to do the second part of the contrast he has set up. The caller, however, having heard the initial 'Yeah but', interpolates a further modifier: 'and other dogs will also' (line 12). This time, the host simply overrides his opponent, pressing on to complete the second contrast part in overlap with the caller's talk.

Thus, there are quite subtle ways in which we can observe callers displaying their orientation to the sceptical uses of the 'You say (X)' component by attempting to resist the contrastive implications being set up by the host. The following extract is a more straightforward example of this form of resistance.

**(11) [G:26.11.88:3:1]**
```
1       Caller: Uh, what was supposed to happen yesterda:y, it
2               was an org- it was an o:rganized lobby of
3               Parliament by: the National Union of Students.
4       Host:   °M:mm,°
```

```
5        Caller:  And the idea was to make, .hh the public of
6                 England, an' Great Britain, .h awa:re, .h of
7                 thee loans proposals.
((. . .))
8        Host:    You say it was an organized demonstration by the
9                 National Union of Students.=[do y-
10       Caller:                               [No it was an or- it
11                was an organized lobby, .hh a:nd a ma:rch, which
12                was supposed to go [to (   )
13       Host:                       [Well you- you can organize a
14                lobby or a march it still amounts to a
15                demonstration=d'you think it got out of hand?
```

Again, the host attributes to the caller a reformulated version of what was originally said. In this case, the caller's description 'o:rganized lobby' (line 2) is transformed into the more confrontational 'organized demonstration' (line 8). The caller detects this substitution and seeks to combat it in lines 10–12, by reasserting his own milder version and adding further modulating components: that the lobby was accompanied by 'a ma:rch', which was 'supposed' to conduct people to a particular location. In this way, what the host implies was a militant demonstration is reasserted as a legitimate and peaceable protest: the lobby is shown to be the central activity, and it is implied that the march was stopped by outside forces (which the caller later describes as 'a breakaway group') from reaching its destination.

However, the host again displays clearly his intention to go on and complete the contrast in spite of the caller's interjection (lines 13–15). But rather than simply ignoring or overriding the interpolation, he begins by assimilating the caller's more cautious version within his own: 'You can organize a lobby or a march it still amounts to a demonstration.' He then rapidly goes on to produce the second contrast part: 'd'you think it got out of hand?' by which, of course, he seeks to undermine the caller's original claim that the lobby was 'organized'.

There are thus two sorts of evidence of how callers orient to the contrastive and the sceptical nature of the 'You say X' device. First, the use of continuers demonstrates callers' recognition that such units can and indeed should project some further talk from the host. Secondly, callers' occasional attempts to modify hosts' reformulated attributions shows that they also recognize the potentially damaging scepticism achieved through this device, and resist by reasserting their own more cautious versions.

## Analysing phenomena: further issues

In the foregoing we have illustrated a basic three-stage model for building an analytic account:

- First, identify a potential object of analytic interest – a conversational device or a sequence-type.
- Second, produce a formal description of an empirical example, concentrating in particular on the sequential environment, in order to try and define what the device or sequence-type is doing.
- Third, return to the data collection to refine the description until it becomes a generalized account.

Our discussion has focused on the second two, more analytic stages. Less attention has been given to the question of what 'a phenomenon' is for CA. We will end this chapter by discussing this issue and some other, related questions, including the attitude of conversation analysts towards quantifying phenomena in reporting their findings.

### Different types of phenomena

First of all, it may be noted that in our discussion of the studies by Drew (1987) and Hutchby (1992a), the sorts of phenomena that are analysed are different in a variety of ways. For instance, Drew discusses a particular kind of response to a particular kind of action (a po-faced response to a tease). Hutchby, on the other hand, looks at a special kind of turn-format which is used to accomplish a certain interactional effect ('You say X' as an indication of the speaker's scepticism).

Similarly, on the one hand, Drew's po-faced responses do not take any generalized form. Rather, each of the examples he discusses is quite particular: there are no defining characteristics of po-faced responses in themselves, but the collection is built up through each response being analysed in terms of what it is a response to (i.e., a tease). Hutchby's device, on the other hand, takes a much more regular form; indeed, it is the form itself which accomplishes the interactional work. This, of course, is the point of demonstrating that recipients recognize the sceptical work being done even before the 'What about (Y)' part of the device. However, note that although the device itself is described in a formal way, in each of the cases we have discussed the way that the device appears is different. For instance, Hutchby (1992a) treats both the utterance, 'You say you would not force people . . .' and the linguistically quite different, 'You talk about the rights of people to choose . . .' equally as instances of the 'You say (X)' phenomenon.

A further point that emerges here is that Drew's analysis relies on his (and his readers') ability to recognize commonsensically where a 'tease' occurs in his data, and where a response may seek to treat the tease 'seriously' as opposed to going along with the tease. Hutchby's analysis relies less on this sort of commonsense interpretation, with the collection being built more on the basis of linguistic occurrences of 'You say . . .' and its variants in his data. However there is still, of course, a commonsense element in the identification of when a speaker is being 'sceptical', or a recipient is displaying 'recognition' of possible scepticism.

Do these differences constitute a problem in the CA method? Is it problematic that devices can be identified in quite divergent ways, or that building a collection to identify a phenomenon relies in such a way on the analyst's commonsense understanding? The answer is no, for a number of reasons. First, and most importantly, as we have tried to emphasize, it is not the phenomenon as a linguistic object which is the focus of interest for CA, but the interactional work being accomplished via turns at talk. So whether devices are identified by means of their formal features (e.g., an item such as 'Oh' [Heritage, 1984b], or a construction such as 'You say [X]') or purely in terms of their sequential placement in relation to some other turn (e.g., a reaction to a tease) is irrelevant as long as the analysis focuses on regularities in how the items in a collection achieve their interactional effects.

Second, it is clear that even when the device in question is described in relatively abstract terms, such as the 'You say (X)' device, no two cases are exactly the same. As we have said, there are great disparities between the ways in which the examples in the study by Hutchby are actually verbalized. However, the analytic account focuses on the regularities and therefore develops a more formal or abstract description of the phenomenon that is of interest.

But it is important to bear in mind that both in Hutchby's paper and in Drew's, as in CA generally, the analysis is actually carried out on a case-by-case basis. Each instance in the data corpus is treated in its own right, attending to its particular as well as its general features. This is because in the real world, in the course of naturally occurring interaction, the cases that were recorded were themselves produced on an individual basis. Participants in talk-in-interaction produce their utterances, and understand those of others, in the here-and-now. The regularities in talk which we can identify when, as analysts, we locate a phenomenon or device and observe its use in a collection of instances can thus only be described if we build an account that is more general, while continuing to pay close attention to the particularities.

## The role of commonsense knowledge

This brings us to the further question of the role of commonsense knowledge in developing analyses. It is inevitable that the analyst's commonsense knowledge will be brought to bear, first of all because as analysts of talk-in-interaction we are, for the most part, members of the same culture as the people we are studying. (There are exceptions to this, which we come to below.) Indeed it is difficult to imagine how it would be possible to do conversation analysis on data involving interactants whose language the analyst did not understand. For instance, of the studies we have mentioned only Schegloff's (1968) analysis of summons–answer sequences in telephone openings conceivably does not rely on understanding the actual words that are spoken. Whatever the word people used to answer the phone, that initial sequence would still be crudely analysable in terms of the telephone ring as a 'summons' and the receiver's first turn as an 'answer' (although that interpretation itself would rely on cultural knowledge about what telephones are used for, presumably).

But Schegloff's paper is anomalous in that respect. Both the other studies mentioned above, as well as the vast majority of available CA work, rely fundamentally on the analyst's ability to understand, and to come to some informed interpretation of, what it is that the participants in the data are doing. Of course, as we have emphasized, the aim is actually to come to an understanding of what the participants themselves take it they are doing; but in order to do that, we need to have some access to the interpretive and inferential resources which the participants are relying upon. In other words, it is absolutely necessary that conversation analysts are either members of, or have a sound understanding of, the culture from which their data have been drawn.

This is emphasized by Moerman (1972, 1977, 1988), whose research represents one of the most systematic attempts to apply CA to a culture which is foreign to the researcher; namely, Thai culture. Himself an American, Moerman (1988) remarks that doing research on a culture and language in which the researcher is not native foregrounds the amount that we have to rely on cultural knowledge, for otherwise the practices of interactants may not be understandable at all. But he also points out that when researchers focus on their native language (as conversation analysts mostly do), there is no less a reliance on cultural knowledge – it is simply that such knowledge is more commonsensical and therefore makes things seem more natural than they may be in cultures with which we are less familiar. Moerman in fact argues that conversation analysts should become more overtly aware of the culturally contexted nature of all talk-in-interaction, not just the supposedly 'exotic' or alien.

## The relevance of culture

Some work in CA does make explicit reference to cultural specifics. The kinds of points made tend to focus on two issues: the existence of cross-cultural similarities in conversational practices, and the nature of inter-cultural differences in certain practices. For instance, Moerman (1988) found systematic similarities in techniques for establishing reference to others in Thai and American conversation. In earlier work, Sacks and Schegloff (1979) had found that there are two basic rules for referring to other persons in Anglo-American interaction: first, use as few descriptive terms as possible; and second, seek the recipient's alignment in the description. These rules can be seen to operate in the following extract:

**(12) [Sacks & Schegloff 1979: 19]**
```
1    A:      . . . Well I was the only one other than the uhm
2            tch Fords? Uh, Mrs Holmes Ford? You know
3            uh [the the cellist?
4    B:          [Oh yes. She's she's the cellist.
5    A:      Yes.
6    B:      Ye[s
7    A:         [Well she and her husband were there . . .
```

Speaker A makes three attempts to establish reference to a couple named Ford (lines 2–3), each of them focusing on different ways that the recipient might be able to recognize who is being referred to: 'the Fords', 'Mrs Holmes Ford', and 'you know, the cellist'. The aim is to establish recognition at the first attempt; but having failed with 'the Fords?', the speaker then has to think of other suitable alternatives.

The second rule, that the recipient's affiliation should be sought, is found in the 'try-marking' intonation that the speaker uses: that is, using an upward or questioning intonation to invite B's acknowledgement that the reference form has succeeded (indicated by the question marks in lines 2–3). Moerman (1988) takes this description of an American conversational pattern and applies it to conversations in Lue, a Thai dialect, and interestingly finds that both rules apply in a similar way in his data where not only is the culture quite different, but also the language itself is unrelated to American English. Thus, Moerman demonstrates that similar patterns of talk-in-interaction exist in different cultures and distinct languages.

Focusing on differences, Houtkoop-Steenstra (1991) found some basic divergences between the ways that Dutch speakers open telephone conversations and the way Americans typically do. As we noted earlier, Schegloff's (1968, 1979b, 1986) work in this area has identified a robust pattern in American English telephone calls, in which the answerer's first turn takes the form of 'Hello' or some equivalent answer to the summons issued by the telephone ring. The second sequence following the summons–answer sequence is an 'identification/recognition' sequence, which may take the form of the participants exchanging names, or simply greeting each other and relying on voice recognition.

Houtkoop-Steenstra (1991) finds that Dutch speakers tend to answer the phone not with 'Hello' but with a self-identification. For instance:

**(13) [HH:18:245]**
1→  A:     It's Reina de Wind?
2    B:     Hell<u>o:</u>, it's Bren.

**(14) [HH:12:98]**
1→  A:     It's Catrien?
2           (0.7)
3    B:     It's Maarten.

Just as Schegloff (1986) finds that the summons–answer sequence of [(ring) : 'Hello'] is typical for American English calls, so Houtkoop-Steenstra finds that the sequence in which the ring is answered by a self-identification is typical for her Dutch data. Thus, there is a sense in which the cultural context can be important for identifying and understanding differences, as well as similarities, in the patterns of talk-in-interaction.

## Quantification

Mention of these latter studies brings us to our final point: the relevance of quantification in CA. Both these studies of telephone openings base their findings at one level on rudimentary forms of quantification. For instance, Houtkoop-Steenstra (1991: 246) states that 'out of 87 cases . . . 78 [answerers] . . . self-identify in first turn'. And she quantifies her remaining cases in terms of four other categories. Schegloff's (1968) earlier study has its foundation in part in a crude quantification exercise: out of 500 cases, only 499 were covered by the initial hypothesis. Yet for the most part, conversation analysts have a reluctance to treat quantification as the ultimate aim, or even a preliminary stage, of analysis. Indeed, for Houtkoop-Steenstra, her counting of cases is merely a way of strengthening her account of the robustness of her selected phenomenon, rather than an analytic technique in itself.

The reasons for this reluctance are related to the points we have outlined above. Although this chapter has been about the importance of collections in CA, and the ways in which large numbers of instances come to be used in the analysis of a phenomenon or device, we have also stressed the significance of discovering the orderliness of talk from the participants' perspective and the role of commonsense interpretation in generating analyses. Although conversation analysts, like quantitative researchers, engage in developing categories and classifying data extracts in terms of those, both the ways in which those categories are assembled and the role they play in analysis are different from purely quantitative approaches.

CA employs a methodology in which exemplars are used as the basis on which a generalizable description is built (see Hopper, 1989b). This is different from techniques in which a hypothesis is first made and then tested using large collections of data. This is sometimes thought of in terms of the distinction between inductive and deductive research methods. However, the more significant point to stress is that, as we have shown, CA places great emphasis on the close description of empirical examples, and often the analysis of a phenomenon will grow from the careful description of one instance, which then, through the process we have described, becomes a description capable of covering a whole collection of cases.

Conversation analysts use collections in order to reveal systematic patterns in talk-in-interaction across differing contexts and involving varying participants. But that aim is underpinned by a recognition that while there may be regularities across cases, each case is ultimately unique. A related point, which we have mentioned previously and which we come back to in later chapters, is that CA avoids treating the phenomena of talk-in-interaction as statistical variables. Such an approach may seek to show, for instance, that Drew's (1987) po-faced tease receipts are more likely to occur when a participant with a 'serious' personality is involved in the interaction. This could be described as an 'experimental' approach. For CA, such an approach would be to move away from the aim of explicating, on a case-by-case basis, the systematic competencies that participants in naturally occurring talk-in-interaction rely on to understand one another's actions and to generate interactionally appropriate responses.

As an illustration of these distinctions we can consider the quantitative experimental approach as it is adopted in social psychology. In that field, researchers who are interested in interpersonal communication tend to use recorded conversational data (though of conversations recorded in a laboratory setting rather than in naturally occurring interaction) in order to test hypotheses about the nature of speech phenomena (Hopper, 1989a). These hypotheses are tested using statistical techniques which involve coding certain speech phenomena into pre-established categories. We can demonstrate the differences between the social psychology (SP) approach and CA by focusing on the issue of speech overlap, and especially 'interruption', since this is an area that has interested both social psychologists and conversation analysts (Drummond, 1989).

In SP, interruption tends to be seen as one type of the more general category of overlapping speech. The aim is to distinguish between these different types in order to count the number of interruptions that occur in a given set of data. Underlying this is a theoretical assumption that interruption can be treated as an indicator of interpersonal factors such as dominance, power, or control. The technique is to code each of a collection of examples of overlapping speech on the basis of pre-established criteria. These criteria can be very extensive. For instance, in one of the most well known systems, the 'Simultaneous Speech Coding System' (Roger, Bull and Smith, 1988), interruptions are divided into basic 'simple' and 'complex' forms, and then these types are again subdivided into no less than 17 distinct sub-types of interruption.

In another well-known study, Beattie (1983) classifies all 'attempted speaker switches' in his data corpus on the basis of three criteria. First, the success of the attempt (i.e., whether or not the incoming speaker succeeded in gaining the floor); second, whether or not there is simultaneous speech; and third, whether or not the first speaker's utterance is complete at the point when speaker change takes place. Thus, a category such as 'simple interruption' is defined as a successful speaker switch, in which there is some simultaneous talk, but the first speaker's utterance is not completed.

From a CA perspective, these approaches can lead to the premature categorization of an interactional event as a sub-type of interruption, when closer analysis would lead us to see a different kind of orderliness in the example. For instance, while many SP studies of interruption have focused on the occurrence of simultaneous speech as the basis of interruptions, Jefferson shows how large amounts of simultaneous speech which look like interruptions in fact occur in the environment of legitimate transition–relevance places. Thus, these may not be appro-priately describable as interruptions at all, but rather as attempts to gain the floor which show close attention to the local sequential contexts of talk-in-interaction. As Jefferson puts it:

> The overlap could . . . be seen as a byproduct of two activities: (1) A recip-ient reasonably, warrantedly treats some current utterance as com-plete . . ., and starts to talk, while (2) the current speaker, perfectly within his rights, keeps going. (Jefferson, 1986: 154)

For instance, in the following extract, a focus purely on the existence of simultaneous speech would lead a coder to code Doreen's utterance in line 5 as an interruption. Notice, however, precisely what is happen-ing in the talk at that point:

**(15) [Her:0II:2:7:5]**

```
1     Doreen:    Yes well pop in on the way back 'n pick it
2                up
3     Katie:     °Thhank you ve'y much° eh ha- how are you
4                all. [Yer a little ti:red] °nah°
5→    Doreen:         [Oh wir all fi:ne, ] Yes I'm jus:
6                sohrta clearing up
```

Although Doreen's turn overlaps some continuing talk by Katie, to describe this as an interruption would miss the fact that it occurs at a legitimate transition–relevance place: namely, after Katie's inquiry, 'how are you all.' In fact, what happens is that Katie goes on to provide a candidate response to her own inquiry, 'Yer a little ti:red'. So that while one speaker starts to talk at a legitimate place, as opposed to an interruptive one, her talk ends up looking like an interruption because the first speaker, equally legitimately, carries on talking.

Other instances which appear more clearly interruptive can also be described as quite orderly if we focus not on the appearance of the extract but on the local sequential context of the talk:

**(16) [UTCL A21:4]**

```
1     Pam:       O:h that's what I really need is a lid.
2     Gloria:    For your cake pan?
3     Pam:       Ye:s.
4                (.)
5     Pam:       So that no roaches will stick on
6                the [on the frosti:ng.]
7→    Gloria:        [O::h-  I  kno:w] what you're talking
8                about . . .
```

Here, Pam's utterance begun in line 5 is certainly not complete when
Gloria starts to talk in line 7. So on one level, this could be classified as
an interruption. But in another sense, it is clear that Gloria's turn is an
example of what Jefferson calls 'recognitional onset' of overlapping
talk. That is, Gloria has evidently caught the gist of what Pam is saying
– that she needs a cake tin lid to keep the roaches off – and starts her
talk at that point in order to demonstrate cooperatively her recognition
of the point. Rather than being a disruptive interruption, then, this
case is more appropriately describable as a display of close cooperation
between the two participants.

The point here is that by focusing purely on the coding and counting
of instances, the SP approach is in danger of counting as 'interruptions'
things that may not be that at all. This is not to say that such things as
interruptions somehow do not exist (see Hutchby, 1992b). But the focus
on quantification tends to lead the analyst away from considering,
closely and on a case-by-case basis, how the participants themselves are
orienting to one another's actions.

In this chapter we have introduced some of the principal conversation analytic techniques used for developing robust accounts of conversational phenomena. The focus has been on how conversational
devices and other sorts of phenomena are located in large collections of
data. The following chapter comprises the second part of our discussion of techniques for analysing phenomena. There, we turn to look at
procedures involving a sustained analytic focus on extended sequences
of talk, including the widely used technique of single case analysis.

# 5

## Analysing Data II: Extended Sequences and Single Cases

This chapter focuses on further ways in which the analysis of data can be approached. What we are concerned with here is the analysis of extended sequences of talk, and relatedly, the technique of single case analysis. Thus, the focus shifts away from finding recursive features in collections of data, and towards the techniques of seeing significant interactional detail in the ongoing production of singular sequences of talk-in-interaction. In that sense, we now become more centrally involved with exemplifying the 'conversation analytic mentality': the distinctive way of seeing the world of talk-in-interaction that the conversation analyst develops in the course of working through specific pieces of data.

For the most part, the sequences discussed so far have been relatively short, and each turn has been analysed as doing essentially one action. But obviously this is not always the case. Turns at talk are often very long, and accomplish many different actions. At the same time, conversational sequences themselves can be much more extended than the ones discussed in the last chapter. A technique that can be applied in the analysis of extended sequences of talk is 'single case analysis'. In contrast to the analysis of collections, this technique involves tracking in detail the production of some extract of talk, which can be drawn more or less at random from any interactional context, to observe the ways in which particular conversational devices are used in its production. Unlike the building of collections, then, single case analysis is not necessarily aimed at producing new findings (although

that can be an outcome), or at generalizability. Rather, it is more like
a test-bed for the robustness of findings generated using the more systematic techniques described in Chapter 4. As Schegloff (1987b: 101)
puts it, one principal aim is 'to assess the [analytic] capacity of [CA],
using its past results'.

In the second part of the chapter we turn to a common form of talk-
in-interaction which involves not only relatively extended sequential patterns, but also extended single turns at talk: storytelling. Of course, we
all recount stories on a routine basis, about what happened to us during
the day, or what we saw on the way to and from work or University, or
whatever. We might think that these stories are merely ways of relaying
information or of entertaining our friends or partners. But viewing
stories using the conversation analytic mentality shows that they are in
fact highly organized social phenomena, the methodic production of
which is finely tuned to display the teller's orientation to the specific
details of the current interactional context.

## Analysing single episodes

Single case analysis involves looking at a single conversation, or section
of one, in order to track in detail the various conversational strategies
and devices which inform and drive its production. In his original lectures on conversation, Sacks (1992) used this technique often, stressing
that the fundamental aim of CA is to be able to describe, adequately
and formally, singular events and event-sequences. Analysing singular
sequences can be a key starting point in research, and even by beginning
with relatively innocuous data, this technique can be used to discover a
great deal about how the 'technology of conversation' (Sacks, 1984b:
413) operates in particular instances. Furthermore, single case analysis
shows how general features and patterns in talk, described using the collection technique, can be seen to inform the turn-by-turn production of
talk in singular sequences of events.

In one sense, the kind of research described in Chapter 4 itself
involves the detailed analysis of single cases. The patterns that we
looked at there are not seen just as patterns: they are regularities observable across a range of singular instances. To return to Schegloff's (1968)
paper on telephone conversation openings, the reason why that paper is
significant is not simply because Schegloff took one deviant case seriously enough to reformulate his analysis so as eventually to describe a
pattern which accounted for all 500 cases in his data. Rather, the significance lies in why that was done. As Schegloff himself writes:

Although the 'generalisation' did not apply in [one] case, [the participants] had also achieved, somehow, the outcome in question (getting a telephone conversation underway). How? . . . [The second account] was found because one had to respect the fact that the 500th case was also, and equally, orderly for its participants, even though it was anomalous in the aggregate. (Schegloff, 1987b: 102)

To illustrate further, Schegloff invites us to consider lectures as interactional occasions:

Lectures . . . have familiar organisational forms and practices which recur with great regularity on the multiple occasions on which they are delivered. But if a lecturer should begin producing bizarre behaviour, it is unlikely that those present would find it sufficient to set this aside as just a statistical anomaly. It would not suffice to consider that all the previously attended lectures followed one or another canonical form; that there was bound to be a case which deviated; and that this was it. Rather, observers find themselves making some sense or other of what is going on, and find some way of conducting themselves that deals with the situation. On reflection, of course, that is what is done on each of the ordinary such occasions in which persons participate. They find on each singular occasion whether and when to laugh, when to nod or knit the brow, whether and when to applaud, when and how to leave early if it is a bore . . . (Schegloff, 1987b: 102–3)

In other words, although conversation analysts are interested in the patterned nature of talk-in-interaction, it is recognized that the locus of order is always the single case. What we want to do in this section is to show how this aspect of the conversation analytic mentality can be brought to bear on one apparently trivial fragment of naturally occurring interaction, with some interesting and sociologically relevant results.

We focus on the following extract from a telephone conversation between two women, 'Nancy' and 'Edna' (both are middle-aged, middle class white Americans, though that information is provided for background only: it does not play any further part in our analysis). We begin at the very start of the telephone call (Edna is the caller).

**(1) [NB:II:2:1–2]**

```
         ((Ring))
1   N:   Hello:,
2   E:   .hh HI::.
3        (.)
4   N:   Oh hi:::='Ow are you Edna,
```

```
 5   E:    FI:NE yer LINE'S BEEN BUSY.
 6   N:    Yeah (.) my u-fuhh! h- .hhhh my fa:ther's wife
 7         ca:lled me,h .hhh So when she calls me::, h I
 8         always talk for a lo:ng ti:me cuz she can afford it
 9         an' I ca:n't.hhh[hhhhh[huh]
10   E:                    [↑OH::[ ::: ]: my [go:sh=Ah ↑th]a(gh)t=
11   N:                          [ ↑AOO::::hh! ]((falsetto))
12   E:    =my phone was outta order:
13         (0.2)
14   N:    n[:No::?
15   E:     [I called my sister an' I get this busy en then I'd
16         hang up en I'd lift it up again it'd be: busy.
17         (0.9)
18   E:    .hh How you doin'.
19   N:    .t hhh Pretty good I gutta rai:se.h .hh[hh
20   E:                                          [Goo:[ud.
21   N:                                               [Yeh
22         two dollars a week.h
23         (.)
24   E:    Oh [wo:w.
25   N:       [↑Ih:::huh hu[:h huh,
26   E:                    [Wudee gun: do with it a:ll.
27   N:    Gol' I rilly I jis' don't know how Ah'm gunnuh
28         spend all that money.
29         (0.2)
30   E:    Y'oughta go sho:pping,
31   N:    .hhhh Well I should but (.) yihknow et eight
32         dollars a mo:[ n:th:,  anything  I'd ] buy'd, be using=
33   E:                 [hm hmm hm-mm-hm. ]
34   N:    =up my raise fer 'alf [ a  YEA:R: ] ((smile voice))
35   E:                          [  Ye:a:h.  ]
36   E:    .hhhhh Bud j's lef' t' play go:lf he's gotta go tuh
37         Riverside . . .
```

What happens here is on one level entirely trivial. Edna calls her friend Nancy, and indicates that she has had some trouble getting through. Nancy then complains about a paltry pay rise she just received; then as the extract ends Edna announces that her husband, Bud, has gone to play golf. What could be more commonplace? However, using the conversation analytic mentality we can come to see how the activities which make up this fragment are delicately accomplished through the use of interactional techniques which both transcend this particular conversation, yet at the same time are specifically designed for use within it.

So how do we go about using the findings of conversation analytic studies in order to explicate the underlying interactional organization of this fragment? One technique is simply to focus on some point in the talk and attempt to explicate the interactional work that is being done, and the conversational resources being used in that work. We will focus first of all on Edna's utterance 'FI:NE yer LINE'S BEEN BUSY' (line 5). Later, we will look at the second half of the extract, following Nancy's utterance 'Pretty good I gutta rai:se' (line 19). One reason why we focus on these two turns is that both are done in response to an entirely conventional 'How are you?' inquiry (Nancy's ''ow a:re you Edna' in line 4, and Edna's 'How you doin'' in line 18), yet both take very different forms. A second reason is that each of the utterances constitutes a form of complaint: yet these complaints are accomplished in different ways, which in turn have specific consequences for the talk which immediately follows. A number of CA studies can be brought to bear in helping us to understand how those utterances are designed to achieve the interactional effects that they do.

Let us note to start off with, then, that the fragment begins with a version of the standard telephone conversation opening described by Schegloff (1968, 1986): a summons–answer sequence of (ring) + 'Hello:?', followed by an exchange of greetings: 'HI::' + 'Oh: hi:::'. This in turn is followed by the initiation of a how-are-you sequence: 'Oh: hi:::='ow a:re you Edna' + 'FI:NE . . .'.

To get a sense of how routine this form of opening is, note the almost identical structure of the opening we discussed briefly in the previous chapter:

**(2) [HG:1]**

|   |        | (Ring)            |
|---|--------|-------------------|
| 1 | Nancy: | H'llo?            |
| 2 | Hyla:  | Hi:,              |
| 3 | Nancy: | Hi::.             |
| 4 | Hyla:  | How are yuhh=      |
| 5 | Nancy: | =Fi:ne how er you, |
| 6 | Hyla:  | Oka:y,            |

This opening exemplifies what has been identified as the four 'core sequences' that are characteristic of telephone conversation openings in Western (and some non-Western) cultures:

- The *summons/answer sequence* (lines 0–1): This consists of the telephone ring (the summons) and the answerer's first 'Hello'.
- The *identification/recognition sequence* (lines 2–3): This is accomplished in extract (2) as the caller recognizes the called party's 'Hello',

and uses a vocal signature to identify herself and invite reciprocal recognition.

- The *greetings sequence* (lines 2–3): In extract (2), this is accomplished simultaneously with identification/recognition; but in other calls, the participants may need to identify each other before engaging in greetings.
- The *initial inquiries sequence* (lines 4–6): Following greetings, participants regularly engage in an exchange of 'How are you's. These may lead straight into a first topic: for instance, if a response to a 'How are you' inquiry is either very negative ('Terrible') or overly positive ('Fantastic!'), the inquirer may ask 'Why?' Alternatively, as in extract (2), the responses can be neutral ('Fine' or 'Okay') and then first topic needs either to be introduced or solicited.

In his large-scale study, Schegloff (1986) found this core set of sequences to be present in various forms and permutations throughout his data collection.

Like the two speakers in example (2), Nancy and Edna are friends who call each other up on a regular basis. Thus, in both examples, the caller (Edna in (1), Hyla in (2)) takes it that there is no need to identify themselves; rather, they assume that the answerer (a different 'Nancy' in each case) can recognize them by means of the sound of their voice alone. Consequently, the greetings exchange is minimal and the speakers rapidly move into the ensuing 'how-are-you' exchange.

Here, however, the two calls start to differ. A major difference is that the how-are-you exchange in extract (2) is completed in what is the standard way for such an exchange (that is, two adjacency pairs, adjacent to each other: 'How are you'/Response + 'How are you'/Response), whereas in extract (1) that little sequence of two adjacency pairs is disrupted after the first response. Edna, instead of returning the how-are-you inquiry after her response, '<u>FI</u>:NE', produces a comment about the fact that she has apparently been struggling to get through: '<u>FI</u>:NE yer LINE'S BEEN BUSY'.

What interactional work is this utterance doing? Clearly, one way of viewing this statement is as a form of mild complaint. Edna is complaining, in an indirect way, about the fact that she has been unable to get through; in fact, she later implies, the situation had been so bad that she thought her 'ph<u>one</u> wuz <u>outta order</u>' (lines 10–12). Yet why does she produce this 'complaint' in the way she does: by stating a fact – the line's been busy – rather than objecting more overtly? We can account for this using a study by Pomerantz (1980) of the interactional strategy of 'fishing'.

Pomerantz notes that while speakers may request information in a straightforward way – for instance, by saying, 'Are you coming to the party tonight?' – another routine way in which requests for information are made is indirectly. One technique is to provide a factual report on the relevant events seen from the speaker's point of view, in order to 'invite' the recipient to provide the sought-after information by telling their side of events. So, with the party example, you might say, 'I hear Jeff's having a party tonight' as a way of fishing for information about whether your co-interactant has been invited. Pomerantz refers to these fishing statements as 'my side' tellings.

In telephone conversation, a common form of 'my side' telling is one which reports on the answerer's failure to answer their phone, as a way of fishing for information about where the answerer was, or who she was talking to. Clearly, this sort of information is open to being treated by its holder as entirely private; that is, it could be said that it is none of the caller's business why the phone was not answered. Therefore, there are good reasons why such information should be sought indirectly. As Pomerantz shows, by producing a 'my side' telling, a speaker implies that they are intrigued to know more, but does not put the recipient in the position of having either to answer or find a reason for not answering, as would be the case with an explicit request.

In this sense, as Pomerantz (1980: 194) says, 'the design of the "my side" telling poses this problem for the recipient: to determine what the co-interactant is suggesting or meaning in and through describing "my side".' A significant feature of 'my side' tellings is thus that they provide an environment in which the next turn proof procedure becomes especially relevant. In the turn following a 'my side' telling, the recipient displays her understanding of what the prior speaker was intending.

To return to our example, then, Edna's utterance 'yer LINE'S BEEN BUSY' is a clear example of a 'my side' telling: it reports the state of events from Edna's point of view as a person trying to make a telephone call. But if she is intending this as a form of mild complaint about the length of time she has been trying to get through, there are good reasons to use such a fishing device to do so, since there may be much more negative interactional implications associated with a more direct formulation.

But what exactly leads us to characterize this utterance as a complaint? As Pomerantz points out, discussing the same exchange, there is nothing in the formulation of Edna's utterance itself which necessarily makes it into a complaint: 'Certainly one possibility is that it is "merely" [Edna's] sharing of her experience of trying to get through to [Nancy]. Such a telling may also be done as an elicitor of information, for example, Were you talking on the phone and with whom.'

However, she notes something quite specific about the way Edna's utterance is formulated:

> Those possibilities do not exhaust what can be heard as possibly 'behind' the telling. This telling, which formulates the 'my side' report as a product of the speaker's *repeated* attempts to get through (note the tense of the description), is hearable as a comment on the length of time the line was busy . . . (Pomerantz, 1980: 195)

It is this aspect which Nancy orients to as important in the construction of her response. We see this in the way that she reacts in the next turn by providing an account for the length of time the line has been busy: 'my fa:ther's wife ca:lled [and] when she ca:lls me::, I always talk fer a lo:ng ti:me cuz she c'n afford it en I ca:n't.'

Thus, by focusing in detail on this utterance, on the sequential environment in which it is produced, and the sequential implications which operate in the next turn, we begin to see two things. First, the way in which the speaker in this singular instance utilizes a general conversational resource in order to engage in a specific, locally situated activity; and secondly, the way in which conversation analytic studies of such general resources can be brought to bear in explicating the interactional organization of singuar sequences. We can pursue these themes further by looking at a second instance of a 'complaint' in this extract, this time accomplished using quite different resources.

The talk occasioned by Edna's complaint goes on for a few more turns. It peters out when, after further talk by Edna about the number of calls she's been trying to make, there is no response from Nancy: merely a 0.9-second silence (line 17). This silence is broken by Edna returning eventually to the business of the how-are-you exchange (which, somewhat like an adjacency pair into which an insertion sequence has been slotted, has thus retained its conditional relevance): 'How you doin'' (line 18).

In line 19, Nancy's response to Edna's inquiry begins: 'Pretty good'. This, it turns out, is a significantly different kind of response to 'How are you?' than Edna's earlier 'Fine'. Indeed, the way Nancy responds to Edna's 'How you doin'' can be seen to be consequential for the particular kind of activity that follows: complaining about her raise. We can expand on this using another analysis of a general conversational resource.

As part of a major analysis of talk about troubles, Jefferson (1980) focused on responses to how-are-you inquiries, and began from Sacks' (1975) remarks that 'Fine' represents the conventional response to

'How are you'; it is a 'no-problem' response. 'Pretty good', on the other hand, represents what Jefferson (1980) describes as a 'downgraded conventional response'. Although it appears very similar to 'Fine', one kind of work which 'Pretty good' does that 'Fine' does not do is to suggest or foreshadow bad news. Basically, Jefferson (1980) shows that if a speaker has some bad news to report or some trouble to tell, they can use 'Pretty good' in this sequential environment in order to set up a trajectory in which the trouble might be elaborated on. By contrast, use of 'Fine' in this position, although it may be followed by news of some sort, tends not to be followed by bad news.

Adumbrating bad news, then, is a potential property of a 'Pretty good' response to 'How are you'. It is only potential, because bad news may or may not follow. The claim is not that 'Pretty good' is always followed by bad news, only that that is one of its routine uses. Moreover, even when there *is* bad news, it may not be told straight away. For instance, Jefferson (1980) discusses cases where the troubles talk adumbrated by a 'Pretty good' response at the beginning of a conversation does not emerge until some minutes into that conversation. This potentiality makes it a perfect kind of resource for Nancy to engage in complaining about her raise ironically. Its ambivalence also makes it a good place for us to trace analytically the sequential trajectory of how it is understood.

The first mention of the raise immediately follows the 'Pretty good' response; it takes the form of a straightforward, unelaborated announcement: 'I gutta rai:se'. At this stage, then, the news that is being offered is, it appears, good news. And Edna indeed understands that to be the case, as exhibited in her response in line 20: 'Goo:ud'. It is only in the next two turns (lines 21–4) that the sense of Nancy's news being not so good in fact emerges. But notice that there is nothing in Nancy's next turn itself – 'Yeh two dollars a week' – which overtly suggests that Edna may need to revise her initial understanding of the news. She does not say, for instance, 'It's not that good – it's only two dollars a week'. Rather, her turn begins with 'Yeh', and then goes on to name the amount. In other words, the turn implicitly does the work of making the news ironic: it is left up to Edna to recognize the significance of 'two dollars a week' and so to detect the irony in Nancy's talk.

Now we come to the crux of the issue. Edna's reinterpretation of the announcement appears in the next turn, in line 24. Here, in the same way that her initial reaction was fitted to the form of the announcement as good news, this second reaction, a downward-intoned 'Oh wo:w', equally is fitted to the new, revised status of the news. The fact that the turn begins with 'Oh' is significant in itself. As another collection-based analysis (Heritage, 1984b) has shown, the discourse marker 'Oh' routinely performs the interactional work of displaying that 'its producer has undergone some kind of change in his or her locally current state of knowledge, information, orientation or awareness' (p. 299). Edna's use of the item therefore connects with the way she is exhibiting a new understanding of her coparticipant's talk. More importantly, the particular kind of new understanding being exhibited is marked in how the 'wow' is said. The downward intonation (shown by the period in the transcript) marks the negative status that the raise deserves, just as an upward and animated inflection ('Oh wow!') would mark the news in a positive way (see Local, 1996; and our discussion in Chapter 9).

Following that, and Nancy's burst of laughter in line 25, there is a sequence in which both speakers now adopt a heavily ironic mode of talking. Edna sustains the joke about the paltriness of the raise by asking, 'Wudee gun: do with it a:ll' (line 26) and by suggesting that Nancy 'oughta go sho:pping' (line 30). Nancy's responses are similarly ironic: for instance, 'Gol- I rilly I jis' don't know how Ah'm gunnuh spend all that money' (lines 27–8).

These two complaint sequences repay close analysis partly because they are very well-bounded. The first begins with a response to a how-are-you inquiry, and ends with the eventual production of a return how-are-you. The second sequence begins with a response to that inquiry, and ends when Edna explicitly changes the subject to mention that Bud (her husband) has just left to play golf (line 36). As we have shown, there are many features of this extract which illustrate the ways in which attending to the turn-by-turn organization of singular instances can lead to revealing insights into the orderliness of interaction. By focusing on the sequential management of complaints in these instances, we have illustrated two central themes in CA. First, that there is a close relationship between particular social actions and the sequential resources by which they are accomplished. Secondly, we have seen how the pervasive orderliness of interaction can be detected in singular sequences, simply by describing, in detail, the turn-by-turn unfolding of talk.

Another aspect of talk-in-interaction which repays detailed single case analysis is the activity of storytelling. In the following section, we introduce some of the key findings which conversation analysts have made about the interactional organization of storytelling, by means of an analysis of a single case of a story told in telephone conversation.

## Storytelling sequences

Stories involve extended, multi-unit turns at talk. One of the issues that arises when we begin to think about stories told in conversation is how we can subject such extended turns to analysis using the fundamentally sequential perspective of CA. This raises both empirical and methodological questions. We address some of the methodological questions in Chapter 7, when we discuss the ways in which a CA perspective can be applied to extended, monologic utterances such as those where speakers recount stories about personal experiences in response to interview questions. However, most CA work on stories has focused on a second issue: the fact that stories are not produced in a vacuum, but their telling is always situated within interactional and sequential contexts. Given the overarching concern of CA with the sequential organization of talk, the analysis of stories merges into the analysis of storytelling, which in turn becomes a focus on the production of storytelling sequences.

The linguists Labov and Waletsky (1966) were among the first to show systematically that stories told in conversation could be subjected to formal analysis. Their approach primarily involved soliciting stories from subjects by means of an interviewer asking them informally to recall any 'life-threatening experiences' they may have had. By looking at the overall structure of these stories as recounted in such a 'semi-natural' situation, Labov and Waletsky were able to show that unscripted stories have formal structures which can be analysed in a way similar to classical linguistic analyses of written stories such as fairy tales.

However, Labov and Waletsky's study took a fundamentally linguistic approach: they were interested in 'recurrent patterns characteristic of narrative from the clause level to the complete simple narrative' (1966: 12). Consequently, they focused on the story as a unit viewed, for the most part, in isolation from the surrounding sequential context in which it was produced. But from a CA perspective, one of their most interesting observations, which they mention only in passing, is that the production of a story in fact always occurs in some specific interactional context.

At around the same time as this study was produced, Sacks was developing an alternative analysis of the ways stories in conversation can be built, which focused on the question of interactional contexts. Sacks' concerns centred around two issues. First, how do stories get to be told in the first place? That is, how do speakers who want to tell a story go about starting to tell it? Given that most stories told in conversation are not produced in response to such a question as 'Have you ever been in a life-threatening situation?', how do putative storytellers establish an audience for their telling? The second issue, correspondingly, is: how do story recipients respond to the storytelling? This includes the kinds of actions produced by recipients during the storytelling itself; as well as the question of how the end of a storytelling is established. Both these processes turn out to involve highly systematic conversational phenomena.

We can illustrate these phenomena, again, by means of a single case analysis of a story told in the course of a telephone conversation. The following extract is one on which we have previously commented, in chapter 3. There, however, we focused on it principally in terms of how it is transcribed; whereas here we are concerned with how the storytelling is put together in sequential terms. Prior to the beginning of the extract, Lesley has been trying to persuade Joyce to accompany her to a meeting, which Joyce has declined but in a vague way, without providing any reason. It seems that this declination would be an appropriate point at which to conclude the call. Lesley, however, carries on the conversation in the following way.

**(3) [Holt: Xmas 85:4:2–4]**

```
 1   L:    Are you not feeling very [we:ll,
 2   J:                             [°(  )°
 3         (.)
 4   J:    No I'm all ri:ght
 5         (.)
 6   L:    Yes.
 7         (0.6)
 8   J:    °Ye:s I'm all right,°
 9   L:    °Oh:.° .hh Yi-m- You know I- I- I'm broiling about
10         something hhhheh[heh .hhhh
11   J:                    [Wha::t.
12   L:    Well that sa:le. (0.2) At- at (.) the vicarage.
13         (0.6)
14   J:    Oh ye[:s,
15   L:        [.t
16         (0.6)
17   L:    u (.) ihYour friend 'n mi:ne was the:re
18         (0.2)
19   J:    (h[h hh)
20   L:      [mMister:, R:,
21   J:    Oh y(h)es, °(hm hm)°
22         (0.4)
23   L:    And em: .p we (.) really didn't have a lot'v cha:nge
24         that (.) day becuz we'd been to Bath 'n we'd been:
25         Christmas shoppin:g, (0.5) but we thought we'd better
26         go along t'th' sale 'n do what we could, (0.2) we
```

```
27                hadn't got a lot (.) of s:e- ready cash t'spe:nd.
28                (0.6)
29      L:        In any case we thought th' things were very
30                expensive.
31      J:        Oh did you.
32                (0.9)
33      L:        AND uh we were looking round the sta:lls 'n poking
34                about 'n he came up t' me 'n he said Oh: h:hello
35                Lesley, (.) still trying to buy something f'nothing,
36                .tch! .hh[hahhhhhhh!
37      J:                 [.hhoohhhh!
38                (0.8)
39      J:        Oo[: : :[ : L e s l e y ]
40      L:          [OO:. [ ehh heh heh ]
41                (0.2)
42      J:        I:s[ n 't ]    [he
43      L:           [What] do y[ou sa:y.
44                (0.3)
45      J:        Oh isn't he drea:dful.
46      L:        °eYe::s.°
47                (0.6)
48      J:        What'n aw::ful ma:[::n
49      L:                          [eh heh heh heh
50      J:        Oh:: honestly I cannot stand the man it's just
51                (no[:    )
52      L:           [I thought well I'm gon' tell Joyce that, ehh heh
```

The story here consists of Lesley's recounting of the social insult or 'squelch' inflicted on her by 'Mr R' (in his implication that she is using a charity sale to hunt for bargains) and the circumstances surrounding that. One way of seeing this is as an extended turn which runs from line 12, when she introduces the context for the story ('that sa:le . . . at the vicarage'), to line 35, when she recounts the squelch ('still trying to buy something f'nothing'). However, it is not simply a single turn of extended length: as we can see, at various points her recipient, Joyce, produces utterances which 'break up' the story turn (lines 14, 21 and 31). We return to this point shortly. First, we need to address the question: How does this story come to be told? In other words, how is the story occasioned in the sequential unfolding of the talk?

## Story prefaces

In a series of lectures on storytelling in conversation, Sacks (1992, Vol. 2: 222–68) began with a basic observation: 'Stories routinely take more than one turn to tell' (p. 222). By this, he meant to draw attention to the fact that in order to tell a story, the prospective teller has to engage in work to align their co-interactant as a story recipient. There are various reasons for this. One is that stories are designed in numerous ways 'for' their particular recipients, and the telling provides opportunities for recipients to react to, display understanding of, or otherwise become involved in the telling. We discuss some of these features as they can be found in our focus extract later.

More importantly, the telling of a story involves the teller in keeping possession of the conversational floor for longer than the basic rules of turn-taking ordinarily allow. That is, the storytelling turn consists of more than one turn-constructional unit, and there has to be some way of indicating to the recipient that such an extended turn is underway, in order for them to refrain from taking the floor themselves at what might otherwise be a legitimate transition relevance place. The most routine way of accomplishing this is to produce a story preface. This is a turn in which a speaker, often indirectly, proposes to tell a story. Following the preface, the recipient can then respond by indicating whether they wish to hear the story; and finally, the story can be told with the recipient appropriately aligned. The canonical format for story prefaces is thus a three-part structure:

| TELLER | Story preface |
| RECIPIENT | Request to hear story |
| TELLER | Story |

For example:

**(4) [Trio:2:1:1]**
(A calls B, who is an employee at 'Bullocks' Department Store)
1→  A:     Well I thought I'd jus' re- better report
2             to you what's happened at Bullocks today
3→  B:     What in the world's happened?
4    A:     Did you have the day off?
5             (.)
6    B:     Yah?
7→  A:     Well I:- (.) got outta my car at fi:ve thirty . . .   ((Story continues))

By indicating that she'd 'better report what's happened', A proposes to tell a story. In line 3, B appropriately aligns herself as a story recipient by inviting A to go on and tell 'what in the world's happened', which A then proceeds to do.

Sacks (1992, Vol. 2: 157–87) makes a number of observations on this sequence in terms of how it sets up the story to follow and aligns the recipient in the appropriate way. For instance, 'I thought I'd just re-better report to you what's happened at Bullocks', displays that speaker A is designing this telling specifically 'for' her recipient. Given that Bullocks is B's place of work, but not A's, then her reporting of something that happened there on what she believes to be B's day off (note the way she checks this in line 4) is a way of doing the activity of 'showing that I had my mind on you' (p. 174). This is a common feature of recipient design in conversational storytelling. We find another, more explicit example of it towards the end of extract (3), our focus extract:

**(3) [Holt: Xmas 85:4:2–4]** Detail
```
48    J:      What'n aw::ful ma:[::n
49    L:                        [eh heh heh heh
50    J:      Oh:: honestly I cannot stand the man it's just
51            (no[:     )
52→ L:             [I thought well I'm gon' tell Joyce that, ehh heh
```

Having told her story, and gone with her recipient through an extended response sequence, Lesley makes an announcement which claims that, even at the time the events were happening, she was thinking of Joyce as a suitable and in fact necessary recipient of this story.

Returning to extract (4), there are further features of interest in the way the story preface is designed. Note that the speaker actually executes a self-repair in the course of this preface; she begins to say 'I thought I'd just re-' (the last sound being hearable, in the context of our knowledge of what she goes on to say, as a start on the word 'report'), but then changes that to a formulation which brings to the forefront the urgency and importance of the story: 'I thought I'd . . . better report to you what's happened'. This way of putting it also implicates the recipient as someone who actually has some stake in this story: she is not just any recipient, but one to whom the events had 'better' be reported. When speaker B produces the second part of the story prefacing sequence (i.e., request to hear the story), she too orients to the seemingly momentous nature of this story, thereby situating herself as a suitably awed recipient. She does this by saying, not simply, 'What happened?', but 'What in the world's happened?', thereby focusing on the momentousness of these (so far undisclosed) events. (In fact it turns out that A had seen a policeman wielding a 'great big long gun' outside the store where B works, but could not discover why he was there. Subsequently the two participants engage in a series of phone calls involving a third person who also works at the store but did not, like B, have the day off, in an attempt to discover what was happening.)

Aligning recipients, then, is one of the key functions of story prefaces. But it is not the only significant function. They can also be involved in another key aspect of conversational storytelling: indicating to the recipient what kind of story this will be. This is important because one of the interactional tasks of a story recipient is to respond to the story in appropriate ways once it is over. Thus, the recipient needs to have some idea of what it will take in order for the story to be complete: in other words, an idea of the likely payoff or punchline for this particular story.

This element of story prefaces is illustrated well in the preface which occurs in our focus extract:

**(3) [Holt: Xmas 85:4:2–4] Detail**
```
9    L:     °Oh:.° .hh Yi-m- You know I- I- I'm broiling about
10          something hhhheh[heh .hhhh
11   J:                    [Wha::t.
12   L:     Well that sa:le. (0.2) At- at (.) the vicarage.
```

Lesley's story preface acts as a clue for the recipient as to what kind of story is projected, and thus, how Joyce should be listening for the story's 'point' and her reaction to it. Lesley's choice of 'I'm broiling about something' over other, equally usable alternatives such as 'I'm dying to tell you what happened at the vicarage sale', or 'I just thought I'd better report what happened at the vicarage sale' (recalling extract (4) above), acts as an indication not just of the 'tellability' of this story at this particular moment, but also of how Lesley herself feels about the events to be reported: the phrase suggests a simmering or agitated state set off by the 'something' in question.

In that sense, 'I'm broiling about something' indicates to the recipient how she might monitor for an appropriate conclusion to the story. In a word, it poses a question for the recipient: 'What kinds of things might the teller legitimately be broiling about?' The kinds of things to which 'broiling' may be a relevant reaction might include having been insulted, embarrassed, made to feel foolish, belittled, and so on; in other words, just the kind of social 'squelch' which Lesley's story reports Mr R inflicting on her.

Having noticed that, we might then note that the very way in which the story is responded to on its completion links back very neatly to the way it was introduced in the preface. That is, the sharp intakes of breath and exaggerated, indignant 'Oooh's have an almost onomatopaeic connection to the state of 'broiling' (which the Shorter Oxford English dictionary defines as 'to subject to high heat' or 'to be in a confused state, a turmoil'). They are sounds which are reminiscent of the sudden release of pressure, or the expulsion of steam. In this way, the coordinated verbalized reactions of Lesley and Joyce can be seen as concomitant with the physical reaction ('broiling') which Lesley has described herself as undergoing as a result of the story's events.

These last few points are of course speculative: there is little systematic evidence in the transcript itself which would unequivocally confirm such an interpretation of Lesley's use of 'broiling'. However, our remarks here relate to an issue with which Sacks was concerned in the later part of his original lectures on conversation: something he referred to as the 'poetics' of everyday talk (Sacks, 1992, Vol. 2: 291–331). Often, in looking repeatedly at a particular segment of talk, Sacks noted that the analyst can begin to find certain poetic resonances and relationships between the words used. He speculated that there may be a principle of 'locally historical searches' that speakers use in coming up with their words. They may somehow rely on echoes of words produced moments earlier to cue other words or phrases. In the lectures Sacks discussed a number of intriguing cases to support this notion.

This way of proceeding may seem to go against the rigorous reliance on the next-turn proof procedure which we have stressed in previous chapters. However, what it in fact does is to illustrate a significant benefit of single case analysis: that it provides the analyst with an entirely open opportunity to develop and explore analytic themes and ideas. As Sacks put it:

> When we start out with a piece of data, the question of what we are going to end up with, what kind of findings it will give, should not be a consideration. We sit down with a piece of data, make a bunch of observations, and see where they will go. (Sacks, 1984a: 27)

One implication of this is that we should not initially feel constrained in the observations we make by what commonsense might suggest is possible or not. In the very first of his lectures, Sacks was at pains to point this out to his students:

> When people start to analyse social phenomena . . . then, if you have to make an elaborate analysis of it – that is to say, show that they did something as involved as some of the things I have proposed – then you figure that they couldn't have thought that fast. I want to suggest that you have to forget that completely. Don't worry about how fast they're thinking. First of all, don't worry about whether they're 'thinking'. Just try to come

to terms with how it is that the thing comes off. Because you'll find that
they can do these things. . . . So just let the materials fall as they may.
Look to see how it is that persons go about producing what they produce.
(Sacks, 1992, Vol. 1: 11)

### Recipient's actions during the storytelling

We noted earlier that the story turn itself is not a single unbroken utterance, but one which is punctuated by turns from Joyce, the recipient.
However, these turns cannot be seen as utterances which 'break up' the
story turn, to use our earlier words. They are sequentially organized features of the storytelling itself. Obviously, the 'Wha::t' in line 11 functions as the second part of the story preface sequence. Let us now turn
to Joyce's next two utterances: 'Oh ye:s' in line 14, and the similar 'Oh
y(h)es' in line 21.

Like the 'Wha::t', but in a different manner, these two turns are
invited or solicited by Lesley. Recall in the last chapter that we briefly
discussed some generalized, cross-cultural procedures by which speakers seek to establish mutual recognition of the identity of someone or
something they are referring to. This comes under the heading of recipient design (Sacks and Schegloff, 1979): the way in which all turns at
talk are in some way designed to be understood in terms of what the
speaker knows or assumes about the existing mutual knowledge
between him or her and the recipient. In Chapter 4 we observed that in
the following extract, Speaker A makes three attempts to establish
mutual reference to a couple named Ford (lines 2–3), each of them
focusing on different ways that the recipient might be able to recognize
who is being referred to:

**(5) [Sacks & Schegloff 1979: 19]**
```
1    A:    . . . Well I was the only one other than the uhm
2          tch Fords? Uh, Mrs Holmes Ford? You know
3          uh [the the cellist?
4    B:       [Oh yes. She's   she's the cellist.
5    A:    Yes.
6    B:    Ye[s
7    A:       [Well she and her husband were there . . .
```

Having failed to establish mutual reference with the general term 'the
Fords?' (line 2), the speaker then proceeds to more specific labels: 'Mrs
Holmes Ford' – which again does not immediately work – and finally
'the cellist'. Note that it is this third reference which appears to be most
closely designed in terms of the two participants' mutual knowledge:

when B finally recognizes who is being referred to, she herself affirms that recognition (line 4) by repeating the categorization: 'she's the cellist.'

There are close similarities here with our focus extract:

```
12→ L:      Well that sa:le. (0.2) At- at (.) the vicarage.
13          (0.6)
14   J:     Oh ye:s,
```

And a moment later:

```
17→ L:      u (.) ihYour friend 'n mi:ne was the:re
18          (0.2)
19   J:     (h[h hh)
20→ L:         [mMister::, R:,
21   J:     Oh y(h)es,
```

On both these occasions Lesley makes successive attempts to get Joyce to recognize (a) the context of the story, and (b) its key protagonist. It is notable that both her first attempts are very vague: 'that sa:le' (line 12) and 'Your friend 'n mi:ne' (line 17); also, that both these attempts fail. The first, 'that sale', could potentially refer to any sale in any place, although clearly Lesley believes that Joyce is capable of pinpointing the precise sale in question, perhaps because of its recency, the fact that it had been discussed in a previous conversation (this is the first mention of it in this particular call), or some other aspect that gives it salience. Equally, Lesley's first mention of the key protagonist in the story (line 17) is extremely vague: 'Your friend 'n mine'. While this is a conventionally ironic way of referring to someone who is not a friend at all, it leaves the recipient a lot of work to do in order to establish which person exactly is being mentioned.

One other thing to notice about Lesley's turn, 'Your friend 'n mi:ne was the:re', is its slight upward intonation (indicated by the underlined colon in 'the:re'). Sacks and Schegloff (1979) observed that one way of attempting to achieve the most economical form of reference is for speakers to use upward intonation, which they called 'try-marking' (since it is a way of marking a try at establishing mutual reference). Speaker A in extract (5) uses try-marking three times (indicated in the transcript by question marks), and a similar phenomenon is found in our focus extract.

A further thing to observe is that a pause follows this try-marked reference (line 18). This appears to be a place in which Lesley is monitoring for a response from Joyce indicating that she has 'got' the reference.

In the absence of any such indication, Lesley then produces her next attempt, which is also try-marked: 'Mister::, R:,' (line 20): note again the underlined colon. At this point, Joyce recognizes the referent (line 21), and the story subsequently proceeds.

Thus, in this case, 'interjections' into the storytelling turn can be seen to result from interactionally organized forms of invitation by means of which Lesley, rather than merely recounting the incident, is actively seeking to involve Joyce in the telling. Furthermore, this segment illustrates the carefully designed ways in which storytellers may display that they are designing their telling for this particular recipient (see Goodwin, 1984). Notice, for instance, the way that both of Lesley's attempts to establish reference are designed to point up the common knowledge of the interactants. In the first case this is done by the use of pronouns: 'that sale . . . at the vicarage'. Implicit here is the claim not only that Joyce knows about the sale, but also that she knows about the vicarage in question.

In the second case, Lesley twice uses euphemisms rather than a name; furthermore, each of those figurative references in turn foregrounds common knowledge: 'Your friend and mine', and the familiarism, 'Mister R'. A final point on this is that Joyce not only recognizes the person being referred to as 'Mister R', but appears to do the correct kind of recognition for what turns out to be the point of this story. That is, by appending a slight laugh to her affirmation: 'Oh y(h)es, °(hm hm)°', Joyce exhibits that she sees Mister R in the appropriate way; that is, as someone who may be expected to have done something amusing, embarrassing or possibly insulting.

Conversation analysts, then, consider stories not just as single turn narratives, but as multiple-unit turns which occur in concrete sequential contexts. One thing that is clear about storytelling sequences is that they can be relatively extended, as compared, say, to the classical adjacency pair structure. But as we have seen through this discussion of a single storytelling sequence, it is possible also to show that other structures – for instance, story preface sequences, or recognitional sequences – are used in specific ways in putting together a storytelling sequence. In other words, one of the main objectives of a CA approach to storytelling as a conversational phenomenon is to analyse how the various structural patterns in talk can be deployed as the 'building blocks' for other, more extended sequences.

This takes us back to an idea mentioned briefly in Chapter 1: that the resources of talk-in-interaction are both context-sensitive and context-free. What we have done in this and the preceding chapter is to demonstrate how that feature of conversational resources can be seen empirically, and how it informs the analytic procedures of CA. In Chapter 4 we focused on the building of collections of similar extracts which are organized using certain techniques to demonstrate the existence of patterns in interaction. This procedure relies on the idea that different conversationalists, at different times and in different situations, have available essentially similar resources for accomplishing their actions. These resources (such as the po-faced receipt of a tease, for instance), while they are not tied to the specific occasion of their use, are nonetheless utilized in a way which attends to the unique features of that local occasion. In this sense, talk-in-interaction can be described as an abstract, structural phenomenon, without going against the idea that participants are knowledgeable agents who are not somehow 'caused' to act by that structure but actively use it to accomplish particular communicative actions.

In a similar way, the present chapter has demonstrated how abstract structural resources such as the story preface sequence, or sequences for inviting a recipient's reactions or establishing mutual reference to a third party, are used in locally situated ways to accomplish activities such as telling a story. We also demonstrated how conversation analytic studies of structural patterns themselves can be fruitfully deployed in making sense of how participants are managing interaction in single cases or extended sequences.

In conclusion, it is important to say that while these chapters have aimed to introduce some of the key 'how to' techniques in CA, it has not been our aim to provide an exhaustive account of all the possible research practices employed by conversation analysts. This is because, for one thing, there are simply too many minor variations to make such an exercise worthwhile; also, specific techniques which work well for one researcher will not necessarily work in the same way for another. Therefore, what we have done is introduce the basic means of beginning on a piece of CA research. For the beginning researcher, thinking in terms of systematic, formal similarities between data extracts which appear to be involved in certain classes of social action is perhaps the most useful starting point. But as we have shown in this chapter, a great deal can also be learned simply by sitting down with a transcript, and the associated tape, and trying to describe, turn by turn, what is going on in the talk. However trivial it may appear, the lesson is that like any stretch of talk, *this* stretch of talk is an orderly, methodic accomplishment. Approaching data in terms of 'What are the participants doing here?', 'How are they accomplishing that?', and 'How do they display the orderliness of the talk for each other?' is at the root of the conversation analytic mentality, and will virtually always yield results.

In the following chapters, we turn away from issues specifically to do with the process of analysis and towards the question of how a conversation analytic approach can be applied to a wide range of important topics in the organization of social life. We begin in chapter 6 with an account of how CA approaches the nature of interaction in institutional and workplace settings.

# Part III IMPLICATIONS

# 6

# Talk in Institutional Settings

Beginning with the publication, in 1979, of Max Atkinson and Paul Drew's book *Order in Court* (Atkinson and Drew, 1979), a distinctive wing of conversation analytic research grew up that concerned itself specifically with talk-in-interaction in so-called 'institutional' or workplace settings. This type of CA research, to which we turn our attention in the present chapter, has become widely practised, and major collections of studies now include those by Boden and Zimmerman (1991), Drew and Heritage (1992), Button (1993), Clayman and Heritage (2002) and Heritage and Maynard (2006). A recent overview of CA work on institutional interaction was produced by Arminen (2005).

Of course, it will be recalled that Sacks' earliest explorations of talk-in-interaction, outlined in Chapter 1, drew upon data from calls to a suicide prevention centre: in other words, an institutional setting. Later, he also drew significantly from recordings of a series of group therapy sessions for teenagers labelled as 'delinquent', another institutional context for talk (Sacks, 1979). Similarly, Schegloff's early paper on telephone call openings (Schegloff, 1968), which we described in Chapter 4, used data from calls to a police station, which can be seen as another institutional setting. However, a key point is that these early investigations did not pay any systematic attention to the 'institutional character' of the talk; rather, they were primarily concerned with establishing the kinds of features of orderliness in talk that was to become CA's hallmark, without bothering too much about the particular social contexts in which that talk was occurring.

The distinctiveness of the wing of CA that is concerned with institutional interaction is found, therefore, in its willingness to explore the connections between talk and its social contexts. In line with the general approach in CA, where participants in interaction are seen as actively accomplishing the orderly nature of conversation itself, a characteristic argument is that the procedures participants deploy in the production of institutional forms of talk are centrally involved in the reproduction of the 'institutional' nature of institutions themselves. We have seen how participants can be observed to display an orientation to the rules of turn-taking for conversation, thereby constituting the very activity of 'having a conversation', as opposed to, say, 'doing an interrogation'. By focusing on the relatively specialized ways in which turn-taking and turn-design are accomplished in institutional settings, conversation analysts show how participants similarly constitute 'non-conversational' interactions by the same process of displaying an orientation to the relevance of specific types of activity.

We therefore begin this chapter by looking at how CA approaches the issue of participants' orientations to institutional contexts. In later sections, we move on to address a series of related issues such as the different forms of interaction in institutional settings that can be discovered, focusing mainly on three influential lines of research: those concerned with courtroom interaction (Atkinson and Drew, 1979), with medical interaction (Heritage and Maynard, 2006) and with interaction in the broadcast media (Hutchby, 2006).

## Orienting to context: the comparative approach

As we have seen, a central feature of CA is a focus on the turn by turn unfolding of talk-in-interaction. This approach is linked to the view that participants themselves use that sequential development as an interpretive resource in order to make sense of one another's actions. In analysing talk-in-interaction, then, CA places great emphasis on the immediate sequential context in which a turn is produced.

But there is a broader sense of 'context' which can be invoked. Talk does not occur in a vacuum. It is always, somehow, situated. These situational contexts range from chance meetings in the street, through conversations with friends and family members, to larger-scale organizational settings such as workplaces, schools, and various kinds of service institutions, including even more specialized settings such as doctors' consulting rooms, courts of law, or TV and radio studios. The question is, what can CA's essentially local idea of context tell us about these wider social contexts?

To answer this question we need to understand what characterizes institutional interaction itself. As Goffman (1961) once pointed out, institutions are things that social scientists spend a great deal of time trying to describe and explain, but which they have not found a very apt way of classifying. CA has found one way round this problem. As far as CA is concerned, what characterizes interaction as institutional is to do not with theories of social structure, as in most sociology, but with the special character of speech-exchange systems that participants can be found to orient to.

This idea has its roots in the seminal paper on turn taking by Sacks et al. (1974). In that paper, the authors proposed that different forms of talk could be viewed as a continuum ranging from the relatively unconstrained turn-taking of mundane conversation, through various levels of formality, to ceremonial occasions in which not only who speaks and in what sequential order, but also what they will say, are pre-arranged (for instance, in wedding ceremonies). By selectively reducing or otherwise transforming the full scope of conversational practices, concentrating on some and withholding others, participants can be seen to display an orientation to particular institutional contexts.

This involves moving beyond a commonplace conception of context, in which the contexts of interaction are thought of as 'containers', which people enter into and which, at the same time, exert causal influences on the behaviour of participants within them. This is an assumption which underlies a good deal of work in sociology and sociolinguistics (Coulter, 1982; Schegloff, 1991). However, it raises the problem of the 'cultural dope' (Garfinkel, 1967). Basically, the 'container' view of context fails to pay sufficient attention to the active knowledge that participants have of the production of their behaviour. Rather than seeing contexts as abstract social forces which impose themselves on participants, conversation analysts argue that we need to begin from the other direction, and see participants as knowledgeable social agents who actively display for one another (and hence, also, for observers and analysts) their orientation to the relevance of contexts.

This is not to deny that the wider social contexts of interaction may have an overarching relevance for the participants. Intuitively, we know that a lively sense of context routinely informs our actions in the various social scenes of everyday life. For instance, if we were to call a radio phone-in programme, it is unlikely that in the midst of that activity we would suddenly be under the impression that we were calling a friend about a dinner invitation. In general, it seems, we 'know what we are doing', and are aware of the social settings for our actions.

But for conversation analysis, this intuitive view is inadequate. By relying on the private realm of individual awareness, it fails to account for the essentially public means by which participants display for one another their orientation to context and their understanding of each other's actions. As in mundane conversation, CA looks for a proof procedure which will show how participants make available for each other (and hence for the analyst too) the relevance of an institutional setting. That proof procedure is found in the observable details of talk-in-interaction.

CA has developed a distinctive means of locating participants' displayed orientations to institutional contexts. This is done by adopting a broadly comparative perspective in which the turn-taking system for mundane conversation is treated as a benchmark against which other forms of talk-in-interaction can be distinguished. By 'mundane' conversation, of course, we refer to a technical category which is defined by a turn-taking system in which the order, size and type of turns are free to vary. By contrast, other, more institutional forms of talk-in-interaction involve either the reduction or the systematic specialization of the range of practices available in mundane conversation.

The significance of this approach is that it succeeds in revealing what is distinctive about interaction in different types of environment. This is the most basic way in which CA aims to locate participants' active orientations to institutional contexts. Using this method, two basic types of institutions have been defined. They are described as formal types and non-formal types (Heritage and Greatbatch, 1991). The formal types of institutional setting are represented by courts of law (Atkinson and Drew, 1979), many kinds of interview, particularly the broadcast news interview (Clayman, 1988; Heritage, 1985; Heritage and Greatbatch, 1991) but also job interviews (Button, 1992), by some more 'traditional' or teacher-led styles of classroom teaching (McHoul, 1978), and most sorts of ceremonial occasion. Non-formal types include more loosely structured, but still task-oriented, lay/professional encounters such as GPs' consultations (Frankel, 1990), counselling sessions (Perakyla, 1995), various other kinds of social work encounters (Heritage and Sefi, 1992), business meetings (Boden, 1994), service encounters in places such as shops (Lamoreux, 1988/9), radio phone-in conversations (Hutchby, 1996a) and so on. We can look at each of these basic types in more detail.

## Formal institutions and question–answer sequences

The distinctiveness of formal types of institutional settings is based on the close relationship between the participants' social roles and the forms of talk in which they engage. As Heritage and Greatbatch (1991: 95) put it:

> The institutional character of the interaction is embodied first and foremost in its form – most notably in turn-taking systems which depart substantially from the way in which turn-taking is managed in conversation.

Studies of settings such as courtrooms and broadcast news interviews have focused on the ways in which participants orient to a strict turn-taking format. Atkinson and Drew (1979) coined the notion of 'turn-type pre-allocation' to characterize the organization of interaction in these settings. Turn-type pre-allocation means that participants are normatively constrained in the types of turns they may take according to their particular institutional roles. Typically, the format involves chains of question–answer sequences, in which the institutional figure asks the questions and the witness, pupil, or interviewee is expected to provide the answers. This format is oriented to by participants, but at the same time normative rules operate which mean that participants can be sanctioned if they refuse to stay within the boundaries of the question–answer framework.

For example, in the following extract from a televised news interview, which is one major type of formal institutional setting (see Clayman and Heritage, 2002), the fact that the interview format is produced via norms rather than external constraints comes to the surface. The interviewee (IE) begins accusing the interviewer (IR) of misrepresenting him in a previous broadcast and demands to know why, while the interviewer overtly requests that the interviewee observe the norms by allowing him to play the 'interviewer' role itself, that is by asking questions:

**(1) [Greatbatch, 1988: 421–2]**

```
1   IE:    despite the fact there were fou:r major factories
2          that you knew about,=despite the fact there was a two
3          hundred and thirty million capital investment programme
4          that you knew about,=.hhh that we dealt in companies you
5          stated and restated toda::y, .hhh despite the fact that
6          ninety one per cent of our companies are still there:,=
7          and only the marginal ones which you knew were sold, .hhh
8          and you e:ven mislead people by suggesting for instance
9          that we owned the Parisian publishing house Brooke.
```

```
10→          Why.=
11   IR:    =s-s-s-Sir James I['m so sorry (   ) I'm so s-
12   IE:                    [No,=I'm asking a question now.=
13→ IR:    =It's more conventional in these programmes [fo:r
14   IE:                                             [Well I
15          don't mind ab[ out  convention. = ]I'm asking you why
16→ IR:                  [me to ask questions,]
17          (.)
18   IE:    you distorted those facts.
```

Here, we see that the interviewer appeals to the 'convention' that he should ask the questions, while the interviewee explicitly disregards that convention and persists in attempting to ask a question of his own. Such breakdowns in the normative conduct of the news interview are rare, but their occurrence brings to the surface the extent to which the characteristic question–answer structure of the interview is an active accomplishment of the participants rather than a pre-existing factor that constrains their behaviour.

The question–answer pre-allocation format is only a minimal characterization of the speech exchange system for formal types of institutional interaction. As Atkinson and Drew (1979) point out, any of a range of actions may be done in a given turn, provided that they are done in the form of a question or answer. For instance, consider the next extract, which is taken from the transcript of a rape trial.

**(2) [Levinson, 1992: 83]**
```
1    A:    You have had sexual intercourse on a previous
2          occasion, haven't you.
3    B:    Yes.
4    A:    On many previous occasions?
5    B:    Not many.
6    A:    Several?
7    B:    Yes.
8    A:    With several men?
9    B:    No.
10   A:    Just one?
11   B:    Two.
12   A:    Two. And you are seventeen and a half?
13   B:    Yes.
```

Here, A and B are respectively the defence attorney and the alleged rape victim. As we see, they restrict themselves to producing questions and answers, and by this restriction of turn-taking behaviour, we gain a powerful sense of context simply through the details of their talk.

However, when we look more closely at the questions asked by speaker A, we find that they are of a peculiar type. Searle (1969) introduced a distinction between two types of question: 'real' questions which are designed to inform the questioner about something which he or she does not know, and 'exam' questions which are designed to test the answerer's knowledge about something which the questioner already knows. The questions in extract (2) seem to represent neither of these types. First of all, they are not designed to inform the questioner. When asking about B's sexual experience, or about her age, it seems clear that A knows the answers already. Neither, though, are the questions designed to test B's own knowledge. Rather, they are designed to get B to admit to something: namely, to having had sexual intercourse with 'several men' at the age of seventeen and a half.

By these means, the questions are designed to construct, piece by piece, a certain social image of B: as a woman with 'loose morals'. Levinson (1992) observes that it is not any one question in particular which accomplishes this, but rather the juxtaposition between the questions as a series (especially in the last case, in line 12) and their answers. In other words the style of questioning is itself a significant part of the participants' displayed orientation to the context of a courtroom.

Participants' displayed orientation to pre-allocated turn-taking systems such as the question–answer format can have important implications for the specifically 'institutional' character of actions in formal settings. One of the most significant of these is the fact that in settings such as courtrooms and broadcast news interviews, powerful constraints operate to restrict the distribution of rights to express a personal opinion on the matter being discussed. In both settings, questioners (that is, attorneys or interviewers) are required to avoid stating their opinions overtly. Rather, their task is to elicit the stance, opinion or account of the one being questioned; but to do so at least technically without bias or prejudice. This is because both courtroom and broadcast news talk are intended to be heard principally by an audience: the jury in a trial court, and the public in broadcast news. For different reasons, the audience in each case is supposed to draw inferences and make judgements about the one being questioned without undue influence from the questioner. As well as constraints on the form of questioners' turns, then, there are restrictions on their content, in that a questioning turn should not be hearable as putting forward a personal opinion.

However, questioners clearly have ways of undermining this constraint. We have already observed how the questioner's strategies in extract (2) serve to construct a negative social image of the witness, and hence are implicitly critical in their assessment of her behaviour. In broadcast news, interviewers can similarly produce talk that is critical and challenging towards interviewees by adopting various kinds of strategies. For instance, they can embed critical or evaluative statements within questions; or they may cite the 'facts' so as to emphasize their contrastive relationship with an interviewee's statement; alternatively, they may attribute opposing points of view to others, and then offer them for comment (Pomerantz, 1988/9). These strategies enable interviewers to take up critical stances on their own behalf; yet through being framed within a question, allow them formally to adhere to the journalist's norm of neutrality (Clayman, 1988, 1992).

## Analysing conduct in the news interview

Within the CA framework, a wide variety of aspects of news interview conduct have been analysed. These range from the basic ways in which the turn-taking format is managed (Greatbatch, 1988), to the means by which interviewees shift the agendas that interviewers seek to pursue (Greatbatch, 1986); from the ways in which interviewers display their journalistic objectivity in questions (Clayman, 1988, 1992), to the means by which debate and disagreement are managed in the context of panel interviews (Greatbatch, 1992). Recently, Clayman and Heritage (2002) published the first full-length treatment of news interviews from a conversation analytic standpoint.

As noted above, one of the key issues here is that, in their role as questioners, interviewers are required to avoid stating their views or opinions on the news. Rather, their task is to elicit the stance, opinion or account of the one being questioned, but to do so at least technically without bias or prejudice. This is bound up with the professional journalistic ethos of neutrality, in which journalists (including broadcast journalists) are seen as acting in the interests of a wider public in extracting information from individuals in the news. But from a conversation analytic point of view, such a practice is of additional interest because it is bound up with the means by which broadcast news interviews are produced for the benefit of an 'overhearing' audience (Heritage, 1985). This involves the withholding, by interviewers, of certain kinds of turns that routinely occur in question–answer sequences in other contexts of social interaction.

In many types of question–answer adjacency pair, in ordinary conversation as well as institutional settings such as classroom teaching (McHoul, 1978), there occurs a third position slot in which the questioner acknowledges or evaluates the answer. Thus, in standard information-seeking questions, we may find the sequence *question–answer–acknowledgement*, while in the kind of knowledge-testing questions asked by teachers we may find the sequence *question–answer–evaluation*. In news interviews, there is generally no third turn acknowledgement or evaluation; rather, the standard sequence is *question–answer–next question* . . . and so on. (One exception to this, the case of *question–answer–formulation*, is discussed below.) The general avoidance of third-position acknowledgements and evaluations thus acts as one of a number of noteworthy features of the question–answer chaining sequence that is specific to news interviews.

It is also the case that news interviewers routinely and systematically minimize their use of the kind of continuers, receipt tokens and newsmarkers (such as 'uh huh', 'right', 'yeah', 'oh really?' and so on) that, as we saw in Chapter 5, are regularly found in ordinary conversation (Heritage, 1985). Such items do the work of situating their producer as the intended, and attentive, primary recipient of the talk being produced by an interlocutor (Schegloff, 1982). Hence, by withholding their production, news interviewers effectively preserve a sense in which it is the audience, rather than themselves, who are the primary recipients of the interviewee's talk.

As Heritage (1985: 100) summarizes it, the withholding of acknowledgements, evaluations and continuers is significant in the design of talk for an overhearing audience for two main reasons:

> First, their production would identify prior talk as news for questioners (who are usually fully briefed beforehand or may be required to appear so) rather than the overhearing audience . . . for whom it is, putatively, news. Second, by their production of these receipt objects . . . questioners identify themselves as the primary recipients of the talk they elicit [and] audiences could . . . come to view themselves as literally the overhearers of colloquies that, rather than being produced for them, were being produced and treated as private.

This does not mean that interviewers do not possess opinions, or that they do not sometimes find ways of inflecting their questions so as to evaluate an interviewee's response or convey a particular stance on an issue or on the conduct of an interviewee's talk on the issue. For this reason, Clayman (1992) stresses that we should prefer the term 'neutralism' over 'neutrality' in discussions of news interview talk. While 'neutrality' implies that the interviewer *is*, somehow, a neutral conduit using questions to extract relevant information from interviewees (an interpretation often favoured by news professionals themselves), 'neutralism' foregrounds the fact that news interviewers actually *achieve* the status of 'being neutral' through a set of specialized discourse practices.

One such practice is the 'footing shift'. Goffman (1981) used the concept of footing to describe the varying ways in which speakers are able to take up positions of proximity or distance with respect to the sentiments expressed in an utterance. Distinguishing between the *animator* (the producer of the utterance), the *author* (the person whose words are actually being uttered) and the *principal* (the person whose viewpoint, stance, belief, etcetera, the utterance expresses), Goffman noted that at any moment in talk, the animator can exhibit differing degrees of authorship and principalship regarding the words he or she is speaking.

Clayman (1992) adopted this concept to examine how broadcast news interviewers use footing shifts in order to give the appearance of formal neutrality. The following examples illustrate.

**(3) [Clayman, 1992: 169]**

```
1    IR:    Senator, (0.5) uh: President Reagan's elected
2           thirteen months ago: an enormous landslide. (0.8)
3→          It is s::aid that his programs are in trouble,
4           though he seems to be terribly popular with
5           the American people. (0.6)
6→          It is said by some people at thuh White House
7           we could get those programs through if only we
8           ha:d perhaps more: .hh effective leadership
9           on on thuh hill an' I [suppose] indirectly=
10   IE:                          [hhhheh ]
11   IR:    =that might (0.5) relate t'you as well:. (0.6)
12          Uh what d'you think thuh problem is really.
13→         is=it (0.2) thuh leadership as it might be
14          claimed up on thuh hill, er is it thuh
15          programs themselves.
```

Here, the interviewer begins by stating a statistical fact about President Reagan's election victory (lines 1–2), and at that point he takes up the footing of animator, author and principal. But when he comes to more controversial issues (challenging the effectiveness of the President's programs and his leadership), he shifts footing so that he is no longer author, and principalship becomes ambivalent (line 3 and line 6). In other words, he *redistributes authorship* for the position that lies behind his eventual question. Note that even when the question gets asked (lines 13–15), after the statement-formulated preamble, the footing shift is sustained: 'the leadership **as it might be claimed** up on the hill . . .'.

The next extract shows how interviewers may repair their turns in order to insert a footing shift which turns the utterance from one in which they begin by expressing an opinion, to one where that opinion is attributed to others.

**(4) [Clayman, 1992: 171]**
```
1    IR:    How d'you sum up thuh me:ssage. that this
2           decision is sending to thuh Soviets?
3    IE:    .hhh Well as I started- to say:: it is ay- one
4           of: warning an' opportunity. Thuh warning
5           is (.) you'd better comply: to arms control::
6           agreements if arms control is going to have
7           any chance of succeeding in thuh future.
8           Unilateral compliance by thuh United States
9           just not in thuh works . . .
((Some lines omitted))
10→ IR:    But isn't this- uh::: critics uh on thuh
11          conservative- side of thuh political argument
12          have argued thet this is::. abiding by thuh
13          treaty is:. unilateral (.) observance (.)
14          uh:: or compliance. (.) by thuh United States.
```

Having begun, in line 10, to ask a question the wording of which heavily implies that he will be both author and principal of the view behind the question, the interviewer breaks off and then initiates self-repair in order, once again, to redistribute authorship, this time to 'critics . . . on thuh conservative- side'.

Clayman's (1992) argument is that the use of footing shifts enables the interviewer to fulfill two professional tasks simultaneously: to be adversarial, while remaining formally neutral. Interviewers routinely use footing shifts when they want to put forward provocative viewpoints for discussion, when they want to counter an interviewee and put the other side of an argument, or when they want to foster disagreement among interviewees on panel programs. If they did any of these things while retaining a footing of animator, author and principal, they would inevitably be taking up positions on these issues. With the footing shift, they can avoid this.

Another technique for producing talk that is critical and challenging towards interviewees, and which is also bound up with the production of talk for an overhearing audience, is that of 'formulating' the gist or upshot of the interviewee's remarks, usually in pursuit of some contro-versial or newsworthy aspect. Heritage (1985: 100) describes the prac-tice of formulating as:

summarizing, glossing, or developing the gist of an informant's earlier statements. Although it is relatively rare in conversation, it is common in institutionalized, audience-directed interaction [where it] is most commonly undertaken by questioners.

This practice of summarizing or glossing is used as a means of packaging or repackaging the central point made in an interviewee's turn for the benefit of the overhearing audience. In Heritage's (1985) study of formulations in news interviews, he found that the practice could be used both in a relatively benign, summarizing role ('cooperative recyclings'), and also as a means by which the interviewer seeks to evaluate or criticize the interviewee's remarks ('inferentially elaborative probes'). The following extract provides an illustration of the latter type of use:

**(5) [TVN: Tea]**

```
1    IE:    What in fact happened was that in the course of last
2           year, .hh the price went up really very sharply, .hhh
3           and uh the blenders did take advantage of this: uh
4           to obviously to raise their prices to retailers. (0.7)
5           .hhh They haven't been so quick in reducing their
6           prices when the world market prices come down. (0.3)
7           .hh And so this means that price in the sh- the
8           prices in the shops have stayed up .hh really rather
9           higher than we'd like to see them.
10          (0.7)
11→ IR:     So you- you're really accusing them of profiteering.
12   IE:    .hhh No they're in business to make money that's
13          perfectly sensible.=We're also saying that uh: .hh
14          it's not a trade which is competitive as we would
15          like it.=There're four (0.2) blenders which have
16          together eighty five percent of the market .hhh
17          and uh we're not saying that they (.) move in
18          concert or anything like that but we'd like the
19          trade to be a bit more competitive.=
20→ IR:     =But you're giving them: a heavy instruction (.) as
21          it were to (.) to reduce their prices.
22   IE:    .hh What we're saying is we think that prices
23          could come down without the blenders losing their
24          profit margins
```

The interviewee here is the Chairman of the Price Commission, who is being interviewed about the Commission's report on tea prices. Looking at the two arrowed IR turns (lines 11 and 20), what we find is an emergent dispute over what IE can be taken as 'actually saying'. In line 11, for instance, the interviewer formulates the long turn in lines 1–9 as 'accusing [the blenders] of profiteering.' Since the interviewee had not himself used the term 'profiteering', this formulation can be described as inferentially elaborating a claim proposed to be implicit in IE's remarks.

A central sequential feature of formulations is that they make relevant in the next turn a response in which a recipient either agrees or disagrees with the version being put forward. Thus, although their use seems to move the inteview out of its formal question–answer–next question structure, in fact interviewees routinely treat formulations as if they were themselves first parts of a 'formulation/response' adjacency pair. As we see, in extract (5)'s case, IE disagrees with the 'profiteering' formulation (line 12) and moves on to address another issue, lack of competitiveness. In line 20, the interviewer formulates these remarks, again using much stronger terms than the interviewee; and once again (in lines 22–4), IE puts forward a weaker version of his argument than the 'heavy instruction . . . to reduce prices' referred to in the formulation. As Heritage (1985: 100) summarizes it:

> The interviewer's two formulations . . . restate the interviewee's position by making overt reference to what might be treated as implicated or presupposed by that position . . . Further, in this case and many others like it, the interviewee is invited to agree to a characterisation of his position that overtly portrays him as critical of, or in conflict with, some third party.

Formalized speech exchange systems can also impact on the management of more overt disputes, as detailed in Garcia's (1991) analysis of mediation hearings in a small claims court, and in Greatbatch's (1992) study of the panel set-up in some broadcast news programmes, where a number of participants with varying stances on an issue act jointly as interviewees with the interviewer as chair.

In both these environments, disagreement is an intrinsic feature of the encounter. In Garcia's data, the official task of the mediator is to hear and arbitrate between two sides in an ongoing dispute which arose in circumstances external to the hearing, and which is now being put forward for an independent judgement. In a similar sense, Greatbatch notes that in panel interviews, interviewees are selected precisely on the basis of their differing standpoints on issues. Panel formats thus 'allow interviewers to facilitate combative interaction through the airing of disagreements between the interviewees themselves' (Greatbatch, 1992: 272).

However, the specialized distribution of speaker roles and rights in both settings leads to the disputes taking distinctive forms. In both settings, an institutional agent (the arbitrator in Garcia's data, the interviewer in Greatbatch's) is accorded a central mediating role, with two main consequences. First, the institutional agent is allotted the task of eliciting, through questions, the position or version of events supported by each antagonist. Consequently, oppositional turns are generally not adjacently positioned, since each side's opportunity to put forward its case needs to follow an intervening question from the mediator.

Consequentially, opposing sides in the dispute tend not to address their disagreements directly to each other, but instead to direct their talk at the mediator as a third party. Garcia (1991) points out that in mediation hearings, this feature takes the form of a sanctionable norm. Disputants who shift into direct person-to-person opposition will be required by the arbitrator to redirect their utterances to him or her, and return to referring to codisputants in the third person. In the case of panel interviews the convention is less stringently observed. Interviewers may allow interviewees to argue with each other directly for short periods of time. But as Greatbatch (1992) shows, there are various ways in which the interviewer retains overall control of the course of the dispute, and at any point he or she may re-establish the mediated format.

These studies illustrate clearly how formal institutional interaction involves 'specific and significant narrowings and respecifications of the range of options that are operative in conversational interaction' (Heritage, 1989: 34). The specialized turn-taking systems found in formal types of institutional setting show us how participants orient to the relevance of an institutional context. But formalized speech exchange systems also have an impact on the ways in which social activities such as disputing or generating controversy are accomplished in these settings.

## Non-formal institutions: tasks, identities and turn design

We have spent some time discussing settings in which interaction is characterized by a strict question–answer turn-taking format. However, the category of formal institutional interaction incorporates only a restricted number of institutional settings: mainly the court in session, various forms of interview, and some of the more 'traditional' pedagogic environments. Far more widespread are what Heritage and Greatbatch (1991: 97) refer to as 'non-formal' types, 'commonly occurring in medical, psychiatric, social service, business and related environments'. In such settings, much less uniformity in the patterning of conduct is evident. The interaction may be more or less explicitly directed towards carrying out official tasks such as diagnosing illness (Heath, 1992) or making decisions about clients' health or welfare needs (Heritage and Sefi, 1992; Bergmann, 1992). As a result there may emerge 'aggregative asymmetries in the patterning of activities between role incumbents (e.g., as between doctors and patients in the asking and answering of questions in private consultations)' (Heritage and Greatbatch, 1991: 97). But typically these official tasks and activities are managed within turn-taking frameworks that allow for considerable variation, improvisation and negotiation in terms of the participation status or 'footing' (Goffman, 1981) adopted by lay and professional participants alike.

For this reason, Heritage and Greatbatch (1991: 98) referred to non-formal types of institutional interaction as having a 'quasi-conversational' character. As they say: 'When considered in turn-taking terms, at least, the boundaries between [non-formal] forms of institutional talk and ordinary conversation can appear permeable and uncertain.' It is important to acknowledge what is *not* being claimed here. The term 'quasi-conversational' does not mean that there are no significant differences between turn-taking procedures in non-formal institutional interaction and in conversation. Rather, the 'permeability' and 'uncertainty' of the boundaries between these two general frameworks makes those boundaries often very difficult to identify in principled analytical terms. The 'aggregative asymmetries' referred to above are not provided for on the basis of normative constraints on participation opportunities for speakers in given institutional roles. Therefore, participants' orientations to context, as a result of which these patterns of asymmetry emerge, must be located in other aspects of talk.

How can we approach this task? One way is to look at how the same interactional task can be accomplished in systematically different ways in different settings. We can illustrate this by means of some data used in an analysis of interaction in one non-formal institutional setting: telephone calls to a radio phone-in broadcast (Hutchby, 1996a). Comparing the opening sequences of these calls with opening sequences in everyday telephone calls, we find further evidence of how orientations to context can be displayed in the details of talk.

In general, telephone openings are a useful thing to study, for the following reason. Since participants do not have visual access to one another, in order to be sure with whom they are interacting they need to engage in purely verbal forms of identification and recognition (Schegloff, 1979b). Thus, the way speakers design their first utterances will begin to reveal how they categorize themselves in relation to the other. This categorization issue is a key one in conversation analysis, because categories of personal identity and of reference to others are necessarily selective. There are innumerable ways in which we could legitimately describe ourselves and our relationship to someone else with whom we might be interacting. For instance, on the telephone, someone may present themselves as a 'friend' (calling another friend), a 'colleague' (calling a workmate), an 'inquirer' (calling a service agency), a 'family member' (calling another family member), and so on. Similarly, those who pick up the phone in any of these scenarios will aim to present themselves in the appropriate way, possibly using aspects of the caller's talk as a cue to what their own identity is for the purpose of the present conversation. Thus, by examining the design of the talk we can locate the relevant identities to which speakers are orienting at that moment (Schegloff, 1991).

Looking at extract (6), it is clear that the two participants in this telephone conversation rapidly establish their identities as 'friends':

**(6) [HG:1]**

```
1              ((phone rings))
2      N:     H'llo?
3      H:     Hi:,
4      N:     HI::.
5      H:     How are yuhh=
6      N:     =Fi:ne how er you,
7      H:     Oka:[y,
8      N:         [Goo:d,
9              (0.4)
10     H:     .mkhhh[hh
11     N:           [What's doin',
```

One thing to notice here is that the two speakers establish one another's identity, and start chatting about 'What's doin',' (line 11) without exchanging names at all. Hyla (the caller) recognizes Nancy's voice as Nancy answers the phone in line 2. Hyla's first utterance, 'Hi:,' in line 3, exhibits that recognition; and at the same time, invites Nancy to recognize the caller's voice (note that she does not self-identify by saying, 'Hi, it's Hyla'). After Nancy's enthusiastic return greeting (line 4), they move into a 'How are you' exchange without needing to check their mutual recognition in any way. Following that, Nancy invites Hyla to introduce a first topic by saying 'What's doin'' (Button and Casey, 1984).

This opening sequence can be described in terms of the four 'core sequences' that Schegloff (1986) found to be characteristic of mundane telephone call openings (recall that we discussed Schegloff's work on telephone openings in Chapter 5). This set of sequences enables callers and answerers economically to establish their relevant speaker identities, and to negotiate the initial topic that the call will be about.

Turning to a non-formal institutional setting, the talk radio show, we find a strong contrast in the form of opening sequences. Rather than passing through a set of four relatively standard sequences, calls on talk radio are opened by means of a single, standard two-turn sequence, which is exemplified by extract (7):

**(7) [H:21.11.88:6:1]**
(H = Host, C = Caller)
```
1    H:    Kath calling from Clapham now. Good morning.
2    C:    Good morning Brian. Erm:, I:: I also agree that
3          thee .hh telethons a:re a form of psychological
4          blackmail now. .hhh Because the majority of
5          people I think do know . . . ((continues))
```

Here, identification and recognition, greetings, and topic initiation are accomplished in rapid succession in two turns occupying lines 1 and 2. In line 1, the host announces the caller, and then provides a first greeting which invites her into the speaker role for the next turn. In line 2, after returning the greeting, the caller moves without ado into introducing her 'reason for the call'. Typically for this setting, that reason consists of her expressing an opinion on some issue: 'I also agree that thee .hh telethons a:re a form of psychological blackmail'.

Clearly, the kinds of tasks and issues around identification and first topic that are involved in calls on talk radio are different from those arising in mundane conversational calls. In everyday telephone calls, prior to the talk getting started, it is not unequivocally clear for either participant who will be talking at the other end. Nor is it clear, at least for the answerer, that there will be any specific reason for the call. It is for these reasons that the core sequences are used locally to negotiate mutual identification and the introduction of a first topic.

On talk radio, by contrast, caller and host are, for all practical purposes, pre-identified before talk even begins. This is because callers, who of course have called the host specifically, typically first encounter a switchboard operative who takes details of their name, and passes these on to the host, who in turn first encounters each caller as an item on a list of callers waiting to get on the air. Once that has happened, the expectation of the host is that the caller has called in with something specific to say, and so it is not strictly necessary for the initial topic to be solicited.

The basic difference, then, is that in mundane telephone talk, participants need to select from among an array of *possible* relevant identities and a range of possible things that the call may be about. The structure of the opening in extract (6) allows those tasks to be done. In the institutional setting of the talk radio show, the opening is designed in such a way that the participants can align themselves in terms of given institutional speaker identities ('host' and 'caller'), and move rapidly into the specific topical agenda of the call (for a more detailed discussion, see Hutchby, 1999).

If we look more closely at the construction of the opening turns, we find more detailed evidence of the participants' orientations to the specialized features of their interaction. Here are some further examples:

**(8) [H:23.1.89:2:1]**

```
1   H:   Bob is calling from Ilford. Good morning.
2   C:   .hh Good morning Brian. (0.4) .hh What I'm phoning
3        up is about the cricket . . .
```

**(9) [H:30.11.88:10:1]**

```
1   H:   Mill Hill:: i:s where Belinda calls from. Good
2        morning.
3   C:   Good morning Brian. .hh Erm, re the Sunday
4        o:pening I'm just phoning from the point of
5        vie:w, .hh as a:n assistant . . .
```

**(10) [H:21.11.88:11:1]**

```
1   H:   On to Philip in Camden Town. Good morning.
2   C:   Yeh guh morning Brian. Erm (.) Really what I
3        wanted to say was that I'm fascinated by watching
4        these telethons by the anuh- amount'v
5        contradictions that're thrown up by them . . .
```

**(11) [H:2.2.89:12:1]**

```
1   H:   Michael from Uxbridge now. Good morning.
2   C:   .h Er, g'morning Brian. .hh Emm:, I have some
3        advi:ce that might be, a little bit more practical,
4        to people . . .
```

In these opening sequences, the design of each turn exhibits clearly the speaker's orientation to the specialized nature of the interaction. For instance, the host's first turns already have an institutional quality to them in that they are constructed as announcements. In most types of telephone call, the answerer's first turn is an answer to the summons represented by the telephone's ring. We thus find typical responses such as a

simple 'Hello?' (see extract 6); or, more commonly in Continental countries (Houtkoop-Steenstra, 1991; Lindstrom, 1994), self-identifications in
which the answerer recites their name. In institutional settings, once again
answerers self-identify, but this time usually in organizational terms: e.g.,
'Police Department', 'Sociology', or 'Simpson's car hire, how can I help?'
In the talk radio data, the host begins by identifying not himself but the
*caller*: e.g., 'Kath calling from Clapham'.

This apparently has not always been the case. In examining recordings of an American talk radio show broadcast in 1968, Hutchby
(1996a) found that the host answers the telephone using the more conventional organizational self-identification format (line 2):

**(12) [BCII: Red]**
```
1    H:     Thirteen minutes before ten o'clock here o:n
2→          W.N.B.C., ((click)) Good evenin:g, W.N.B.C:,
3           (0.3)
4    C:     A:h. (0.2) Is that Brad Crandall?=
5    H:     =Yes sir good evening.
```

Possibly, callers in this early form of talk radio got straight through to
the host, without first encountering a switchboard and being put on
hold or on call back, as tends to happen now. (Possible evidence for this
in the transcript is the ((click)) in line 2, where the host may be opening
the channel to the incoming caller.) Nonetheless, this example serves to
point up the way in which the host's first turn in extracts (7)–(11), in
which the caller's name and geographical location is announced, displays that it is designed principally for reception by the overhearing
audience. By constructing this turn as an announcement, the host
exhibits an orientation to the broadcast nature of the conversation.

Callers' turns too are designed to fit the institutional properties of the
talk radio show. In each case, callers introduce topics on which they
propose to offer opinions: 'What I'm phoning up is about the cricket';
're the Sunday o:pening'; or 'Really what I wanted to say was that I'm
fascinated by watching these telethons'. But there is a sense in which
those topics get introduced not just as topics but as issues. One way this
is done is by referring to them using the definite article: 'the cricket', 'the
Sunday opening', and so on. Using this form of reference, callers can
provide their topics with a sense of being generally recognizable. As
Clark and Haviland (1977) observed, to refer to a topic with the definite
article is to invoke some degree of shared knowledge between speaker
and recipient(s). This way of introducing topics constructs them as
given themes in the public domain. In this sense, callers specifically

introduce topics which are the 'right' kind of thing to be discussing in the public sphere of a talk radio show.

This point is illustrated further by the fact that callers do not phone in about personal or private problems and complaints; not, at least, unless these can be explicitly related to an identifiable public concern. For instance, in the following extract the caller begins by stating that 'We've got a real problem here'; but that problem is immediately linked to the public issue of 'dogs fouling our footways':

**(13) [H:2.2.89:4:1]**
```
1    H:      And good morning to Ma:ndy from Ruislip. Good
2            morni[ng.
3    C:            [Good mor:ning Brian. .hhh We've got a real
4            problem he:re with dogs fouling our footway,
```

In various ways, then, the design of turns and sequences allows us to locate the participants' orientations to context in non-formal institutional settings such as talk radio, where the type and order of turns are not pre-allocated. Our remarks here fit with research in a wide variety of these settings, where, as Drew and Heritage (1992b: 28) report:

> Systematic aspects of the organisation of sequences (and of turn design within sequences) having to do with such matters as the opening and closing of encounters, and with the ways in which information is requested, delivered, and received . . . emerge as facets of the ways in which the 'institutionality' of such encounters is managed.

## Bricolage and the institutional shape of interaction

In his work on AIDS counselling as institutional discourse, Peräkylä (1995) suggested that a term which captures this ad hoc moulding of resources to hand in order to shape the interaction in light of institutional concerns is *bricolage*. *Bricolage* derives from the French verb *bricoler*, meaning 'to tinker', and a *bricoleur* is someone who is adept at utilizing materials in ways that they were not originally intended in order to create something new. Peräkylä (1995) suggested that the emergent asymmetries found in his data of counselling sessions for patients taking an HIV test could be accounted for on the basis of a *bricolage* arrangement. The turn-taking itself, he found, is quasi-conversational, yet uniformities emerge whereby counsellors tend either to ask questions, or produce post-response information statements directed at clients; while clients tend to restrict themselves to answering the questions put by counsellors. This pattern he accounted for not in terms of a normative specification of the relationship between the roles of counsellor and client and the activities of asking/informing, on the one hand, and answering on the other. For example, as Peräkylä (1995: 75–87) showed, when clients do ask questions this is not sanctioned or treated as a departure from the institutional norm by counsellors. *Bricolage* enables counsellors and clients to locally construct a pattern of turn-taking using stock conversational resources marshalled in the light of the particular circumstances of AIDS counselling.

Studies which show related features while not using the term *bricolage* include Frankel's (1984, 1990) and Heath's (1992) analyses of consultations between physicians and their patients. Beginning from the basic level of the organization of turn-taking in medical consultations, these conversation analysts have shown how patients are often complicit in maintaining a situation in which the doctor is able not only to determine the topics that will be talked about, but also to define the upshots and outcomes of those discussions.

For instance, Frankel (1984, 1990) observes that while there is no institutionalized constraint against patients asking questions and initiating new topics, overwhelmingly these two activities are undertaken by doctors and not by patients. His analysis reveals that this asymmetry emerges from two tacitly negotiated features of the talk. First, doctors tend to ask certain kinds of questions, usually information-seeking questions which require strictly factual responses. By this means, they routinely open up restricted options for patients to participate in the encounter. Patients are situated as the providers of information about their current physical state; and not, say, as individuals who can contextualize their state of physical health within a broader narrative of life events (Mishler, 1984). Yet at the same time, patients themselves orient to and reproduce this asymmetry in participation options when they seek to offer additional information to the doctor. Frankel (1984) shows that this new information is offered almost exclusively in turns which are responses to doctors' questions. By this means, patients 'ensure that the new information, if it is going to be dealt with, will be handled via a physician-initiated obligation package, i.e., question–answer sequence' (Frankel, 1984: 164).

In a similar vein, Heath (1992) shows how asymmetries are oriented to by patients during the consultation, as patients systematically withhold responses to doctors' announcements of a diagnosis. Given that the diagnosis represents a piece of 'expert' knowledge which the doctor passes on to the patient, then by withholding responses other than acknowledgement tokens such as 'yeh' or 'um', patients display their orientation to the expert status of the doctor. Heath shows that this withholding is even done when the patient has an opportunity to respond through the doctor leaving a gap following the announcement of diagnosis, as in the following extract:

**(14) [Heath, 1992: 242]**
(Physical examination)
```
1    Dr:    Yeah.
2           (0.3)
3    Dr:    That's shingles.
4           (1.2)
5    Dr:    That's what it is:
6           (0.6)
7    Pt:    Shingles.
8    Dr:    Yes.
```

The doctor provides the diagnosis in line 3, then pauses for over a second (line 4); then reiterates that the diagnosis has been made (line 5). After a further pause, the patient responds simply by repeating the diagnosis (line 7), at which point the doctor reconfirms it. Thus, the diagnosis is produced over a series of turns alternating with pauses, in which there is no response from the patient other than a single-word repetition of the doctor's conclusion.

As Heath (1992) notes, the only times when patients do respond more fulsomely occur either when the doctor mitigates or expresses doubt about the diagnosis, or when the patient appears to have an opinion about what may be wrong and this turns out to be incongruent with the diagnosis. In the first kind of case, typically, patients respond with turns in which they stress their own lack of knowledge and often present their own or others' guesses about the problem, as in the next extract:

**(15) [Heath, 1992: 248]**
```
1    Dr:    Well there's a marked er:: (.) conjunctivitis
2           on both si:des there mister Banks, erm:
3    Pt:    °er°
4           (0.2)
5    Dr:    .thhhhh What set it off I wouldn't know:
6    Pt:    I wouldn't either I thought it was hay: fever or
7           somit like this:
```

The patient responds to the initial diagnosis with a very brief acknowledgement (line 3). Subsequently, the doctor remarks that he 'wouldn't know' what caused the condition (line 5). After this, the patient responds by, first, announcing his own lack of knowledge, then secondly, mentioning his guess that it was hay fever.

In the second kind of case, patients respond to the incongruence between their own thoughts and the doctor's opinion by using newsmarkers such as 'Is it?' or 'Oh really?', which then lead to the doctor reconfirming the diagnosis. The following extract is an illustration:

**(16) [Heath, 1992: 250]**

```
1    Dr:    It's not a vein: (.) it's a muscle in spa:s[m.
2    Pt:                                              [Is it?
3    Dr:    Yeah.
4    Pt:    Oh.
5    Dr:    And I think what's causing it to be in spasm . . .
```

Here, the patient has previously suggested (in data not shown) that the problem is related to 'a vein'. In line 1 of the extract, the doctor contrasts his diagnosis with the patient's suggestion, asserting that 'it's a muscle in spa:sm'. This is responded to with a newsmarker (Jefferson, 1981), 'Is it?' (line 2); and the subsequent reconfirmation (line 3) receives the change-of-state token (Heritage, 1984b) 'Oh' (line 4).

In these ways, patients preserve, in the design of their turns at talk, the fundamentally asymmetrical nature of the medical consultation. As Heath (1992: 262) writes:

> By withholding response, patients not only provide the doctor with the opportunity of developing the consultation as they so wish, but preserve the objective, scientific, and professional status of the diagnosis or medical assessment; the silence or acknowledgement operating retroactively to underscore the significance of the practitioner's 'opinion' of the condition. . . . Even in cases where the doctor displays uncertainty in diagnosis, and thereby encourages discussion of the medical assessment of the condition, it may be observed how the patient's contribution preserves the contrasting status of the two versions of the illness and in particular embodies the subjective and lay standpoint of their own opinion.

In this chapter we have begun to introduce some of the extensions and applications of the conversation analytic approach. By moving outside the domain of mundane conversation to look at more specialized forms of talk, the researchers discussed here have made significant inroads into an understanding of how institutional contexts function which goes beyond conventional sociological and sociolinguistic notions of context as a container for action. By focusing on the distinctive nature of the speech-exchange systems which are oriented to by participants in such settings, and on other aspects of the design of talk, CA demonstrates that institutional contexts are the ongoing accomplishment of the participants in their interactional conduct, rather than external constraints which cause certain forms of conduct to occur.

# 7

# Conversation Analysis and Research Interview Data

The interview is one of the most widely used research instruments in the social sciences. Focused or conversational interviews are a cornerstone of qualitative social science research, as they allow the respondent and interviewer to explore in depth issues and events that guide the research. Interviews are also important in the collection of data for statistical research; for example, national and local government questionnaire surveys are often conducted in interviews in people's homes or over the telephone. Much of our knowledge about the social world is therefore derived from analysis of data generated during interviews.

Social science research methods textbooks routinely provide advice about how to recognize and minimize the influence of interpersonal variables that might 'bias' the interview or distort its findings. They discuss how problems may arise if the interviewer's gender, ethnicity or class background is different to that of the respondent; and they describe how the respondent's desire to assist in the research, or seek approval from the interviewer, may lead them to produce the kind of responses they think the interviewer wishes to hear.

However, from the perspective of conversation analysis, there are important features of the *interaction* between interviewer and interviewee which tend not to be addressed. The way turns are exchanged, the methods by which misunderstandings and other troubles are repaired, or the effect of letting misunderstandings go unrepaired, and so on, may also impinge upon the organization of the interview, and therefore influence the nature of the information subsequently collected. However careful we might be to ensure that interpersonal factors do not 'contaminate' a research interview, information obtained from interviews can never be gathered in an interactional vacuum, and for this reason it is not only fruitful but necessary to examine the interactional organization of interviews.

The fact that research interviews are not just neutral data gathering tools but are social encounters mediated through language and interaction has led conversation analysts to consider, in Maynard and Schaeffer's (2002: 9) terms, the research interview's *interactional substrate* – [the] basic skills for engaging meaningfully' in interviews. This line of research has generated a number of important findings about the organization of activities during interaction in the standardized interview. For example, Maynard and Schaeffer (2002) describe a three-turn 'interviewing sequence', consisting of question–answer–acknowledgment turns. They also show how problematic moments in the interview are underpinned by systematic departures from this sequence. Other studies have examined the interactional practices of interviewers who cultivate a 'friendly' or 'personal' interviewing style (Houtkoop-Steenstra, 1997), the use of laughter in the development of rapport (Lavin and Maynard, 2002), the organization of repair in survey interviews (Moore and Maynard, 2002), and the ways in which people refuse to participate in telephone surveys (Maynard and Schaeffer, 1997).

We will focus on interaction in three types of interviews, and use each to illustrate a different dimension of the application and outcomes of a conversation analytic approach. First, we will look at standardized or structured interviews, in which the interviewer simply administers a questionnaire or survey to the respondent. This is the most formal kind of interview setting. The interviewer follows the (usually computer based) survey or questionnaire much like a script. To ensure consistency across interviews, the interviewer does not ask questions which are not written in the survey, nor is there an opportunity to develop lines of inquiry raised by the interviewee's responses. CA research has revealed some of the interactional difficulties that can arise from the attempt to ensure standardization across interviews.

We will then examine semi-structured interviews. Here the researcher will ask a set number of questions, but may vary both the way in which they are asked, and the order; moreover, he or she does not follow a strict survey or questionnaire, and is therefore at liberty to explore issues generated in the course of the interview. We will use data from a social psychological project on youth identities to explore some of the interactional dynamics surrounding respondents' uptake of the researcher's questions in semi-structured interviews.

Finally, we will look at focused or unstructured interviews in which the interviewer may simply invite the respondent to consider a range of broad issues, or to talk freely about specific events. In these open-ended interviews, respondents may produce lengthy and (largely) monologic accounts, anecdotes and narratives. We will consider narrative descriptions from open-ended interviews to allow us to make some remarks about the interactional design of extended accounts. (Many of these issues are relevant also to interaction in focus group interviews in social science research; useful discussions can be found in Myers, 1998 and S. Wilkinson, 2006; Puchta and Potter, 2004, examine the interactional dimensions of focus groups in market research).

## The structured interview

In a structured interview the interviewer administers a survey to a respondent, and then codes the answers into a number of pre-set categories. The numbers entered into each category then provide the social scientist with the basis for statistical analysis. Because it is necessary to have standardized data for statistical analysis, it is imperative that the interviewer ask the respondents the same questions in the same way in the same order every time. Consequently, for many social scientists, this interview format is regarded as an essentially neutral instrument for data collection.

Recent studies, however, have shown that the process of administering such a survey is itself an interactional event. The interviewer and respondent will be co-present, and the interviewer will elicit the required information by asking the respondent questions written down on the survey or questionnaire. Consequently, the structured interview actually relies upon very basic features of conversational interaction: turn-taking, question–answer sequences and so on. Moreover, because it is necessary to produce standardized answers, the participants in the structured interview also have to suppress some essential characteristics of mundane conversational interaction. So, although the interviewer may appear to be engaging in everyday interaction, the nature of their task is such that they also have to violate certain conversational procedures (Houtkoop-Steenstra, 2000; Maynard et al., 2002). This may have important consequences for the nature of the information actually being recorded.

To illustrate how features of ordinary conversational interaction are constrained in structured interviews, we will discuss one of the earliest

CA studies of interview interaction: Suchman and Jordan's (1990) analysis of recordings of interviews in the General Social Survey and the National Health Survey in the United States.

In a structured interview, the interviewer must pose the same question in the same way to different respondents: consequently the person (or group) who produces the survey has to ensure that each question must be designed to accommodate everyone who may have to answer it, and it must address a wide range of possible circumstances. Survey questionnaires, then, are not recipient designed, but audience designed (Houtkoop-Steenstra, 1995: 104). The upshot is that questions can become awkward and clumsy. For example:

**(1) [Suchman and Jordan 1990: 233]**
| 1 | I. | During those two weeks, did anyone in the family receive |
|---|---|---|
| 2 | | health care at home or go to a doctor's office, clinic, |
| 3 | | hospital or some other place. Include care from a nurse |
| 4 | | or anyone working with or for a medical doctor. Do not count |
| 5 | | times while an overnight patient in hospital. |
| 6 | R: | (pause) No:: |

Because questions have to be exhaustive they may contain many clauses, and it is not unusual for a respondent to answer a question after an initial clause. But because of the requirement to ask questions the same way on each occasion the interviewer has to continue with the rest of the question, even after the respondent has answered it (see also Houtkoop–Steenstra 2000):

**(2) [Suchman and Jordan 1990: 234]**
| 1 | I: | Was the total combined family income during the past twelve |
|---|---|---|
| 2 | | months, that is yours, your wife's, Judith's and Jerry's more or |
| 3 | | less than twenty thousand dollars. |
| 4 | R: | More |
| 5 | I: | Include money from jobs, social security, retirement income, |
| 6 | | unemployment payments, public assistance and so forth. Also |
| 7 | | include income from interest dividends, net income from |
| 8 | | business or rent, and any other income received. |
| 9 | R: | More. it was more income. |

In everyday interaction, speakers may monitor and attend to the immediately prior sequence of utterances, or information revealed in earlier stages of the conversation. Subsequent contributions to a conversation can be designed to take account of these prior interactional events, or previously disclosed information. However, the professional interviewer has to disattend this local context. They are not allowed to incorporate inferences available from prior turns into the design of subsequent questions. Suchman and Jordan cite an instance in which an interviewer is asking a respondent about health problems. Having established that the respondent has a form of skin complaint brought on by playing the violin, the interviewer asks 'When did you last see or talk to a doctor or assistant about the dermatitis under the neck?' (Suchman and Jordan, 1990: 233). The respondent answers that she did not see a doctor in relation to this problem. Some turns later, however, the following sequence happens:

I:    Were you ever hospitali[zed::for
R:                            [No

In mundane conversation, a participant would have been able to infer that if a co-participant had not even seen a doctor because of a skin problem, then it was highly unlikely that it was a serious enough condition to warrant institutional care, and a question about hospitalization would not have been asked.

These features of structured interviews may become very irritating to the respondent, leading to a strong desire to finish the interview as soon as possible – an attitude that is hardly going to maximize the effectiveness of the interview as an information-gathering instrument. However, there are more pressing dangers from the suppression of mundane conversational procedures. For example, not only are the questions structured prior to the interview, but so are the kinds of answer that the respondents can give. That is, interviewers are not free to take account of how the respondents may wish to answer the question because responses have to be recorded in terms of the categories or coding schemes built into the survey which is being administered. For example, the following segment comes from part of an interview in which the respondent is being asked to assess the appropriateness of the amount of money being spent on problems in big cities.

**(3) [Suchman and Jordan 1990: 234–5]**

| 1 | I: | . . . solving the problem of big cities |
|---|----|----|
| 2 | R: | Ahm:: (long pause) Some questions seem to be ((little laugh)) |
| 3 |    | hard to answer because it's not a matter of how much money, |
| 4 |    | it's- |
| 5 | I: | Alright, you can just say whether you think it's too much, |
| 6 |    | too little or about the right amount, or if you feel you |
| 7 |    | don't know you can:: say that of course. |
| 8 | R: | Ah from the various talk shows and programs on TV and in |

9            the newspapers, ah it could be viewed that they're
10           spending maybe the right amount of money. but it isn't
11           so much the money that they're spending it's the other
12           things that-
13    I:     Well do you think we're spending too much too little, or
14           about the right amount.
15    R:     Ahm, I'll answer I don't know on that one.

In this case the respondent tries to formulate an answer to the question that is premised on the idea that the allocation of financial resources is not the major issue. However, because the interviewer needs to have an answer which fits the categories available, she constrains the respondent's actions so that the respondent eventually produces a 'don't know' answer, whereas it is clear from the preceding talk that she does indeed have an opinion on the topic. In this case, then, the respondent's actual opinion, which she tried to volunteer, was lost.

Often, respondents will provide a narrative or anecdote as a way of illustrating an answer. But because of the requirement to furnish standardized answers, the interviewer must ignore these stories. It is possible, however, that these stories may actually contradict the answer that has been given. Consider the following extract which comes from an interview with a doctor.

**(4) [Suchman and Jordan 1990: 236]**
1    I:     When you think about other doctors in general, how would
2           you compare yourself to them. Are you very similar or different?
3    R:     I think I'm pretty similar to most doctors.
4           Except that a lot of doctors try to stay right in the mainstream
5           of medicine. They don't like to be out, away from the drug-
6           oriented type of medical treatment. In other words, you have a
7           problem. you have drug for it. and that'll take care of it. Or
8           surgery or something. Cut it off. and you'll be fine ((laughs))
9           And most doctors have that attitude. Then there's a small group
10          that believe in the reason that you have doctors in the first
11          place. And that is that we're more holistic. So we can use a
12          more natural approach. The hippocratic approach. So I think
13          I'm more like that group

Here the interviewer is faced with two contradictory answers, and she has a problem. If she accepts the first answer, she will be attributing to the respondent an opinion with which he clearly disagrees. If she takes account of his subsequent explanation, and pursues a response in the light of that, then she may end up with an uncodifiable answer (both 'yes' and 'no'); furthermore, she will be transgressing the norm that the interviewer should actively ignore 'irrelevant' parts of the respondent's utterances.

Suchman and Jordan's paper is important for the following reasons. First, it demonstrates very clearly that even standardized survey interviews are rich interactional events; and that, as Schegloff observes, this interactional dimension is 'inescapable' (Schegloff, 2002: 152). Second, drawing on CA studies of ordinary talk, they begin to provide a formal analytic description of the ways in which interaction in structured interviews departs from procedures in everyday conversational exchanges. Third, and perhaps most important, their analysis identifies some of the implications of these departures. Suchman and Jordan show that in an attempt to ensure that the interview is a neutral and objective instrument, there are requirements that the interview proceeds in a certain way. However, these requirements lead the interviewer into trying to conduct an exchange that has the superficial appearance of a conversational encounter without many central characteristics of talk in everyday settings, for example being able to design utterances for their recipients, clarifying misunderstandings, allowing inferences available from prior utterances to shape subsequent turns, and so on.

Analysts have begun to show how the imposition of these verbal parameters can lead to the respondents' annoyance and disinclination to co-operate fully with the interview (Maynard and Schaeffer, 1997). But a more serious consequence of these requirements is that the nature of the talk may impinge significantly upon the information recorded. That is, Suchman and Jordan show that it is not the case that verbal exchanges in a structured interview are simply a means of eliciting information; rather, these restricted forms of conversational interaction can impact upon the decision as to what information the respondent is actually offering by way of an answer. In short, the information collected in structured interviews may not be disentangled from the organization of the talk through which the interview was conducted.

It is important to situate these kinds of findings in a wider debate about the role of the survey interview, and the requirement to produce standardized data. For example, Suchman and Jordan (1990: 240) argued that the designers of questionnaires should accept that 'the survey interview is fundamentally an interactional event', and that the interviewer should be permitted to clarify questions and engage in a limited form of recipient design. Others, however, are less optimistic about the value of survey interviews because the kind of answers people may provide have an indeterminate relationship to the commonsense, tacit knowledge which informs peoples' real life conduct. An overview of these debates and positions can be found in Maynard et al., (2002).

## Semi-structured interviews

In the previous section we noticed how an analysis informed by findings from conversation analysis could reveal how the absence of everyday interactional procedures may lead to significant problems in structured interviews. In this section, we will begin by describing how discursive practices that are common to everyday talk can be deployed in the context of a semi-structured interview. As we stated in the introduction to this chapter, in a semi-structured interview, the interviewer is not reading questions from a written list. Consequently the 'same' questions may be worded differently on each occasion. We will consider some data from Widdicombe and Wooffitt's (1995) study of semi-structured interviews provided by members of youth subcultures, such as punks, skinheads, rockers and goths. They used a conversation analytic approach to investigate the first exchanges in their interviews. Before we examine their analysis, however, it is necessary to discuss the background to their study.

Initially the interviews were not collected as data for a conversation analytic study of interaction between interviewer and respondents. The interviews were conducted as part of Widdicombe's doctoral research to test a theory known as Social Identity Theory, which tried to explain the processes of group membership and identification. She wanted to find out if this theory could be used to reveal why young people joined youth subcultures. To test the theory, it was necessary to devise an interview schedule which encouraged the respondents to declare their subcultural affiliation right at the start or early on in the interview. Interviews were conducted 'in the field' at rock concerts, on city streets, in shopping malls – any venue or place where members of subcultures were known to gather.

Widdicombe and Wooffitt argue that there were good grounds to assume that the respondents would realize that the reason they were approached for an interview was their visibility as members of a specific subculture. In short, they looked the part. Consequently, respondents could infer that the interviewer was inviting them to speak as 'punks' or 'goths' rather than, say, as 'women', 'students', 'people out shopping', or whatever other kind of categorization could logically apply.

The opening question was designed to elicit a subcultural self-categorization. In some cases the respondents did immediately affirm the relevance of that kind of social identity. However, in many cases, the respondents' first turn in the interview was in fact a question. For example:

**(5) [1R:M:T5SB(RRF)]**

```
            ((Tape starts))
1    I:     how would you descri:be (.) yourself
2           and your appearance and so on
3           (.)
4    R:     describe my appearance,
5    I:     yeah
6           (1.0)
7    R:     su- su- slightly longer than average hair
            ((goes on to describe appearance))
```

**(6) [1P:F:T7SA(KR)]**

```
            ((Tape starts))
1    I:     RIght how would you describe your sty:le,
2           (0.6)
3    R:     how would I describe [the style
4    I:                          [yeah
5           (0.4)
6    R:     well (0.4) it's:: (.) different it's
7           usually dirty and ((continues))
```

In these cases, the respondents' first turns have the character of 'questions-seeking-clarification/confirmation'. This was a recurrent phenomenon in the data. Instead of trying to explain these responses in terms of Social Identity Theory, Widdicombe and Wooffitt wondered if there might be an interactional basis for the respondents' production of these kinds of utterances.

Instead of producing the relevant conversational action – a self-identification in terms of a subcultural category – the respondent has produced a request for clarification. This is an entirely different kind of action, and which has significant implications for the trajectory of the interaction.

To illustrate, consider again extract (5). By producing a request for clarification the respondent has also initiated an insertion sequence. As we have previously seen, an insertion sequence is simply a spate of inter-action that is nested in or embedded in an overarching conversational framework.

**(5) [1R:M:T5SB(RRF)]**

```
            ((Tape starts))
1    I:     how would you descri:be (.) yourself         Q1
2           and your appearance and so on
3           (.)
4    R:     describe my appearance,                       ins.Q2
```

| 5 | I: | yeah | **ins.A2** |
| 6 |   | (1.0) |   |
| 7 | R: | su- su- slightly longer than average hair | **A1** |
|   |   | ((goes on to describe appearance)) |   |

Significant sequential implications follow from the production of this insertion sequence: through this action the respondent is able to re-characterize the business of that part of the interview. Note that the first part of the insertion sequence borrows some words from the interviewer's prior turn, but deletes other words. So we find that the component 'describe yourself' has not been recycled as 'describe myself' but 'describe my appearance'. In this sense, the respondent's turn in line 4 formulates a *version* of the interviewer's prior utterance. And that version is crucial because it is designed to make available certain inferences about the social identity of the speaker. By producing a turn in which he does not address those parts of the prior turn which make relevant, and invite him to confirm, a particular kind of categorical self ascription, he makes available the inference that that kind of identity is not relevant to him. He produces a request for clarification, the kind of which would be produced by any normal, unexceptional person who could not infer what it was about them in particular that had motivated the interviewer to approach them and ask a question concerning style, appearance, and so on. In this sense, this first turn is designed not to invoke the speaker's identity as a member of some subculture, but instead to warrant his identity as an ordinary person. He is in the business of, as Sacks (1984b) put it, doing 'being ordinary'.

As we said earlier, this use of insertion sequences after the interviewer's first question is not an unusual phenomenon. Widdicombe and Wooffitt argue that this is a strategy to resist a way of being seen. Doing 'being ordinary', or at least, through their actions portraying themselves as not belonging to a specific category or group, is a method by which respondents can counter what must be a routine feature of their everyday lives: that by virtue of an inspection of their dress and appearance, other people assume that it is possible to see what kind of person they are. By virtue of a category membership (either attributed by others or offered by the individual), a person's own behaviour can be glossed, interpreted and characterized in terms of what is known and expected about that category. It is therefore always potentially the case that the sense or purpose of a person's actions, beliefs, opinions, and so on, may be understood by virtue of what is known commonly about the category to which the individual can be seen to be affiliated (see also Sacks, 1979).

It is this ever present potential state of affairs which the respondents' first utterances may be designed to resist. By portraying themselves as 'not seeing the category relevance of the interviewer's first turn', the respondents are rejecting the validity of (what they can infer to be) the basis on which they were selected for interview; they are resisting the categorical affiliation that the interviewer's first turn tacitly asks them to confirm. So providing this kind of clarification seeking question is a method of resistance executed in the design of utterances on a turn-by-turn basis.

The production of an insertion sequence therefore allows the respondents to manage the inferential and attributional properties associated with their self-identity. This is a useful resource, which means that when the interviewer subsequently asks explicitly if they belong to a specific category, any acceptance of that label merely constitutes one further dimension of their identity. It provides them with a resource for avoiding outright denial of the subcultural label, while situating the subcultural identity as merely one of (at least) two relevant identities. This is important in the interview context because outright denial of a subcultural affiliation could warrant assertions of deliberate mischief, disingenuousness, or simple perversity. After all, the kinds of dress and appearance of the respondents invite a certain kind of categorical ascription. So the respondents' talk displays their sensitivity to the delicate issue of undermining the criterial relevance of their subcultural identity, while at the same time minimizing the likelihood that a simple denial of the relevance of their subcultural affiliation could warrant unfavourable conclusions about themselves and their behaviour.

There is one more interactional benefit to be gained from initiating insertion sequences in this way. There are other ways of resisting category ascription; for example, the respondents can simply question the legitimacy of the interviewer's first question. In the following extract, the first respondent formulates her negative attitude to the prior question, and thereby resists providing any kind of self-identification.

**(7) [3:NSG:F:T3SA (FP)]**

```
          ((Tape starts: respondents talking to each other
          about Princess Anne for approximately 12 seconds.))
1    I:    can you tell me something about your style and the way
2          you look,
3          (0.7)
4    I:    how would you descri:be yourselves
5          (0.7)
6    R1:   °huhh°
7          (.7)
```

```
8    R1:    I dunno >I hate those sorts of quest[ions uhm<
9    R2:                                       [yeah horrible
10          isn't it
```

The first respondent's utterance, 'I hate those sorts of questions', constitutes a complaint about having to provide a characterization of
herself. Her reluctance to answer the question has therefore become
an explicit feature of the exchange. Although an overt complaint about
the interviewer's question does not necessarily index an imminent
breakdown of the interview, it certainly constitutes a 'trouble' in the
exchange. This is a marked departure from routine conversation in
which participants rely on various interactional practices to minimise
the likelihood of explicit conflict or disagreement. Explicit rejections of
questions can jeopardize the smooth flow of the interview, and can
undermine the relationship between interviewer and interviewee.

The production of an insertion sequence which seeks clarification,
however, does not question the propriety or salience of the prior turn.
Yet it does permit the speaker to establish a spate of talk in which the
likelihood that they will be expected to produce a subcultural self identification is minimized. In this sense, producing an 'ordinary person's'
kind of response via an insertion sequence is a delicate strategy: it
allows the respondents to avoid giving a subcultural identification in
such a way that their resistance does not become an explicit focus of the
exchange.

Before concluding this section it is worth making a few broader
methodological remarks, as they illustrate the power of a conversation
analytic approach to semi-structured interview data. It is important to
remember that the interviews with members of youth subcultures had
not been collected as part of a conversation analytic project. Instead,
they were initially conducted as part of a social psychological project to
assess the utility of a theory of group membership. However, in keeping
with empirical traditions in cognitive psychology it was assumed that
the raw data themselves would not be able to reveal anything significant
about the processes of group affiliation. Instead, the data had to be
transformed: first they were sieved through a coding scheme that transformed them into a form of numerical information. These numbers
were then subject to high-powered statistical tests, the results of which
were then interpreted in terms of Social Identity Theory. Only after this
series of methodological transformations were the data considered to
be suitable to allow the investigator to make inferences about the dimensions of, and processes underlying, for example, group membership and
self-categorization.

happening. Here are two more examples. In extract (9) the interviewee is reporting a vision of her dead husband during his funeral service; and in extract (10) the interviewee describes one of a series of apparitions which appeared in her home.

**(9) [EL:4:29]**

```
1    an' I went in there (.) er:m
2    w- with my mother in law and uhm: (0.4)
3    friends that were with me
4    (1.3)
5    .hhh
6    (.)
7    and I was just looking at the coffin          X
8    and there was David standing there (0.3)      Y
9    he was in Blues
```

**(10) [REW 52]**

```
1    so I I think I remember I 'ad a dish
2    in hand I was out in the kitchen
3    it was different like (.) y' know (.)
4    to this sort've flat (0.5)
5    an' it ws' like a (.) big entrance hall (0.7)
6    with one (.) door (0.5) and then it came
7    straight the way through
8    there was a door there and a
9    door there (0.5) a door there
10   an (0.5) it was a kitchen
11   (1.0)
12   and I was right by this unit part
13   (1.5)
14   an'
15   (.)
16   I were lookin' out that way                   X
17   an' it seemed to be like a figure             Y
18   (.)
19   coming through the hall (0.7)
20   all I could see was the ah (a-)
21   the top part
```

Thus, the data begin to reveal a consistent pattern emerging. The question is, given that this observable pattern exists, what interactional work might it be doing in the context of the interview?

Considering some features of the (X) component in the device enables us to examine how it can be used to address interactional and inferential tasks. We can describe the 'I was just doing X' component as a *state formulation*. That is, it describes a particular state of activity or state of mind that the speaker was engaged in immediately prior to the onset of the paranormal experience. When we look closely at the design features of these state formulations, we find that they are built to accomplish specific kinds of inferential tasks.

A common characteristic of state formulations is that they seem to report very mundane or ordinary activities. Consider the state formulations we have seen so far:

'.hhh as I was going through the doorway'
'I were lookin' out that way'

These are very routine activities. However, it is not necessarily the case that the speakers are reporting these events in this way simply because that is what was happening at the time. These formulations have been designed to have this mundane character. We can find evidence for this when we look at those cases in which the state formulation is used to provide a summary of the speaker's own prior talk. Consider the following extract.

**(11) [DM 7]**

```
1    un' I was thinkin' about religion
2    un' eh (0.5) I was thinkin' well (0.4)
3    (    ) on the lines of it (0.3)
4    I(t)- i- it must be very easy
5    to be Saint Paul because yuh get yer
6    blindin' light on the road to Damascus
7    sort u(v) thing un' eh .hh (0.6)
9    you've no problems (so you) you:: know
10   as far as you're concerned
11   you measure all things
12   according to that experience
13   the experience was exterior
14   to yourself an' so therefore
15   (1.3)
16   you viewed it (0.7) as a star:t
17   (0.5)
18   (>yu know<) >yeah<
19   I were just thinkin'                    X
20   (0.3) er:m
21   and then suddenly I was aware of        Y
22   (0.7)
23   almost (.) the sensation was
24   almost as if a veil was lifted
```

The speaker is describing what he was doing just before the onset of a mystical or revelatory experience. In the first part of the extract he provides a lengthy account of the kind of thoughts which were occupying him at the time, and these concerned his reflections on religious faith which results from a direct personal encounter with a mystical presence. These could hardly be called everyday reflections. However, when he comes to that part of the account in which he makes first reference to the actual phenomenon he is reporting, he builds a very mundane state formulation, 'I were just thinkin'' (line 21).

The speaker in the next extract seems to follow similar design features in the construction of the 'I was just doing X' component.

**(12) [EL 5:39]**
(The speaker here is describing how she had her husband's funeral service video recorded for relatives who were unable to attend the ceremony.)

```
1     I also wanted it video'd for
2     my children: who were
3     (1.7)
4     two and four at the time
5     and they didn't come to the funeral
6     (2.4)
7     so perhaps a wee:k later
8     (1.3)
9     >must've bin about< a week afterwards
10    .h I:: (0.5) put the recording on
11    and was: (0.5) watching it
12    I was obviously extremely upset
13    (0.8)
14    and I was sat on a chair               X
15    (.)
16    uhn:d
17    (0.5)
18    when I looked down David was (.)       Y
19    kneeling at the side of me
```

In this case the speaker is describing how she was watching a video recording of her husband's funeral service – clearly a traumatic and emotional experience. However, when she comes to produce the first reference to the apparition of her husband, her state formulation is the prosaic 'I was sat on a chair' (line 14). Indeed, given these extremely traumatic circumstances, this state formulation seems to be conspicuously routine.

In both these cases the speakers are using their state formulations to provide one of two kinds of summary of their prior talk. 'I were just thinkin" is a gist of 'thinking about personal faith which is verified by direct contact with a deity', and 'I was sat on a chair' is an upshot of watching a recording of the service. In both these cases, then, the speakers gloss over or discard those features of their prior talk that are non-ordinary, emotive or traumatic. This deletion of specific features of their prior talk suggests they are actively constructing their state formulations. Given that we seem to have identified this design feature of (X) components we can ask: what kind of work is being done when state formulations are built in this way?

One consequence of reporting anomalous events is that there is always the possibility that a sceptical recipient may try to reconstruct the reported experience so as to recast it as an ordinary event which may, for example, have been misidentified. (This is a strategy often employed by sceptics when they appear in television documentaries about the paranormal.) In extracts (11) and (12) the speakers reveal a lot of information about themselves. For example, in (11) the speaker is describing in positive terms the kind of phenomenon he subsequently claims to have encountered. Consequently it would be easy to suggest that his experience was a form of wish fulfilment and not a truly extraordinary mystical or revelatory experience. And in extract (12) the speaker's perception of her husband's apparition can be 'explained' by reference to the trauma of reliving his funeral service as she watched a video recording made at the time. It is precisely this kind of information that could be used to build a sceptical or non-paranormal explanation for the events being reported. One function of mundane state formulations, then, is that they ensure that the immediate sequential context for the first reference to the phenomenon is not the kind of personal or biographical detail that could support a sceptical reappraisal of the claimed experience, but a conspicuously 'normal' activity.

In many cases, speakers insert information between the two components of the device. Inspection of these inserted materials reveals that they too work to undermine the possible sceptical reappraisals. For example, one type of insertion deals with the possible retort that when the speaker encountered a phenomenon, they were not in the best position to observe it accurately. In the following extract the speakers are describing one in a series of poltergeist experiences that were centred in the attic of their house. The insertion reveals that the speakers were directly underneath the source of the disturbance they are reporting.

**(13) [ND 7:49]**
1     S1        and then the disturbances started
2              (2.4)

```
3           the first thing we
4           (1.3)
5           really noticed was: (0.5)
6           one night
7           (1.3)
8           in (0.7)
9           I would think September
10   S2     yeah September [seventy six=
11   S1                   [September
12   S2     =it would be
13   S2     yeah that's right
14          (1.5)
15          we were laid (0.7) in the front bedroom    X
16          which was below the front attics            ins.
17          (1.5)
18          and we heard a noise (0.5)                  Y
19          like someone throwing gravel across
20          a piece of (.) hollow hardboard
```

Similar work is done by the insertion in the following case.

**(14) [HS 17]**
```
1    ah came home from work at lunchtime
2    (1)
3    an' I walked into the sitting room door
4    (.)
5    in through the sitting room door            X
6    (1.5)
7    an::
8    right in front of me (.)                    ins.
9    was a sort of alcove (.)
10   and a chimney breast (.)
11   like this (0.7) ((pointing to wall))
12   and a photograph of our wedding             Y
13   (1)
14   came off the top shelf (0.2)
15   floated down to the ground
16   hh completely came apart
17   But didn't break
```

Finally, consider the following case. This comes from a different source: a corpus of naturally occurring telephone conversations. The participants, L and T, are chatting about friends, relatives, and so on. Immediately prior to this extract, L has asked about T's 'haunting', a reference to unusual happenings in a house belonging to one of T's friends. T replies that nothing untoward has occurred recently, but then goes on to say:

**(15) [Holt:.J86:1:2:4]**

| 1  | T: | It's quite funny actually cuz there's someb'dy |     |
|----|----|------------------------------------------------|-----|
| 2  |    | up the road I wz talking to an' uh (0.2) sh'reckoned |  |
| 3  |    | tha(.)t uh: he he bought th'house b't'er bought it off his | |
| 4  |    | sister                                         |     |
| 5  |    | (0.5)                                          |     |
| 6  | T: | A[n' iz sister wz: uh gettin' ready one night= | X   |
| 7  | L: | [Yes.                                          |     |
| 8  | T: | =t'go out.                                      |     |
| 9  | T: | She hadn't been °drhhinking° .hhh              | **ins.** |
| 10 |    | an' the hairspray apparently lifted itself up 'n | Y  |
| 11 |    | went t'the other side a' the dressing table.   |     |

This is a very neat conversational instance of an insertion between the two components of the device that is starkly designed to minimize the possibility of a specific kind of sceptical response to the story. This example is important because it provides clear evidence that the 'I was just doing X when Y' phenomenon, and at least one way it can be used, is not an artefact of the interview situation.

The structural features of the device discussed above seem to furnish a range of resources, some of which we have examined. Analysis of the design of state formulations, and examination of insertions between the (X) and (Y) components, indicates that speakers are using the device to defuse potential sceptical claims about the veracity of the account, or the reliability of the speaker. In short, the device is used for inferential work that is sensitive precisely to the possibility that the account might receive an unsympathetic or sceptical hearing.

It is important to keep in mind that the recipient of the story – in most cases above, the interviewer – does not need to express any scepticism for the speakers to build their accounts to warrant the claimed paranormality of the event. Regardless of the avowed or assumed beliefs of the interviewer, a speaker's utterances may be designed to address a wider, culturally based scepticism. To a degree, Sacks made a similar argument when discussing the ways in which we may invoke or resist membership of certain kinds of categories, even when we have no reason to care about the opinions of the people we are talking to. Observing that people will lie to market researchers about the amount of time they spend watching television, Sacks observes that 'it's interesting in that they're controlling an impression of themselves for somebody who couldn't matter less' (1992, vol. 1: 580).

In this chapter we have considered three kinds of interview data, and illustrated some of the empirical issues that can be examined using conversation analysis. In the structured interview, CA can tell us about some of the important consequences when everyday conversational conventions have to be abandoned because of the need to administer all questions in the same order and with the same wording. And data from unstructured or open-ended interviews can be investigated to reveal the broader organizational devices and patterns through which people structure lengthy narratives and accounts.

There are some methodological features that underpin the application of conversation analysis to all three kinds of interview data. First, there is an emphasis on the identification and description of recurrent patterns in the data; the focus may be on the organization of exchanges between interviewer and respondent, or on the communicative competencies that inform longer sections in a single speaker's turns. Second, it is important to explicate the participants' orientation to the normative properties of the sequential unfolding of the exchange; or, in the case of unstructured interview data, the normative properties of descriptive practices. Finally, we have tried to show that, in all the interview data, it is not the case that respondents are simply imparting information to a passive recipient. Whatever the ostensible topic, context or purpose of the interview, the interviewer and respondent are engaged in social action.

# 8

# Extensions of Conversation Analysis

Conversation analysis is an evolving field of inquiry. Developing from Sacks' initial studies of the organization of calls to a suicide prevention centre, not only has it become established as the pre-eminent social scientific method for the analysis of ordinary conversational interaction, but researchers have extended the principles and practices of CA into the analysis of forms of talk which are far removed from everyday conversation. For example, Atkinson and Drew's (1979) pioneering analysis of courtroom interaction was only the first in a continuing series of studies which focus on talk in institutional and work settings (Arminen, 2005). Furthermore, CA continues to evolve as an interdisciplinary field of study, contributing to questions that emerge in specific discipines but turn out to have a wider relevance.

Like many qualitative research methods, CA is often accused of having little relevance for issues and problems in the 'real world': the world outside of academic social science. This, however, is not a view that we share; and consequently in this chapter, we turn to examine how CA's policies and procedures have been applied in such diverse fields as political communication, human-computer interaction, children's language use, and the treatment of language disorders. In the process, this chapter will illustrate something of the practical implications of the conversation analytic approach.

## The language of political rhetoric

We first consider one of the earliest extensions of conversation analysis: Max Atkinson's work on the rhetorical performance of political communicators (Atkinson, 1984a, 1984b). Atkinson became interested in the relationship between rhetorical figures used in political speechmaking and the occurrence of audience applause. Drawing on CA's approach to turn-taking and transition-relevance, his research suggested that the way in which speakers' turns are constructed may significantly influence the likelihood of applause. By searching for recurrent characteristics of those parts of speeches which immediately preceded enthusiastic audience applause, Atkinson discovered that there were indeed consistencies in the way these successful points were organized and packaged. He identified various rhetorical formats which seemed to be particularly effective at eliciting audience applause. Two of these, *three-part lists* and *contrastive devices*, proved to be particularly efficient.

Indeed, a couple of years later, Heritage and Greatbatch (1986) conducted a major statistical analysis of a large corpus of 476 recorded broadcast political speeches and found that, either singly or in combination, three-part lists accounted for some 12.6 per cent of all 'applause events' in their data base, while contrasts accounted for no fewer than 33.2 per cent (p. 139).

A three-part list is simply a way of packaging a point or position in an argument using a list of three separate items. A contrastive device is similarly a means of packaging a point, where one argument or approach is contrasted with another in such a way that the speaker's favoured position is seen to be superior. Heritage and Greatbatch (1986: 116) argue that such devices are effective in generating applause because of two properties: '(a) [they] *emphasize* and thus highlight their contents against a surrounding background of speech materials and (b) [they] *project a clear completion point* for the message in question.' In other words, as they are being built, they signal when they are likely to end. The devices themselves provide the audience with a cue when to clap and thus allow collective displays of affiliation.

For instance, consider the following extracts from party conference speeches by ex-British Prime Minister Margaret Thatcher. In each case, a point is made by listing three items, after the third of which we see the audience applauding loudly (the transcription convention for applause is a row of x's, with louder applause being signalled by capital X's):

**(1) [Conservative Party Conference]**

```
1    Thatcher:    This week has demonstrated (0.4) that we are a
2                 party united in
3                 purpose                                          1
4                 (0.4)
5                 strategy                                         2
6                 (0.2)
7                 and reso[lve                                     3
8    Audience:         [Hear [hear
9                           [x-xxXXXXXXXXXXXXXXXXXXXXXXXxx-x
                      |              (8 seconds)                |
```

**(2) [Conservative Party Conference]**

```
1    Thatcher:    Soviet Marxism is
2                 ideologically,                                  1
3                 politically                                     2
4                 and morally bankru[pt                           3
5    Audience:                      [xxXXXXXXXXXXXXXXXXXXXXXxx-x
                      |              (9 seconds)                |
```

**(3) [Conservative Party Conference]**

```
1    Thatcher:    There's no government anywhere that is tackling
2                 the problem with more
3                 vigour,                                          1
4                 imagination                                      2
5                 and determination                                3
6                 than this conservative government
7    Audience:    Hear    [hear
8    Audience:            [x-xxXXXXXXXXXXXXXXXXXXXXXXXXXxx-x
                      |              (8 seconds)                |
```

In each case, the audience's applause is coordinated very closely with the production of the third part in the list. In fact, in the first two extracts it is noticeable that the onset of applause overlaps slightly with the final syllable of the third list part.

One of the reasons why three-part lists seem to work in this way is that, as Jefferson (1990) has shown, lists of three are commonplace in ordinary conversation. The following extracts come from Jefferson's (1990) study of the interactional properties of listing, and all occurred in everyday conversation, either on the telephone or in face-to-face interaction.

**(4) [Jefferson 1990: 64]**

```
1    Sydney:    While you've been talking to me I mended,
2               two nightshirts,                                  1
```

| 3 | a pillow case? | 2 |
| 4 | enna pair'v pants | 3 |

**(5) [Jefferson 1990: 64]**

| 1 | Maybelle: | I think if you | |
| 2 | | exercise it | 1 |
| 3 | | an' work at it | 2 |
| 4 | | 'n studied it | 3 |
| 5 | | you do become clairvoyant. | |

Interestingly, in these next extracts speakers have produced two parts of a list, but either have exhausted the relevant items which could be used to extend the list, or cannot find an appropriate word with which to complete it. In each case they nevertheless use an item to complete the list as a three part unit.

**(6) [Jefferson 1990: 66]**

| 1 | Heather: | And they had like a concession stand at a fair | |
| 2 | | where you can buy | |
| 3 | | coke | 1 |
| 4 | | and popcorn | 2 |
| 5 | | and that type of thing. | 3 |

**(7) [Jefferson 1990: 66]**

| 1 | Sy: | Take up m:Metacal er, | 1 |
| 2 | | Carnation Slender | 2 |
| 3 | | er something like that. | 3 |

These extracts tell us something very interesting about three-part lists. In each case the third part is not actually another item like the two that went before. Instead, it is a general term, such as 'and that type of thing'. Where a specific third component does not come to mind, therefore, speakers can use a general term in order to end up with a three-part list. By using these 'generalized list completers' (Jefferson, 1990) speakers in extracts (6) and (7) are displaying their sensitivity to a conversational maxim which runs something like: 'if doing a list, try to do it in three parts'.

This means that in ordinary conversation, when one speaker is producing a list, a co-participant can anticipate that when the third item is produced, then the list is likely to be complete. As Jefferson shows, co-participants recurrently treat the end of the third part of a list as a legitimate place to start taking their next turn.

**(8) [Jefferson 1990: 74]**

| 1 | Matt: | The good actors are all dyin out. |
|---|---|---|
| 2 | Tony: | They're all- they're all |
| 3 |  | dyin out [yeah. |
| 4 | Matt: | [Tyrone Po:wuh. Clark Gable, Gary Cooper, |
| 5 | Tony: | Now all of 'em are dyin. |

Here, Matt's list of good actors who are 'dying out' – 'Tyrone Po:wuh. Clark Gable, Gary Cooper,' – could easily have been extended. Moreover, the 'continuing' intonation with which he produces the third name (indicated by the comma after it) does not indicate that he has necessarily come to the end of his turn. Thus, Tony's decision to start talking in line 5 displays his understanding that Matt's list could be *treated* as complete upon the provision of a third item.

Just as third items in conversation are conventionally taken to be possible utterance completion points, so too are they treated as completion points in speeches. Hearing that a politician is making a list, an audience can use their tacit sensitivity to conventions of everyday conversation to anticipate that it is likely to be completed not after two points, and not after four, but after three. Each individual member of the audience can therefore predict the end of a specific point and is thereby provided with a resource, intrinsic to the speech, through which their behaviour can be coordinated with the other audience members to provide a collective response. (Atkinson also shows that speakers' intonation and upper body movement can sometimes play a part in this signalling of upcoming completion.)

We earlier showed some examples from Atkinson's (1984a) own data, taken from the 1970s and 80s. However, it is not just politicians of that era who are prone to use three-part lists. More recently, in a speech by latter day British Prime Minister Tony Blair on military strikes against Afghanistan, he too uses a list of three factors which summarize 'the dangers of inaction':

**(9) [Blair Oct 2001]**

| 1 | Blair: | The world understands that whilst of course there |  |
|---|---|---|---|
| 2 |  | are dangers in acting as we are, the dangers of |  |
| 3 |  | inaction are far, far greater: |  |
| 4 |  | the threat of further such outrages | 1 |
| 5 |  | the threats to our economies | 2 |
| 6 |  | the threat to the stability of the world | 3 |

Indeed, throughout their victorious election campaign in 1997, the British Labour Party made extensive use of a slogan which simply consisted of a list of three (repeated) items: 'Education, education, education'. Possibly, the rhetorical effectiveness of this slogan is additionally demonstrated by the fact that ten years on, the Labour government were still under scrutiny by the media as to whether they had 'delivered' on this commitment to improve education.

Extract (9) also shows that lists can be used in combination with the other major rhetorical device discussed by Atkinson (1984a): the *contrast* (in this case, between 'dangers in acting as we are' and 'dangers of inaction', lines 2–3). In extracts (10) and (11), we see further examples of contrast devices. These extracts illustrate that close coordination is evident between the completion of a contrast and the audience's applause:

**(10) [Labour Party Conference]**

```
1      Osborn:     the way to fight Thatcher
2                  (0.4)
3                  is not through the silent conformity of the      A
4                  graveyard
5                  (0.5)
6                  but by putting party policies (0.2) powerfully   B
7                  and determinedly from the front bench
8      Audience:   xxXXXXXXXXXXXXXXXXXXXXXXXXXXXXXXXXXxx
              |                  (8.2 seconds)                      |
```

**(11) [Labour Party Conference]**

```
1      Morris:     Governments will argue (.8) that resources
2                  are not available to help disabled people
3                  (1.3)
4                  The fact is that too much is spent on the        A
5                  munitions of war
6                  (0.6)
7                  and too little is spent [(0.2) on the            B
8      Audience:                           [XXXXXXXXXXXX=
9      Morris:     =[munitions of peace.
10     Audience:   [XXXXXXXXXXXXXXXXXXXXXXXXXXXXXXXXX
              |                  (9.2 seconds)                      |
```

Indeed, in extract (11), the audience begins applauding at a point where it is simply clear that the second part of a contrast is being made (i.e., after 'too little is spent . . .'), without waiting to hear what 'too little is spent' on.

The completion point of a contrast device can be anticipated partly because both parts tend to be constructed and presented in the same ways: for example, some words or phrases may be mirrored in both parts. In extract (11), there are several points where the second part mirrors the first:

> too much is spent on the munitions of war
> too little is spent (0.2) on the munitions of peace.

There are several words in common, and in fact the only words that differ are the key contrastive items in each part: 'much' vs 'little' and 'war' vs 'peace'.

The importance of symmetry is demonstrated by the following example which shows the striking effect on audience applause if there are major differences between the two contrastive parts. Here, Mr Heath, an ex British Conservative Prime Minister, is arguing that the influence of the trades unions on government policy-making should be restrained. This anti-union stance was a central theme of Conservative policy at the time Heath made this speech. As he was speaking to an audience of Conservative party members and supporters, we might expect Mr Heath's remarks to receive unequivocal support and enthusiastic applause.

**(12) [UK General Election, 1979]**

| 1  | Heath:     | In my view it is right that the government should         | A |
|----|------------|----------------------------------------------------------|---|
| 2  |            | consider these matters and take them into account.       |   |
| 3  |            | (1.0)                                                    |   |
| 4  |            | What is entirely unacceptable (0.8) is the view          | B |
| 5  |            | that parliament never can (0.6) and never should         |   |
| 6  |            | approve any legislation (0.8) nor should a               |   |
| 7  |            | government pursue any policy (0.8) unless first of       |   |
| 8  |            | all the trades unions themselves (.) approve of it.      |   |
| 9  |            | (0.5)                                                    |   |
| 10 |            | THAT is entirely unacceptable                            |   |
| 11 | Audience:  | Hear [hear                                               |   |
| 12 | Audience:  | [x-xxXXXXXXXXXXXXXXXXXXXXXXXXXXXxxx-x                     |   |
|    |            | \|                    (8 seconds)                      \| |   |

Note here that despite the fact that Mr Heath is espousing a sentiment widely supported by the audience, the end of his point in line 8 is greeted not with closely coordinated applause but, at least initially, with silence (line 9). Indeed, it is only when he 'recompletes' his point (Atkinson, 1984b; Hutchby, 1997) by saying 'THAT is entirely unacceptable', thereby explicitly signalling to the audience that he has finished making a point, that the audience start applauding.

The absence of immediate applause can be seen as arising from the failure of Mr Heath to build a symmetrical contrast. The first part of the contrast is neat and short. The second part, however, meanders somewhat, and clearly does not match the first part. Consequently, when Mr Heath has finished, the audience remain silent: they have not been able to use the design of the contrast to help them anticipate when they should start clapping.

When constructed properly, three-part lists and contrasts, among other devices identified by Atkinson (1984a; see also Heritage and Greatbatch, 1986), project their own completion; and thus they allow the audience to anticipate when the device, and the point being made, will end, thereby ensuring that the audience may provide collective displays of affiliation. In this sense, these rhetorical patterns solve the tricky interactional problem of ensuring that a collection of unrehearsed, disparate individuals can be coordinated in their behaviour as a group.

The appeal of the work initiated by Atkinson is that it exposes to conscious and public scrutiny the largely tacit ways in which language can be used in the organization of public speeches. Although the audiences at political meetings or rallies are, by and large, in support of the person who is speaking, or the party he or she represents, political speeches remain a very important vehicle by which a politician can garner the support and affiliation of a wider audience. Thus, one practical upshot of this work is that it offers resources by which politicians and other public speakers may be coached to put across their messages more effectively. Atkinson himself, in fact, subsequently extended his work into the domain of communications consultancy (see the website of Atkinson Communications at www.speaking.co.uk). Others have used his findings to explore and make recommendations about other forms of persuasive discourse, such as the language of market traders (Pinch and Clark, 1986), management gurus (Greatbatch and Clark, 2005), and advertisers (Myers, 1994).

## CA, human–computer interaction and systems design

We next turn to a completely different area: the specialized application of CA in the field of human–computer interaction, which is itself a subfield of computer science. Despite its name, much of computer science is essentially an engineering discipline concerned with the design and construction of artefacts, albeit often only in computer code. Like practitioners of many engineering disciplines, computer scientists are keen to draw upon ideas from other areas of academic research. The field of artificial intelligence in computer science, for example, has always had a parasitic relationship with cognitive psychology. And software engineers have looked to some branches of mathematics for new approaches to the specification of systems.

Increasingly, operating a computer is a process related to linguistic and interactional techniques. System designers tend to talk of what goes on between computers and their users in terms of 'interaction', 'dialogue' and 'conversation'. Users no longer instruct computers by inserting punched cards or writing lines of programming code. In modern interfaces ordinary language is used to specify operations, make requests, issue commands, and assess their outcomes. The interface is an amalgamation of ordinary English words and phrases, icons, a cursor operated through a mouse, and virtual buttons which can be pressed using the cursor. Consequently, during the 1990s, many system designers became keen to explore ideas from sociology, and conversation analysis in particular (see Button, 1993; Luff, Gilbert and Frohlich, 1990; Thomas, 1995). This reflected the increasing influence of the idea that in order to design computer systems which can either simulate or, more ambitiously, reproduce the nature of human communication, it is necessary to know about the ways in which everyday interaction is organized.

A key moment in this 'turn to sociology' in system design was the publication of Lucy Suchman's *Plans and Situated Actions* (1987), in which she drew from conversation analysis and ethnomethodology to offer a critique of the model of human communication with which most system designers and programmers tend to work.

The prevailing idea within the community of computer systems developers is that the individual is a plan-based actor. Essentially this represents a 'computational' metaphor of human action (Hutchby, 2001a): we act on the basis of intentions and plans, which our co-participants in a given situation have to decipher or compute, in order to understand what we are doing and act in concert with us (Berger, 1997).

It is relatively easy to see how this model can be incorporated in a machine. The computer has 'intentions' and 'plans' also; although in this case they are really the intentions and plans of the programmer. This means that there are two basic problems for computer system design. First, the system must be designed in such a way that the user can adequately comprehend its activities, which generally come in the form of instructions as to what to do in order to get the machine to work in a desired way. To use Suchman's term, computer systems are constructed to be self-explicating machines: the machine is an 'expert' in its own use, while the user is conceived as a 'novice'. The expert-novice metaphor is one that is widely relied upon by designers, and the assumption is that the system should be able to explain its own use to a novice user.

The second problem, however, is much more important: the system itself must be designed so as to comprehend the activities of its user. The assumption here is that users come to the system with goals in mind, and the system needs to have the capability to 'discover' what these are and respond appropriately.

Suchman studied pairs of novice users operating a simple 'expert help' system on a photocopying machine. She was interested in two questions: to what extent can we say that there is successful communication, on the basis of mutual intelligibility, between the users and the system? And what happens when that mutual intelligibility breaks down? How do the participants (users and system) manage that situation?

On the basis of her analysis, Suchman argues that the user models employed in cognitive and computer science depend upon users starting with and sticking as closely as possible to a plan. But actual human interaction, with machines as well as with other humans, is essentially *ad hoc*. This distinction is succintly captured in the title of her book: the difference is one between plans and situated action. Designers attribute plans to users, and systems work well whenever the actions undertaken by the user can be linked to prior assumptions about what the user is doing. But problems soon occur when those assumptions about users' goals and plans do not match with their actual, situated actions.

For example, a user may be aware of what the machine requires her to do to achieve some specific objective; however, the situated actions by which she tries to achieve that objective – particularly, the sense she makes of what the system requires her to do – are not available to the machine. Neither do the user's situated actions match the system's idealized model of the 'plan' that the user has in mind. Furthermore, the user has no access to this model, but has to make sense of the system's requirements within the context of her particular situation and in the light of her understanding of previous actions. At the same time, the system has no access to the 'sense' she has made of those prior actions, on the situated level, and proceeds by assuming that she has understood in the way the designer's user model predicts.

Suchman concludes that a model of interaction based on the idea of people with discrete plans and goals in their heads is unhelpful in the design of interactive computer systems. Instead she suggests that it is necessary to view user interaction with computer systems as an emergent and situated activity. In particular she emphasizes the way in which participants' orientation to the sequential ordering of interaction

provides resources for establishing mutual intelligibility and the identification and repair of troubles in communication.

Suchman's work has had an important impact on the field of system
design. Not only did it propose a strong critique of the model of the
user as plan-following and goal-seeking, but it introduced the significance of conversation anaysis, and sociological approaches more generally, to the community of system developers. To many designers, CA
appeared to provide a coherent and principled view of communication
which avoided many of the problems associated with the model of goal-
driven and plan-led interaction. In particular, it was felt that CA offered
a set of empirical findings which might, by analogy, be applied to the
design of the interface between people and computers. For a designer
of complex computer systems, the interface with the human user often
presents particular difficulties. For practical and commercial reasons,
systems need to have a high degree of usability: it is generally accepted
that interfaces should be easy to learn, quick to operate, give rise to low
rates of error and be pleasant to use. Speech is the optimum medium for
computer interfaces: most people can speak, and speech-based interfaces do not require users to be familiar with keyboards, or skilled in the
physical manipulation of on-screen instructions and icons.

Another reason why CA was so readily adopted by system designers
was that it offered a perspective on human–computer interaction which
is independent of the technology used to implement systems and independent of the specific psychological characteristics of individual users
(Norman and Thomas, 1990). Consequently, while CA has been used
in the design of screen-based interfaces (Frohlich and Luff, 1990) it has
been primarily used by researchers designing speech-based interactive
computers (Wooffitt et al., 1997). Indeed, it seems intuitively sensible for
system designers to consider whether it would be possible to develop a
system that it is informed by some knowledge of the organization of
conversation. (For an illustration of this kind of work see the papers in
Luff, Gilbert and Frohlich, 1990).

However, this is a contentious issue. Some conversation analysts have
been critical about the extent to which CA is a useful resource in the
design of natural language interfaces (for example, Button, 1990;
Button and Sharrock, 1995). The main point of contention concerns
the notion of rules. It is a common assumption that if a computer is to
work it needs to be programmed with formal rules. And it has appeared
to some computer scientists that many of the findings of CA, such as
the turn-taking system and basic sequential phenomena like adjacency
pairs, are amenable to being specified in terms of formal rules which a
computer program could instantiate (Frohlich and Luff, 1990).

Yet CA's perspective emphasizes that people orient to these communicative 'rules' not as causal constraints but as interpretive resources by which to make sense of their ongoing interaction with others. Recall, for example, our discussions of turn-taking and conditional relevance in the early chapters of this book. A basic 'rule' is that on the provision of the first part of an adjacency pair, an appropriate second part is conditionally relevant. However, analysis of occasions in which second parts do not appear shows that speakers use that 'rule' to draw context-tied inferences about the intentions of co-speakers, or about some features of the immediate circumstances, which make sense of that absence: the other person didn't hear, was being reluctant to answer a question or accept an offer, and so on. In this, speakers display an awareness of, or sensitivity to, the 'rule' that following the production of a first pair part, the appropriate second is due.

Furthermore, these rules (or 'norms', 'procedures', 'maxims', and so on) are available only through analytic inspection of the empirical materials which display a sensitivity to them; hence, it is asserted that they are embodied in actions, not determinants of action. Computer scientists have responded that this view rests on a limited appreciation of the sophistication of programming techniques: contrary to the impression that one would gain from most of the literature debating the topic, rule-based computer programs are the exception and alternative designs which include nothing that is recognizably a rule are quite feasible (Hirst, 1991).

However, in the literature which draws upon CA as a resource for the design of interactive systems, there has been an unfortunate tendency to discuss aspects of conversational organization, such as turn-taking and paired actions, in abstraction from empirical materials (for example, Cawsey, 1990; Finkelstein and Fuks, 1990). This tendency has, ironically, resulted in an impoverished appreciation of the complexity of talk-in-interaction among those in the HCI community keen to explore the utility of findings from conversation analytic research.

In recent years this particular extension of CA has been developed in newer directions, including a range of work being done, often in collaboration with innovative companies such as the Xerox Corporation, on the organization of communication in workplaces involving high levels of technological mediation (Button, 1993; Heath and Luff, 2000; Luff et al., 2000). Here, the emphasis has turned from designing particular systems that can 'interact' with humans, to explicating the extent to which complex technological systems successfully dovetail with the organization of human interaction and collaborative task management. In short, do such systems help or hinder human collaborative work?

The principle technique is video analysis, usually combined with some form of ethnographic account of the setting. Typically, the researcher sets up cameras in settings such as airport operations rooms (Goodwin, 1996; Suchman, 1996), telecommunications control rooms (Hindmarsh and Heath, 2000) or tube train coordination centres (Luff and Heath, 2002), in which workers use a whole range of technologies such as telephones, walkie talkies, video screens, monitors, computers, and so on. The recordings are analysed to see when and how the technological media are used in concert with speech and non-verbal communication, with one practical aim being the development of recommendations as to the design of systems that will best facilitate this kind of intensive, multi-layered and technologically mediated work. (For a more extended review of this type of work, see Arminen, 2005: 198–242.)

## Children's talk

We now turn to another area in which CA has had an impact which also extends into practical relevancies: the analysis of children's language use and the interaction between adults and children. For many decades, children's talk has been studied from a wide range of disciplinary backgrounds, including psychology (developmental, cognitive and social), sociolinguistics, anthropology (cultural, linguistic and social), education, and sociology. Within these disciplines, two types of research can be identified. One type prioritizes the development of linguistic skills that children acquire on the way to becoming competent members of the surrounding adult language culture. Much of this research draws on the empirical findings of developmental psychology. The second type prioritizes the linguistic competence that children possess and manifest as part of their membership of the indigenous language cultures of childhood, which can be more or less independent of adults. This kind of research is more likely to draw on findings from sociology and anthropology. A related distinction can be drawn between research which focuses primarily on children's talk in interaction with adults, and that which addresses the talk of children among their peers.

These strands of interest are not necessarily mutually exclusive. In areas such as the study of children's argument, for example, a concern with how children develop skills in argumentation as they grow older often exists alongside, and in mutual interchange with, concerns with how arguing is an arena of social action in which children manage relationships among peers, with siblings and with adults (for example, Maynard, 1985, 1986; Eder, 1991; Sheldon, 1992a, 1992b, 1996). Here, as in many other areas of childhood studies, traditional disciplinary boundaries (such as that between psychological interests in development and cognition, and sociological interests in institutions and social relationships) begin to blur.

In conversation analysis there is now a good deal of research showing how talk and other activities represent resources through which children, as social participants or members of a culture, display interactional competence. CA's interest in children's talk can be related to a wider set of interests in sociolinguistics, linguistic anthropology and social psychology where researchers have sought to determine the specific competencies displayed by children in deploying linguistic resources and managing interaction. Much of this work has been path-breaking in terms of situating children as competent manipulators of complex verbal and interactional resources (key texts include Garvey, 1984; Ochs, 1988; Ochs and Schieffelin, 1979, 1983; Schieffelin, 1990). However, a great deal of it is couched within a developmental framework in which children are seen as passing through stages marked by factors such as the increasing sophistication of sentence structures and the growing ability to engage in complex interactional structures.

This developmental emphasis has also meant that sociolinguistic research has tended to restrict itself to studying children in interaction with adults: in the nursery, the classroom, or in parental interaction. Such an emphasis results in a downplaying of children's talk among themselves and in their own spaces; even though, as Ervin-Tripp and Mitchell-Kernan (1977: 7) acknowledge, 'many of the speech events in which children engage typically occur among children apart from adults, and they are explicitly taught, in many cases, by children.'

Within CA, Marjorie Goodwin (1990) has emphasized how research considering children in their peer groups is therefore vital. Her work illustrates the depth of social and interactional competencies displayed by children as they talk among their peers. Goodwin analysed the talk of children in a Black urban neighbourhood of Philadelphia, recorded as they played on the streets near their homes. The data enabled her to demonstrate a wide range of ways in which children use language actively to create social organization among themselves. These include managing the rules and orders of participation in games; collaborating in complex, multi-party tasks; telling stories and other narratives; instigating accusations and constructing defences; and managing arguments in a variety of contexts.

In the latter case, one particularly interesting example involves a dispute format used, it seems, largely by girls and called 'he-said-she-said', in which one participant accuses a second of having said something derogatory about her to a third person behind the first's back. Unravelling examples of this interactionally complex form of 'instigating', Goodwin reveals the competent construction of a whole set of situated, contingent social identities among the disputants:

> Within the he-said-she-said confrontation, a field of negotiated action, complete with its own relevant history, is invoked through the structure of an . . . accusation . . .; a single utterance creates a complex past history of events, providing operative identity relationships for participants. (Goodwin, 1990: 286)

Studies such as this, in focusing on children's talk among their peer groups in natural settings of social interaction,

> show how language interaction plays a central role in shaping the social worlds in which children exist to a large extent independently of adults. In these settings, children demonstrate communicative skills which have more to do with being proficient participants within their own culture, than with learning how to become competent members of an adult speech community. (Thornborrow, 1998: 135)

Goodwin's (1990) work, and that of Sheldon (1992a, 1992b, 1996), also contribute to another major strand of research on child language, that of addressing gender differences in talk. As both note, there is a strong tendency, following work by Lakoff (1975) and Gilligan (1982), to view male and female patterns of speech as essentially different. Male talk is often thought to be characterized by competitiveness and hierarchy whilst female speech is characterized by cooperation and supportiveness. However, while both Goodwin and Sheldon do indeed reveal certain differences between the girls' and boys' groups in their data, the differences do not support this particular dichotomy. It becomes clear that girls may display just as much adeptness at competition and hierarchy as boys; indeed, close analysis of the talk shows that 'cooperation and competitiveness are not mutually exclusive agendas and often coexist within the same speech activities' (Goodwin, 1990: 284).

Work on peer group interaction is therefore important in revealing more about how talk operates in children's own social worlds. Children also routinely find themselves having to manage the contingencies of adult-controlled institutions, including school classrooms (McHoul, 1978), medical settings (Silverman, 1987), counselling services (Hutchby, 2007), and of course the family itself. These often involve professionals and other organizational representatives whose task it is to interact with children. One of the key themes that has been drawn out in relation to such settings is the way that differing agendas – and in many ways, differing moral imperatives – can inform the participation of adults and children. Part of the relevance of studying these differences is that they can contribute to the ways in which professionals, practitioners and policy-makers themselves understand the social competencies of children.

In a study based on video recording of children in the play section of a kindergarten, Danby and Baker (1998) draw on CA to show how children, while subject to construction in the terms of institutional knowledge and practices, can deploy their own knowledge of institutional regimes to create spaces of autonomy and resistance. Their data reveal the kindergarten children responding to a teacher's intervention in their conflicts by adopting two parallel strategies. In the teacher's presence, they comply with her programmatic attempt to alleviate the conflict and get the children to 'make up'. But once the teacher departs, the children's talk changes as they deploy their own, far less conciliatory, procedures for dealing with conflict. Teacher-defined knowledge in which conflict is a hurtful thing and in which the hurt one must be comforted by the perpetrator therefore exists in parallel with alternative knowledges which are defined by children themselves and deployed in the interstices of the school's regime.

In practical terms, this study raises important issues about the interface between teacher-defined social relations and those affecting children. In a broader sense it can be used to raise questions about attempts made by professionals (and indeed parents) to diffuse conflict by exhorting what they define as more moral codes of behaviour. The key point is that only by examining in detail the children's talk and interaction in the absence of the teacher do we come to an understanding that there is, in fact, a different set of moral models at work for them, as well as how that moral code is instantiated in practice.

Similar themes of resistance and alternative practices animate work by Baker (1982, 1984) on adult-adolescent interaction in educational settings, and by Silverman (1987) on interactions between pediatricians and children in clinical settings for conditions such as cleft palate and diabetes. In each of these environments, albeit in very different ways, the interaction is characterized by adult attempts to ensure changes in behaviour by the child, or to manage and regulate children's behaviours according to professionally defined agendas. Perhaps unsurprisingly, children often resist these attempts. However the authors treat such resistance, when it occurs, as itself an indication of interactional competence.

Silverman, Baker and Keogh (1998) pursue this point in their study of parent-teacher interviews – a space in which children are present but at the same time the objects of discussion between adults. Focusing on cases of silent or non-responsive children in these contexts, they show how silence often follows turns in which adults have proffered advice for future actions (such as 'maybe you can agree to work harder . . .'). The silence, however, is not treated by Silverman et al. as evidence of deficiency but as a competent strategy by which the child can avoid implication in the moral universe being set up between the parent and teacher. In other words, it is a strategy of resistance in this form of institutional setting.

Similar themes emerge in recent research on children's talk in counselling sessions following parental separation or divorce (Hutchby, 2001b, 2002, 2005, 2007). Child counselling sessions are an institutional space expressly designed for the enablement of children's talk. Like all forms of counselling, they provide what Silverman (1996) called an 'incitement to speak' about the 'feelings' generated by the break-up of a family unit. Yet paradoxically, young children (the age range for the study is 4–12 years) are generally brought into counselling at the behest of their parent(s) rather than their own volition. The willingness of children to produce the kind of 'feelings-talk' that counsellors try and encourage therefore varies widely.

For instance, in one study (Hutchby, 2001b) both child and counsellor cooperate extensively in producing talk which actively recruits the researcher's data collection technology (a tape recorder) to bring into play topics which turn out to enable the counsellor to draw out a range of insights into the child's perception of her relationships with each of her parents. By stark contrast, another case (Hutchby, 2002) reveals a child resisting the production of situationally appropriate talk (i.e. feelings-talk) throughout an entire 45-minute session by responding to almost everything the counsellor says with the words 'Don't know'. In this case, once again, rather than adopting a simple view of this child as monosyllabic or excessively sullen, the analysis concentrates on the child's resistance as a competent strategy for evading attempts to produce the kind of talk the counsellor desires as appropriate for the institutional work of counselling. At the same time, looking at the data from a different angle, we are shown how the counsellor's responses to this strategy change as the session unfolds; in particular, how he ultimately finds a way of treating the child's talk as therapeutically relevant. This enables the counsellor both to retrieve the institutional agenda of counselling and to protect or validate the child's interactional competence.

Research on children's language by conversation analysts and others influenced by CA thus prioritizes the linkage between children's talk and social processes. The studies we have mentioned address children's talk in natural settings of social interaction as against the more experimental, test-based approaches used in many forms of psychological research. The preference here is to examine language use not simply in terms of the development or acquisition of cognitive processing skills, but as evidence of the growing ability to manage participation in social interaction. In other words, children's talk is treated as an integral aspect of their general social competence. But at the same time, we have seen how this kind of research can have implications for practical concerns in relation to children in the institutional environments where they regularly interact with adult professionals of different kinds. These include paediatricians, professional carers or nursery staff, teachers, and, for some children, counsellors and therapists. For all these professions, an understanding of children's interactional competence based on the fine-grained detail enabled by CA can be a vital component in the development of effective ways of managing the interface between children's behaviour and institutional agendas.

## The order in 'disorderly' talk

Researchers have also begun to explore how conversation analytic methods and findings can be used to help people who have communication disorders that arise from neurological, physiological or psychological causes (Goodwin, 2003a). CA can be used to provide a formal account of the characteristics of interaction between people with communication difficulties and their families, friends and therapists, thereby illuminating how speech disorders impact in people's everyday lives. Moreover, it may be possible to use conversation analysis to devise therapeutic interventions that are sensitive to the ways in which communication disorders effect people in their everyday interactions with others. In this section we will consider each of these contributions. But first, it is useful to establish the distinctive methodological perspective CA can offer to the study of speech disorders.

Traditionally, the characteristics and consequences of communication disorders are investigated in a range of formal and informal tests. So, for example, people with speech impairments may be asked to tell a story based on stimulus material such as cartoons; or therapists may use standardized interviews to assess speech impairment. Conversation analytic research, however, emphasizes the importance of naturally occurring data, and thus the research focus shifts from individual performance on tasks in clinical or institutional settings to social interaction in which speech difficulties are directly relevant to real life communicative concerns. The use of naturally occurring data also means that investigation of the nature and effect of speech disorders is not based on the examination of utterances removed from their context (as in those accounts of communication disorders informed by speech act theory), but closely examines the sequential organization and context of turn production. And in contrast to reliance on the therapists' intuitions or theoretical accounts, CA emphasizes the importance of the participants' own understandings and orientations as they are displayed in their communicative activities (Lesser and Perkins, 1999; Wilkinson, 1999a). The emphasis on naturally occurring data means that researchers can develop an ecologically valid understanding of how speech disorders actually manifest in people's everyday communication, thereby gaining a real insight to the lived experience of impairment.

The conversation analytic perspective on spoken communication as sequentially organized offers a way of developing a formal, technical appreciation of the problems faced by people with speech disorders. For example, in an analysis of interaction between a speech therapist and person with aphasia (the partial or total inability to produce or understand speech as a result of brain damage caused by injury or disease), R. Wilkinson (1995) shows how confusion over the referent of an adjective, and problems in assisting with a word search, are due to misalignments in the parties' current understanding of the appropriate sequential context for their activities.

In the early part of the conversation the topic was the patient's interest in flower arranging.

**(13) [Wilkinson, 1995]**
('T' is the therapist, 'P' is the patient.)
```
1    T:     how about your flower arranging?
2           (.) °is [that uh°
3    P:          [uh actually: (.) still (.)only now and then,
4    T:     [mm hmm
5    P:     [but uh:m uh:m (0.5) I think me and more more:, (1.8)
6           uh:m >I mean< no. only now and then
7           but maybe (.) °ah: right!° maybe (.) not plain
8           but also speckled and (.) much (.) better
9    T:     [[mm.
10   P:     [[and also (.) uh flowers much (0.2) pretty or
11          something. [>you know?< but uh:
12   T:                [oh right! sounds interesting.
13   P:     >I mean< maybe maybe not I [don't know] you know
14   T:                                [  right  ]
```

| | | |
|---|---|---|
| 15 | | so the speckled flowers is that uhm something [you'd ()] |
| 16 | P: | [n-no  ] |
| 17 | | but no uh:m (0.3) vase |
| 18 | T: | oh::! |

In this sequence it emerges that there is some confusion over the referent of the adjective 'speckled', used by the patient in line 8. The therapist misinterprets this word as referring to 'flowers', a perfectly
reasonable interpretation given that the topic of the talk was flower
arranging. It is only when the therapist explicitly refers to 'speckled
flowers' can the patient see that there is a problem, at which point he
produces a repair and clarifies the referent of 'speckled' as a vase, or
vases (it subsequently transpires that he was talking about painting
vases). The problem can be traced to two events. First, the patient's
utterance in lines 5 to 8 had changed the topic from flower arranging to
painting vases without making that shift explicit. Second, the therapist
attempted to locate the sense of the word 'speckled', and indeed the trajectory of the interaction, by interpreting it in terms of its sequential
and topical context.

Wilkinson makes a similar argument about a sequence which occurs
during a later part of the conversation. The patient has trouble finding
a word when he is providing an account of something that is going to
happen in the future.

**(14) [Wilkinson, 1995]**

| | | |
|---|---|---|
| 49 | P: | and uh:m uh:m last (0.3) m- uh year |
| 50 | | (.) and uhm >very famous< |
| 51 | | not England but (2.0) °hm° (0.8) °terrible° (0.8) |
| 52 | | uh:m (4.0) I think (4.0) uh:m (3.0) |
| 53 | | °not England° but (2.0) °not Scotland° but (.) |
| 54 | | Wales right? |
| 55 | T: | °right° |
| 56 | P: | and uh one:, (1.5) °oh God almighty° (0.8) one (1.0) |
| 57 | | uh:m (3.0) ↓ town. |
| 58 | T: | ((nods)) |

At the start of this extract, when he is providing an account of something that is going to happen in the future, the patient has trouble
finding a word.

It subsequently transpires that the patient is trying to locate the name
of a town. It is noticeable that he tries to engage the assistance of the
therapist by establishing the kind of word he is looking for: 'not
England' and 'not Scotland' indicating that the unforthcoming word is

the name of a place. Eventually, he is able to convey that he is seeking the name of a town in Wales. However, the therapist merely provides minimal verbal and non verbal encouragement to the patient (lines 55 and 58). In keeping with common practice she is encouraging the patient to self repair, even if that process is extended over several turns and takes some time. The following exchange then occurs.

**(15) [Wilkinson, 1995]**

```
59   P:    uh:m (.) and >obviously< uh:m people (0.5) uh
60         every (.) part of the (.) country.
61   T:    mm hm=
62   P:    =uh:m and >sorry< and uh:m (2.0)
63         an- and (3.0) car or van or something (.)
64         what the word? >I mean< what the (1.0) uh:m (1.0)
65         very famous or very, (3.5)
66   T:    are these this people round the country go to somewhere
67         in Wales, with (.) are they=
68   P:    =or [ yes ]
69   T:         [what] what do they go there for?
70   P:    hh [ right ]
71   T:         [is that] to [something] to do with driving?
72   P:                      [ u h:m  ]
73         yes [right right ]
74   T:        [for people ] who (.) dis [abled?]
74   P:                                  [ n o  ] >no no<
```

In this segment the search for a place name has been abandoned as the patient attempts a different strategy to tell his story. Eventually, however, the patient says, 'what the word?' (line 64), thereby inviting the therapist to help him. But it soon becomes apparent that the therapist is having difficulty in helping the patient. For example, when she offers the category 'disabled' as a candidate target of the patient's reference to 'people', the patient is quick to indicate that that is not the group he is talking about. Eventually, the attempt to remedy this trouble is also abandoned.

Wilkinson identifies the basis for the therapist's difficulties in helping the patient in his word search. In a subtle analysis he shows how the therapist's problems lie in the fact that she has not understood the previous part of the patient's narrative in which this word search difficulty is embedded. Consequently two problems become conflated: the patient's search for the appropriate word, and the therapist's lack of understanding of the context in which that search is taking place. Again, then, the root of the problem is contextual: because of the patient's aphasia the therapist does not have access to a necessary understanding of the sequential context for which this particular story is being told; and without that understanding she has no basis on which to offer help appropriate to the patient's efforts to locate a specific word.

Conversation analytic research, then, not only provides important insight into the way in which speech impairment is manifested in social interaction, but highlights some of the competencies through which people with speech disorders may attempt to achieve and sustain meaningful communication. This is further illustrated by two key studies. Heeschen and Schegloff (1999, 2003) studied the interactional properties of what is called telegraphic speech: utterances that are lexically, syntactically or grammatically truncated. Telegraph style speech is usually taken to be a way in which an aphasic speaker can deal with the symptoms of the disorder. Heeschen and Schegloff's analysis of talk between an aphasic speaker and a friend with unimpaired speech, however, showed that telegraph style speech from the person with aphasia had the interactional consequence of eliciting increased cooperative activity from the co-participant. In this sense, it was an interactional resource for the achievement of intersubjective understanding.

Heeschen and Schegloff's studies draw attention to the important role of co-participants in the collaborative achievement of aphasic speakers' communicative success. The importance of the active co-production of meaning by unimpaired co-participants is starkly illustrated in a study by C. Goodwin (2003b), who studied family communication in which one of the participants was a man who had suffered a severe stroke, which left him with movement only in his left arm, and with a vocabulary of three words – 'yes', 'no' and 'and'. In his analysis of video and audio recordings of the family making arrangements for dinner, Goodwin shows how the stroke victim, drawing on his limited vocabulary, non-lexical vocalizations and hand movements, is able to shape the family members' inferences about his preferences, and thereby participate in the arrangements.

The analysis of real life communication between people with speech disorders and family and friends not only identifies the competencies by which they can participate in social interaction, but can also stand as a corrective to claims about communicative abilities made on the basis of more formal tests in therapeutic or clinical settings. This is illustrated in Heeschen and Schegloff's (2003) study. They note how an aphasic speaker, when asked to tell a story based on stimulus materials, displayed a range of speech production difficulties. But when she was interacting in more informal settings, some of these production difficulties seemed less severe (pauses, for example, were shorter than in the story telling tests), and she was also able to use telegraphic speech to deal with some of her problems and elicit cooperation from her recipient to ensure intersubjective understanding. The analysis of her actual interactions offered a different perspective on the nature of her problems – and insight to her interactional competencies – not revealed through formal tests.

Lindsay and Wilkinson (1999) have made a similar argument with respect to aphasic speakers' practices of conversational repair. They studied repair sequences in interaction between aphasic speakers and their therapists, and between aphasic speakers and their spouses. The spouses fully engaged in collaborating for a resolution, exposing the problem and prolonging the attempt at resolution. But speech and language therapists attempted to minimize the interactional implications of speech problems stemming from the speakers' aphasia. The concerns of the speech therapists then, led to forms of repair sequence markedly different to those which occurred in informal communication with significant others. At the very least, this analysis would raise questions about the extent to which the formal therapeutic consultation can reveal the nature of the difficulties that aphasic speakers actually face in their daily life.

Finally, Schegloff (1999b) analysed data from a clinical session in which a patient with surgically separated brain hemispheres is tested by a researcher. He focuses on a sequence in which the researcher indirectly requests that the patient move a little closer to the table around which they are both sitting. Although the patient does not speak during this brief interaction, Schegloff shows how his physical orientation demonstrates close analysis of the researcher's request as it is constructed, and displays a deep understanding of the broader sequential organizations that underpin indirect requests in everyday conversation: interactional competencies which, according to prevailing neuroscientific theories, a person with surgically separated brain hemispheres should not possess.

Conversation analytic research on aphasic speech in naturally occurring settings may provide the basis for reassessing the value of conventionally accepted therapeutic goals. For example, Goodwin (in interview with Dickerson, 2006) has argued that, in the case of communication difficulties arising from severe brain injury, the symptoms may be chronic and permanent, and that we may be over optimistic in trying to develop programmes of intervention which seek to encourage improvement in speech performance. Instead he argues for more research into the way in which family and friends of people with severe speech disorders develop interactional and inferential skills to accommodate people with speech disorders. Drawing on his work on family interactions between a stroke victim and his family (Goodwin, 2003b) he urges that consideration be given to ways in which families may be advised to reshape their patterns of communication to facilitate active participation by persons with speech difficulties.

There may be, then, practical implications from a CA perspective on communication disorders. Wilkinson and his colleagues have developed what they call 'interaction therapy' (Wilkinson et al., 1998). This is designed to help sufferers and their families better understand the nature of the problems aphasia causes, and to identify how these may be accommodated or resolved in routine family conversational interaction.

> In this type of therapy the participants are made aware of their interactional patterns by means of the therapist playing back a video of them in conversation and encouraging discussion about these patterns. In particular the participants are encouraged to discuss whether this pattern is common in their talk and whether it is problematic for them. Suggestions are then given by the therapist as to how these problems may be dealt with, and the participants may also engage in exercises to practice new patterns. (Wilkinson, 1999b: 341)

Conversation analytic research methods may be extremely valuable in providing a deeper insight into the precise nature of the difficulties faced by people with aphasia, and other forms of communication problems. In addition, CA may furnish the basis of forms of speech therapy which address exactly the difficulties faced by people with speech disorders, and which attend to the broader interactional contexts in which everyday communication occurs. Finally, the analytic approach of CA seeks to describe the competencies that inform the production of utterances in interaction; this is true even when one or more of the participants might be regarded as verbally handicapped. While being sensitive to the physiological or psychological difficulties people face, the focus of CA thereby emphasizes the subtle and sophisticated range of skills which people with speech problems nevertheless employ in their interaction with others; a range of competencies which might be lost to an analysis motivated by, and embodying the assumptions of, a model of the speaker as intrinsically deficient (Gardner, 1998). Such an approach to the investigation of speech problems is therefore not only positive, but potentially liberating, in that analysis of interaction involving people with speech problems is not in the first instance propelled or constrained by underlying assumptions of (for example) asymmetry in the cognitive or verbal endowment of the participants.

In this chapter we have reviewed work in a number of diverse areas in which the policies and procedures of CA have been extended and shown to have some relevance in terms of practical concerns for workers in these fields. In each of these fields, we have been able to do little more than provide a sketch of the vast range of empirical work that conversation analysts and those influenced by conversation analysis are doing. Each of these areas represents a lively and ongoing research programme which will continue to develop, and thereby continue to provide evidence and incentive for the extended application of CA's theories, methods and findings.

# 9

# Critical Engagements: Sociology, Psychology and Linguistics

Conversation analysis originated in the disciplinary field of sociology, and many of its current practitioners were trained in that discipline. But increasingly, researchers in related fields such as psychology and linguistics are adopting the CA perspective to frame their own work and to shape their analytical concerns. Crucially, whichever of these disciplines a researcher works in, CA encourages him or her to rethink or respecify some of the core issues and problems of that discipline. CA has developed a highly distinctive theoretical and methodological stance on central issues such as the relationship between events in the world and analytic claims about those events that goes against many of the assumptions that have traditionally underpinned research in the social sciences.

In the first edition of this book, in 1998, we touched on these questions at various points. However, given the enormous expansion since then of CA work and its influence across disciplines, it is pertinent in this new edition to address such issues in a more focused way. Therefore, in this chapter we provide a discussion of CA's relationship to some key questions in the disciplines of sociology, psychology and linguistics. Beginning with an account of how conversation analysis can respond to what might be termed the *sociological agenda* – an analytical agenda foregrounding the importance of 'wider structural issues' such as power – we then turn to how CA suggests a respecification of one of the core themes in psychology, that is, research on cognition and other mental processes. Finally, we examine the developing relationship between CA and linguistics, with a particular focus on how conversation analysis encourages linguists interested in grammatical and prosodic aspects of language use to place these squarely within the context of interaction.

## Sociology: conversation analysis, interaction and power

Despite its origins in the discipline of sociology, conversation analysis is frequently criticized for being unresponsive to what might be called the 'sociological agenda'. These criticisms focus on two related issues. First, there is a claim that CA lacks an adequate sense of the contextualization of utterances within a wider set of social relations and practices. Second, conversation analysts in general are thought to be unwilling to make links between the 'micro' details of talk-in-interaction and the 'macro' levels of sociological variables – class, gender, power, ideology and so forth (see, for example, Bourdieu, 1991; Thompson, 1984).

Although we have called it the 'sociological agenda', it is not only sociologists who raise these criticisms of CA. Indeed, the place where such points have been made perhaps most forcefully is in the area known as *critical discourse analysis*: a perspective that seeks to combine linguistic analysis with sociological theory. As Norman Fairclough, a leading proponent of critical discourse analysis (CDA), puts it, for him conversation analysis is flawed by being actively 'resistant to linking properties of talk with higher-level features of society and culture – relations of power, ideologies, cultural values' (Fairclough, 1995: 23).

To what extent should CA be responsive to these criticisms? To some in the field, it is felt that they amount merely to the claim that CA is flawed because it refuses to base itself on the pre-established agendas of traditional sociology. Especially (but not only) in the American context, these are based on assuming the importance of particular sets of sociological variables for any form of analysis or explanation of social phenomena. But CA's analytical agenda derives from the ethnomethodological position that the relevance of any analytic category needs to be shown to be relevant for members, or participants in interaction, rather than being assumed by the analyst (a point that is discussed at length, along with other critical topics, in the exchanges between Wetherell, 1998 and Schegloff, 1997, 1998; and between Billig, 1999 and Schegloff, 1999a).

The key factor is that CA's position makes it problematic to *begin* by thinking in terms of sociological variables such as power, ideology and so forth, because the traditional sociologist's question is turned around. Rather than asking how social power (for example) affects the nature of the discourse, conversation analysts ask how – and, indeed, whether – the participants in a social scene show themselves to be oriented to that phenomenon in the ongoing course of their interaction.

Such a position, interpreted as a reluctance to engage explicitly with sociological concepts such as power, gender, class and so on, leads to a fundamental difference with CDA, as well as with sociology more generally. While the proponents of CDA are quite comfortable with an approach to discourse that is, as Fairclough puts it, 'informed by . . . social theory insights' (1995: 54), many conversation analysts remain suspicious of what they see as the preconceptions built into such insights.

It is possible to argue, however, that a good deal of work in CA does indeed link the properties of talk with 'higher-level' features of society. In particular, there is a tacit idea of power to be located in much CA work on institutional discourse. Making this idea more explicit is important, not least for challenging the view that CA is merely a 'micro-level' approach with little or nothing to say about the relationship between language use and wider social structures.

Fairclough's (1995) position, and that of CDA in general, is that the analysis of talk must be undertaken not just in terms of the local construction and exchange of turns between participants, but must be related to external structures – historical, social, and ideological – which impact upon the meaning of actions undertaken within the talk. As Fairclough (1995: 54) puts it: 'calling the approach "critical" is a recognition that our social practice in general and our use of language in particular are bound up with causes and effects which we may not be at all aware of under normal conditions.' He goes on:

> Connections between the use of language and the exercise of power are often not clear to people, yet appear on closer examination to be vitally important. . . . For instance, the ways in which a conventional consultation between a doctor and a patient is organised, or a conventional interview between a reporter and a politician, take for granted a whole range of ideologically potent assumptions about rights, relationships, knowledge and identities. For example, the assumption that the doctor is the sole source of medically legitimate knowledge about illness, or that it is legitimate for the reporter – as one who 'speaks for' the public – to challenge the politician. Such practices are shaped, with their common-sense assumptions, according to prevailing notions of power between groups of people. The normal opacity of these practices to those involved in them – the invisibility of their ideological assumptions, and of the power relations which

underlie the practices – helps to sustain these power relations. (Fairclough, 1995: 54)

Such a position suggests, in a way akin to what we described in Chapter 6 as the 'container' theory of context, that power relations and other sociological variables are pre-established features of the context. This viewpoint is also traceable in sociological claims that institutions 'are characterised by . . . hierarchical relations of power between the occupants of institutional positions' and, consequently, in their actions institutional agents 'exercise the power which is institutionally endowed upon them' (Thompson, 1984: 165).

This points to a key difference at the very starting point of analysis. While CA aims to describe the ways that participants display that they *are* aware of specific contextual factors (by observably modifying the ways that they talk, for instance), CDA maintains that there are other factors, external to the situation the speakers are in, and of which the speakers may *not* be aware, that impact on the production of their talk.

However, for CA, this stance leads to a crucial problem. Clearly, since these factors are said to operate outside the awareness of the participants themselves, it falls to the analyst to demonstrate where and how they affect the talk. The problem with this is that such a policy can end up giving too much licence to the analyst to 'read in' the relevance of external factors where there may be no other evidence to support the claim beyond the analyst's assertion (Wooffitt, 2005). By assuming the relevance of these factors before the analysis of data actually starts, the analysis is in danger of becoming a self-fulfilling prophecy.

To illustrate this, let us consider the characteristically asymmetrical nature of institutional discourse as outlined in Chapter 6. Within the question–answer structure that typifies a large proportion of talk in institutional settings (Drew and Heritage, 1992b), questions tend to be asked far more frequently by institutional agents such as doctors, interviewers, teachers, and so on. Many of the asymmetries in institutional discourse can therefore be thought of in terms of the 'power' of institutional agents to establish the participation opportunities of laypersons, and to define the upshots and outcomes of their encounters. It may be claimed that due to their asymmetrical asking of questions, doctors exert power over patients by controlling what will count as an acceptable diagnosis (e.g., 'it's not a vein, it's a muscle in spasm'), while patients systematically defer to that institutionalized power.

However, conversation analysts have cautioned that we need to be careful about how we relate asymmetries in institutional discourse to power and authority (Schegloff, 1991). For instance, policies of simply counting the number of questions, or coding the types of questions asked or answers given, can run the risk of not being sensitive enough to the more basic sense of context stressed by CA: the local sequential context of talk in which utterances are produced. Schegloff (1991) argues that analysts need to take care to understand the basic conversational functions of utterance types before drawing conclusions about relations of authority and power in institutional talk.

We can illustrate this point with the following extract, which is taken from a doctor–patient consultation (Schegloff, 1980). Notice in particular the patient's utterance in line 5:

**(1) [Frankel 4–80: LOG 10750]**

| 1 | Dr: | Very good. (0.4) Very good=lemme see your ankle. |
|---|---|---|
| 2 | | (2.2) |
| 3 | Dr: | pt. .hhh VERY GOOD. |
| 4 | | (1.1) |
| 5→ | Pt: | I wanna ask you som'n. |
| 6 | Dr: | What's that. |
| 7 | | (0.6) |
| 8 | Pt: | pt. .hh (0.5) I have- (0.6) this second toe (.) |
| 9 | | that was broken. (0.4) But I went to the pediatrist |
| 10 | | (.) because I couldn' find a doctor on th' weekend. |
| 11 | | (0.4) An' he said it wasn' broken.=It was. |
| 12 | | So it wasn' (.) taken care of properly. .hh 'n when |
| 13 | | I'm on my feet, I get a sensation in it. |
| 14 | | I mean is anything (th't) can be do:ne? |
| 15 | Dr: | How long ago d'ju break it. |
| 16 | Pt: | Mmh two years. |
| 17 | Dr: | Yih c'd put a metatarsal pad underneath it . . . |

In this extract, the patient's utterance in line 5, 'I wanna ask you som'n', might be seen as a 'request for permission' to speak in the asymmetrical doctor–patient context. In this kind of setting, as we have said, the questioning initiative usually lies with the doctor (Frankel, 1990). Therefore, this could be taken as an example of the patient deferring to the institutional authority of the doctor.

Yet this would represent only a superficial analysis; one which *assumed* that patients defer to the authority of doctors. As Schegloff (1980) shows, the utterance at line 5 is in fact of a quite common type in ordinary conversation, where it functions as a particular kind of item: a 'preliminary to preliminaries'. Basically, utterances such as 'I want to ask you something' or 'Can I ask you a question' indicate that whatever it is the speaker wants to ask, it requires some preliminary background detailing before the question can be answered. Schegloff supports this analysis by observing that, generally, what a speaker does immediately after saying 'Can I ask you something' is *not* to ask a question. The question itself comes after some preliminaries: this is what Schegloff means by the phrase 'preliminary to preliminaries'.

This analysis can be applied to extract (1). The actual question the patient wants to ask comes at line 14: 'I mean is anything th't can be do:ne?' The question follows the preliminary detailing, in lines 8–13, in which the patient relates a background story about what happened to his toe. Thus, what might seem at first glance to be an orientation to having to ask permission to put a question to the doctor, turns out on closer inspection to be an orientation to a common conversational practice whereby a question can be projected following some background details. In other words, it is not enough simply to codify individual utterances on the basis of an assumption about the power relationships in doctor–patient discourse. We need to remain sensitive to the local interactional relevancies that the participants are demonstrably oriented to.

However, this does not mean that CA can say nothing systematic about how asymmetries can be related to power in institutional discourse. Indeed, by focusing on the local management of talk, CA can provide compelling accounts of how power is produced through talk-in-interaction, rather than being predetermined by theoretical features of the context.

One kind of example can be found in some of Drew's work on courtroom interrogation. Drew (1992) observed how the pre-allocated question–answer format of courtroom interaction gives attorneys a certain discursive power which is not available to witnesses, namely, the 'power of summary'. As a questioner, the attorney 'has "first rights" to pull together evidence and "draw conclusions" ' (p. 507); in other words, to define the meaning, the terms, and the upshots of a particular set of answers. This is something the witness cannot do:

> The witness is left in the position of addressing and trying to deal with the attorney's selection of which items to pull together: she has no control over the connections which are made between pieces of information or testimony, nor over the inferences which may be drawn from such juxta-positioning – although she may attempt [in her answers] to rebut those inferences. (Drew, 1992: 507)

This is a kind of power that is available to anyone, in whatever context, who asks a series of questions of a coparticipant. The added significance in the courtroom, of course, is that the witness is systematically disabled from asking any questions of her own, or taking issue with the attorney's final summary.

Let us now consider a more specific attempt to ground an account of power in a conversation analytic framework. Earlier (in Chapter 6) we discussed aspects of some work carried out on talk radio (Hutchby, 1992a, 1992b, 1996a, 1996b). Recall that we described how, at the outset of calls, callers in this setting orient to their role as introducers of topics for discussion. Moreover, we suggested that they introduce topics in such a way that they are treated as 'issues' on which they offer opinions. However, this basic structural feature of talk radio calls, apart from being one way in which callers display an orientation to interaction in an institutional setting, is also closely linked to differences in power between hosts and callers.

The principal activity in these interactions is that of argument. Callers offer opinions on issues, and hosts then debate those opinions, frequently taking up opposing stances in the process. As Sacks observed (1992: Vol. 2: 348–53), arguing about opinions is a basically asymmetrical activity, whatever context it occurs in. There are significant differences between, on the one hand, setting out an opinion, and on the other, taking issue with that opinion. Sacks described these actions respectively as 'going first' and 'going second' in an argument. Sacks proposed that those who go first are in a weaker position than those who get to go second, since the latter can argue with the former's position simply by taking it apart. Going first means having to set your opinion on the line, whereas going second means being able to argue merely by challenging your opponent to expand on, or account for, his or her claims. Thus, while first position arguers are required to build a defence for their stance, those in second position do not need to do so, and indeed are able to choose if and when they will set out their own argument, as opposed to simply attacking the other's.

Sacks observes that in conversation, speakers can often be seen to try and maneouvre their interlocutors into first position, and one of the features of arguments in ordinary conversation is that there may be struggles over who sets their opinion on the line first and who gets to go second. But as Hutchby (1996b) shows, on talk radio, this asymmetry is 'built into' the overall structure of calls. Callers are expected, and may be constrained, to go first with their line, while the host systematically gets to go second, and thus to contest the caller's line by picking at its weaknesses. The fact that hosts systematically have the first opportunity for opposition within calls thus opens to them a collection of argumentative resources which are not available in the same way to callers. These resources are 'powerful', in the sense that they enable the host to constrain callers to do a particular kind of activity – i.e., produce 'defensive' talk.

One set of such resources is a class of utterances, including 'So?' and 'What's that got to do with it?' which challenge a claim on the grounds of its validity or relevance to the matter in question. We can describe these as powerful resources, since one feature of them is that they need not make clear precisely on what terms the claim is being challenged. They may function purely as second position moves, by which the first speaker is required to expand on or account for the challenged claim.

In the following extract the caller is complaining about the number of mailed requests for charitable donations she receives. Notice that in line 7, the host responds simply by saying 'So?'

**(2) [H:21.11.88:6:1]**

| 1 | Caller: | I: have got three appeals letters here this |
|---|---|---|
| 2 | | week.(0.4) All a:skin' for donations. (0.2) .hh |
| 3 | | Two: from tho:se that I: always contribute to |
| 4 | | anywa:y, |
| 5 | Host: | Yes? |
| 6 | Caller: | .hh But I expect to get a lot mo:re. |
| 7 | Host: | So? |
| 8 | Caller: | .h Now the point is there is a limi[t to (   ) |
| 9 | Host: | [What's that |
| 10 | | got to do- what's that got to do with telethons |
| 11 | | though. |
| 12 | Caller: | hh Because telethons . . . ((Continues)) |

As an argumentative move, this 'So?' achieves two things. First, it challenges the validity or relevance of the caller's complaint within the terms of her own agenda, which in this case is that charities represent a form of 'psychological blackmail'. Second, because it stands alone as a complete turn, 'So?' requires the caller to take the floor again and account for the relevance of her remark.

Another second position resource available to the host enables him to try and establish control over the agenda by selectively formulating the gist or upshot of the caller's remarks (recall our discussion of formulations in news interviews above). In extract (3), we see a particular kind of strategic direction of talk, that is related to the argumentative uses of formulations in a setting such as talk radio. The host here uses two closely linked proposals of upshot to reconstruct contentiously the position being advanced by the caller. The caller has criticized the 'contradictions' of televised charity events known as telethons, claiming that their rhetoric of concern in fact promotes a passive altruism which exacerbates the 'separateness' between donors and recipients. He goes on:

**(3) [H:21.11.88:11:3]**

```
1    Caller:    . . . but e:r, I- I think we should be working at
2               breaking down that separateness I [ think ] these
3    Host:                                        [Ho:w?]
4               (.)
5    Caller:    these telethons actually increase it.
6    Host:      Well, what you're saying is that charity does.
7    Caller:    .h Charity do::es, ye[ ::s  I  mean-  ]
8    Host:                           [Okay we- so you]'re (.) so
9               you're going back to that original argument we
10              shouldn't have charity.
11   Caller:    Well, no I um: I wouldn't go that fa:r, what I
12              would like to [see is-
13   Host:                    [Well how far are you going then.
14   Caller:    Well I: would- What I would like to see is . . .
```

In line 6, the host proposes that the caller's argument in fact embraces charities in general and not just telethons as one sort of charitable endeavour. This is similar to the inferentially elaborative formulations that Heritage (1985) discusses. Although the caller has not made any such generalization himself in his prior talk, he assents to this in the next turn (line 7).

However, it turns out that the caller, by agreeing, provides the host with a resource for actually reformulating the agenda in play here. By using a second formulation to describe the upshot of the caller's position, the host proposes that the caller is going back to an argument which a previous caller had made, namely that 'we shouldn't have charity' (lines 8–10).

The caller rejects this further formulation (line 11). But the point is that by relying on his 'second position' ability to formulate the gist or upshot of the caller's remarks, the host can actually attempt to change the agenda in the caller's remarks. Having changed it, he would then be in a position to challenge – and constrain the caller to defend – this new agenda.

Thus, we see a similarity here with Drew's (1992) remarks on attorneys' power of summary, quoted above. Only here, rather than emerging out of a preallocated question–answer turn-taking format, the discursive power of the host emerges in an environment where turn taking is much more 'conversational' (see Hutchby, 1996a: 20–40). What seems to be the case on talk radio is that a form of power emerges in the talk as a result of the way calls are structured overall. In particular, the fact that callers must begin by taking up a position means that argumentative resources are distributed asymmetrically between host and callers. The host is able to build opposition using basic second position resources. The characteristic feature of these resources is that they require callers to defend or account for their claims, while enabling hosts to argue without constructing a defence for an alternative view. At the same time, as long as the host refrains from setting out his own position, such second position resources are not available to the caller.

It is important to stress two points about this discussion of power in discourse from a CA perspective. First, such a view does not lead us back to the container theory in which pre-existing hierarchical features of the context exert causal forces over the available actions of participants. We have emphasized that CA reveals the orientations of participants themselves to the specialized features of institutional interaction. In line with this, the features of power that we have discussed are rooted in oriented-to patterns of action. Hence, the participants could conceivably make things different; although obviously departures from the normative conventions, while possible, would potentially be treated by other participants as accountable and open to challenge.

The second point is that we are not seeking to treat power as a monolithic, one-way process. The exercise of powerful discursive resources can always be resisted by a recipient. In the two studies we have mentioned, strategies of resistance play a key part. Drew (1992) discusses how witnesses utilize the many resources that are available for evading or challenging the strategic implications to be detected in attorneys' questioning. In Hutchby (1996b), it is shown how callers may resist the second position challenges of hosts in numerous ways; and indeed, how callers may take the opportunity to move into second position themselves if hosts elect to move away from the challenging mode and express an opinion on their own part.

As we began by saying, CA is not in favour of the view that power relations somehow preexist and determine the course of actual encounters; nor does it make any *a priori* assumption about factors such as power and ideology operating outside the immediate awareness of participants. However, this does not mean that CA can have nothing to say about such factors. By focusing on the local management of talk-in-interaction CA can in fact provide compelling accounts of how power comes to operate as a feature of, and is used as a resource in, institutional interaction. Indeed, even though the issue is usually left implicit, a good deal of CA can be seen as dealing with a possible analysis of power, where power is viewed in terms of differential distributions of

discursive resources which enable certain participants to achieve interactional effects that are not available, or are differentially available, to
others in the setting.

Thus, while critical discourse analysts and some sociologists claim
that CA is 'resistant to linking properties of talk with higher-level features of society and culture – relations of power, ideologies, cultural
values' (Fairclough, 1995: 23), that in fact is not the case. Rather, CA is
resistant to *assuming* linkages between the properties of talk and such
features of society and culture. The debate between CA and CDA is not
about the *existence* of factors such as power in interaction. Rather, it is
an argument about the nature of claims that can legitimately be made
about the data we gather to analyse language use in social interaction.
This brief discussion about the different approaches to 'critical' issues
taken by CDA and by CA therefore illustrates a central methodological
policy that distinguishes CA from many other perspectives within linguistics, sociology and psychology: an insistence that it is more important to try and explicate the ways that the participants in any interaction
display their understanding of what they are doing than to begin from
theoretically driven assumptions about what might be going on.

## Psychology: conversation analysis, language and cognition

In this section we turn to another domain often driven by theoretical
assumptions to which the CA perspective has offered a major challenge:
the psychological study of mental states. A fundamental everyday,
common-sense assumption is that there are cognitive *processes*, such as
'thinking', 'reasoning' and 'believing'. Another assumption is that there
are psychological or mental *entities* such as 'thoughts, 'knowledge' and
'beliefs'. We take it for granted, also, that these processes and entities
are fundamentally internal phenomena – a feature of our (usually) conscious experience of our minds or selves. And it seems natural to assume
that these cognitive and psychological phenomena are separate from
and independent of our social and public behaviour. They may be disclosed in social contexts, in that we can report our thoughts, verbalize
our memories of events and articulate attitudes and beliefs; ultimately,
though, they are private phenomena. Finally, it seems uncontentious to
assume that cognitive and psychological phenomena determine or
predict social behaviour. We might say, then, that a person's decision to
donate to charity simply reflects their altruistic attitude; or that idiosyncratic expressions and forms of humour simply express aspects of
our personality.

These kinds of assumptions about the relationship between cognitive and psychological phenomena and social behaviour are extraordinarily influential in contemporary western social science. Much sociological research is informed by the idea that people's opinions, attitudes, beliefs, memories and thoughts about issues or events can be accessed and explored through survey questionnaires or interviews. And much contemporary psychology is defined by its attempt to determine experimentally the cognitive basis of behaviour, be that in the study of child development, the nature and role of individual differences, or the relationship between the individual and wider social groups. To illustrate the influence of these sets of assumptions, we can briefly consider the main perspective in the psychology of language.

The psychology of language, or psycholinguistics, explores how we develop, produce and understand spoken and written language. It is concerned with psychological, cognitive and biological processes in the production and interpretation of language, in that it emphasizes that we need brains and mouths and tongues. It does acknowledge that language is used in social settings. But even here, priority is given not to interpersonal or socially organized activities, such as those documented in CA research, but to the underlying perceptual and cognitive requirements of language use; what is significant for psycholinguists about the social setting is the interpretation by a speaker of a hearer's beliefs and knowledge states (for example, Harley, 2001). These beliefs and knowledge states are taken to be independent internal cognitive phenomena that are encoded in language and merely expressed in talk. The actual production of utterances is taken to be of secondary importance to, and largely determined by, underlying cognitive and psychological mechanisms.

In conversation analytic research, however, the key question is not how some stretch of talk reveals, represents or is determined by cognitive processes of the participants, but how are turns designed as actions within sequences of actions? To illustrate this, we can briefly consider psycholinguistic work on pauses, and then compare this to conversation analytic perspectives on silences or gaps in talk-in-interaction.

In psycholinguistics, pauses are seen as indicating some form of cognitive difficulty (the speaker temporarily ceases speaking while he or she tries to locate a relevant next word), or speech planning (the speaker temporarily ceases talking while preparing or structuring the next component of the utterance). Psycholinguistic research argues that within-turn pauses tend to occur before words that are, in the context of the surrounding speech, less predictable, suggesting that pauses may be connected to the cognitive processes involved in accessing less regularly used lexical items; or suggests that pauses are more related to semantic planning than lexical predictability (for an overview, see Harley, 2003: 374). This perspective is markedly different to that developed in conversation analytic research, in which any absence of talk has to be understood in terms of its placement in a sequential organization and its contribution to particular trajectories of social action. The following quote comes from a paper that explores some features of the relationship between conversation analysis and linguistics (discussed at further length below). In this section the authors make some remarks about repair in interaction:

> The practices of repair at issue for CA are discursive and interactional, not cognitive. Initiating repair is an action or a move in interaction, one which claims a problem; that is so whatever may cognitively be the case. Displaying a delay before a next word is a move in interaction, quite distinct from some delay in the 'speech planning process'. (Schegloff et al., 2002: 7)

The focus on the action orientation of utterances – even those which seem on first glance to report some internal psychological state or event – was given expression in Sacks' first recorded lecture, in which he considered the following sequence, taken from a call by a member of the public to the Los Angeles Suicide Prevention Centre.

**(4) [Sacks 1992 Vol. 1: 1]**
A:    This is Mr Smith, may I help you
B:    I can't hear you
A:    This is Mr <u>Smith</u>
B:    Smith

As we discussed earlier in the book, Sacks did not treat B's utterance 'I can't hear you' as a literal description of the speaker's state of knowledge about the co-participant's name, but as an object which, by virtue of its design and its sequential location, performed a delicate interactional task: avoiding giving a name without explicitly refusing to give a name.

Conversation analytic research, then, has developed a radical position on the relationship between cognition and discourse. Analysis focuses on the way that utterances are designed to perform actions in sequentially organized interactional contexts, and no analytic priority is given to (supposedly) underlying mental processes, beliefs and knowledge states. This radical stance is one of the reasons why conversation analytic methods and findings have been adopted by psychologists working in a tradition that has come to be known as discursive psychology (Edwards, 1997; Edwards and Potter, 1992; Potter, 2006).

Discursive psychology is informed by the (broadly social constructionist) position that phenomena traditionally taken to be mental entities, cognitive procedures and psychological processes are discursive practices of, in and for, discourse. As such they are treated as the business of talk, and as such, analysed as *irreducibly* social and pragmatic phenomena (Edwards, 1997; Edwards and Potter, 1992, 2005).

> Discursive psychologists ask: What does a 'memory' do in some interaction? How is a version of the past constructed to sustain some action? Or: what is an 'attitude' used to do? How is an evaluation built to assign blame to a minority group, say, or how is an evaluation used to persuade a reluctant adolescent to eat tuna pasta? (Potter, 2000: 35)

There are clearly some overlaps between the CA perspective and the explicitly anti-cognitivist arguments of discursive psychology. For example, one leading discursive psychologist has argued that the relationship of cognition to interaction should parallel the conversation analytic position on the relationship between talk and its context (see Chapter 6 herein): that is, as something to be realized in the participants' conduct, rather than an analytic given (Potter, 1998). There are, however, important differences.

Conversation analysts reject the determinism of cognition on methodological grounds, arguing that talk-in-interaction is an independent domain of activity, the properties of which are not dependent on psychological (or sociological) variables. This does not mean, however, that cognitive or psychological factors (or indeed, as we have seen, macrosociological variables) are denied: but that, for the purposes of analysis, it is methodologically unsound to assume their relevance prior to the empirical analysis of any spate of interaction. Consequently, some conversation analysts do not reject the idea that there is an independent realm of cognitive processes, and are willing to explore the degree to which cognitive episodes can be detected in or analysed via the normative and sequential basis of interaction (Drew, 2005; Heritage, 2005; Schaeffer and Maynard, 2005).

It has also been argued that CA can provide a corrective to naïve or premature claims about how cognitive processes relate to social action. For example, Maynard (2005) has argued that the analysis of the 'interactional substrate' (Marlaire and Maynard, 1990) via which psychological tests are administered to young children diagnosed with autism exposes not their interpersonal difficulties (which the tests are designed to assess), but hitherto unexpected degrees of interactional sophistication and order. And Wootton's (1997) pioneering video-based study of the interactional skills of very young children allowed him to critique assumptions in cognitive developmental psychology that inform claims about the development of memory. Rather than denying the relevance of underlying psychological processes, these researchers have shown that it may be possible to explore how our knowledge of the social, interactional order may shape our understanding of cognitive or neurological phenomena.

Let us now look in more detail at the relationship between CA and psychology by way of discussing the key research technique of the psychological experiment.

### The practices and outcomes of the psychological experiment

Psychology is primarily an experimental discipline, in that it has modelled itself on the natural sciences, and adopted the methodological principles which have informed physics, chemistry and biology. Consequently, the psychological experiment is a scientific activity designed to test hypotheses derived from wider psychological theory about people's behaviour, cognitive functioning or interpretative and evaluative processes. However, the design of most psychology experiments requires the experimenter and the experimental participant to interact verbally. The experimenter may have to provide instructions; and the participant may have to report their sensations, reasoning, perceptions, and so on. Consequently, whatever the scientific rationale for experimentation generally, and the scientific goals of any specific experimental procedure, the experiment is a social encounter realized through the participants' use of language. The production of psychology as a science, then, is largely rooted in talk-in-interaction. This raises two important issues: how is language used in the psychology experiment? And, perhaps more importantly, does the language through which laboratory procedures are conducted influence the outcome of the experiment? Is experimental psychological science in some sense an artefact of interactional or discursive practices?

Some psychologists have explored the impact of the communication between experimenter and participant in the psychology laboratory. Perhaps the key work was Martin Orne's investigation of the 'demand characteristics' of the experimental setting: interpersonal processes which may influence the behaviour of the research participant (Orne, 1962). Orne wanted to examine how potentially robust experimental artefacts, unconnected to the variables the experiment was designed to

study, may arise when experimental participants consciously or unconsciously change their behaviour as a consequence of trying to infer the
experimenter's reasons for asking them to perform certain tasks. Orne
argued that demand characteristics are an important aspect of the psychological laboratory. Unlike experimenter effects, which can be con-
trolled for via double blind experimental protocols in which the
experimenter does not know the hypothesis being tested, demand characteristics are ubiquitous, and potentially undermine the ecological
validity of any experimental design.

Orne identified the communication between experimenter and
participant as a key component of the emergence of demand characteristics. The emergence of conversation analytic techniques provides a
valuable resource by which we can examine the communicative processes which underpin psychology laboratory experiments. To illustrate, we will consider some empirical observations from an analysis of
experimenter-participant interaction in parapsychology experiments
on extrasensory perception (Wooffitt, 2003, 2007; Wooffitt and
Allistone, 2005).

Although the concept of extrasensory perception (ESP) is contro-
versial, there have been numerous laboratory-based attempts to assess
the evidence for these and other ostensibly parapsychological abilities,
some of which have been discussed in prestigious mainstream science
journals (for example, Bem and Honorton, 1994). One experimental
design is known as the ganzfeld procedure (Honorton et al., 1990;
Hyman and Honorton, 1986). A common version of the ganzfeld pro-
tocol has three participants: the experimenter, a receiver (a member of
the public), and a sender (either another experimenter or friend/relative
of the receiver). The experiment has three main phases. During the
*sending phase* the sender tries mentally to send or project images of a
target video clip that is shown several times. During this period the
receiver is asked to report verbally whatever images or sensations they
are experiencing. This report is called their mentation. The mentation
report is noted by an overhearing (but at this point, non-participating)
experimenter in another room. After the sending period, the experimenter and receiver discuss the mentation, called the *mentation review*.
Finally, there is the *judging phase*. The receiver is shown four video clips:
the target and three others. On the basis of the images and sensations
experienced during the sending phase, the receiver has to nominate
which clip they think the sender was trying mentally to project.

The mentation review is an important part of the experiment. If ESP
is occurring, the receiver's mental imagery and conscious experiences
during the sending period may provide insight as to how anomalous

cognitive processes interact with routine cognitive functioning. In the review the experimenter checks the accuracy of her record, and allows the receiver to add further information about their imagery. Experimenters will make a note of any additional information or observations offered by the receiver about their earlier imagery.

The interaction between experimenter and receiver in the review has some robust sequential properties. The experimenter reads through her notes in a step-wise manner. After each item has been read out, experimenters withhold moving to the next item for about one second, thus providing a series of 'slots' in the interaction in which the receivers can correct the experimenter if necessary or, where relevant, add further information about their earlier imagery or reflect on its significance, and so on. In most cases however, receivers 'pass' on these slots for correction and expansion, either by saying nothing or by indicating their ongoing recipient status by the use of continuers such as 'mm hm', 'yeah' and 'uh huh'. Note in the following example the series of pauses following each of the experimenter's turns. The receiver says nothing until the 'mm hm' in line 16:

**(5) 01–47**
('E' is the experimenter, 'R' is the receiver)
```
1    E:    .hh next an a:pple.
2          (0.5)
3    E:    and then a ha:nd again.
4          (0.4)
5    E:    .hhhh a strange face with bulging ey:es and
6          teeth grinning.
7          (1.0)
8    E:    next you had the impression of a ↑magazine and the
9          edge of the magazine
10         (0.6)
11   E:    next a toadstool
12         (0.8)
13   E:    .h and then an underwater scene,
14         (0.6)
15   E:    and there were worms heading towards a chest?
16   R:    mm hm
```

Occasionally, receivers do provide more information. In extract (6), the experimenter first introduces the imagery 'boat=in=the=water= leaving=a=wake'; the subject uses 'm:m::' to confirm the item and to pass on the opportunity to expand. The next imagery item, 'a pile of something?' does, however, generate further participation.

**(6) [01–05]**

```
1    E:    ˙hh boat=in=the=water=leaving=a=wake,
2    R:    m:m::
3          (0.6)
4    E:    (tk) ˙hh a pile of something?
5          (1.1)
6    R:    >˙h yeah< it was like a pile of pla:tes or:: ˙ (0.7) um::
7          (1.1) °something like that°
8    E:    °okay:?° (0.5) ˙h a fro:g(h) >a big one?<
```

This extract illustrates the properties of a recurrent organization of item expansion sequences. On hearing the experimenter announce the mentation item, the receiver produces an initial and unequivocal confirmation; they then offer further information. So, in extract (6), the receiver identifies the objects in the pile. She then says 'something like that' more quietly than the preceding talk, which marks the 'general adequacy' of the prior description. This also stands as a (candidate) closing component of the expansion turn. This closing component is matched by the experimenter's immediate 'okay:?' produced with a rising or 'questioning' intonation. The absence of any further receiver contribution in response to the try-marked 'okay:?' is treated by the experimenter as licence to return to the stepwise progression through the mentation imagery, and he introduces the next item (a frog).

The absence of further receiver talk after a try-marked 'okay' is common throughout the corpus used for this study; it stands as the end of an expansion sequence and marks the progression to the next imagery item to be considered. On occasion, though, experimenters respond to receiver expansion in other ways. In the next example, E uses 'm:hm' in line 9, and again in line 17:

**(7) [01–21]**

```
1    E:    °°˙(n)hh°° °o:kay,° (tk).hh and then I think the final
2          thing you said was uh:: (.) ˙h something like a chair (.)
3          >in< in a pyramid?
4    R:    °(n)hh° yeah, >saw the< (.) the triangle thing again and
5          then (.) °.h°>something< which reminded me of like, (.)
6          um, (0.5) .h an upright chair like um:, (1.5) °(n)hhh° (.)
7          um:? >°so-°< like a black chair,
8          (1.4)
9    E:    m:hm
10         (0.5)
11   R:    not like the one I'm sitting on or °anything° jus:::t °uh:°
12         (3.5)
13   R:    >I don't know,< it was >sort of< °uhm:(h)° (2.1) >like a
```

```
14              s-< like a sort of padded chai(hh)r or something °.h° >it
15              was just< from the side that I saw it, so >it was like<
16              an ell shape (.) °.h° [that =
17    E:                            [°mhm°
18    R:        = suggested a °chair:
```

In this extract the experimenter introduces the last item from the receiver's report of their imagery during the earlier sending phase of the experimenter, the 'chair in a pyramid'. The receiver produces an unequivocal confirmation 'yeah,' and then provides more information. There is, first, a report of the immediately prior imagery 'the triangle thing again' and then the receiver tries to detail the imagery by reference to an associated everyday object '>something< which reminded me of like, (.) um, (0.5) .h an upright chair'. At this point in the turn the receiver says 'like um:,' which would suggest that the turn at that point is incomplete. There follows a gap of 1.5 seconds and then, after some non-lexical contributions, the receiver says '>°so-°< like a black chair,'. This characterizes how the report of the chair was related to the imagery. When this final component of the turn is complete, the receiver stops speaking.

There are good grounds for assuming that the receiver has completed his expansion turn: he has provided further detail, and the final part of the turn was designed as an upshot or conclusion to prior talk, thereby signalling the terminal status of that component. And in the subsequent 1.4 second gap the receiver does not initiate further talk, or take an audible inbreath, which might suggest the onset of a next turn component. However, there is no immediate experimenter response to the completion of the expansion turn. Moreover, when the experimenter does speak, he does not use 'okay' to exhibit his recognition of the likely completion of the expansion turn, but offers instead 'm:hm' (line 9).

Continuers such as 'mm hm' and 'uh huh' do particular kinds of work. Speakers use them to pass on opportunities in which turn transfer could be initiated, thereby publicly displaying their producer's continued recipiency within the interaction (Jefferson, 1984; Schegloff, 1982). Routinely, then, continuers are taken to exhibit the expectation that there is more to come in the prior speaker's talk. As such, they are resources by which co-participants can facilitate another's production of an extended turn. This is what happens in extract (7); after the experimenter's 'm:hm', the receiver continues to talk about the imagery.

The receiver's post-continuer talk about this imagery, however, is noticeably more circumspect or hesitant than the initial expansion turn. The turn starts with an account of what the imagery is not like (line 11).

There is also an explicit doubt marker 'I don't know' (lines 10 and 11). Potter (1997) and Wooffitt and Widdicombe (2006) have shown that 'I dunno/ I don't know' can be used on occasions when speakers are making sensitive or slightly controversial claims, and have grounds for assuming that co-participants may be unsympathetic to or dissatisfied with the kind of report or account they are making. 'I don't know' formulations allow the speaker to mark their own scepticism or uncertainty about what it is they are claiming, thereby displaying some degree of alignment with an anticipated sceptical response. Similarly, the post-expansion turn is more noticeably marked by perturbations and hesitations (such as intra-turn gaps, word stretching, and so on). Finally, the receiver offers a recollection of his imagery which reports his partial perspective (the imagery was perceived in consciousness from a side view) and which emphasizes that the phenomenological experience was of an 'L' shape which merely *suggested* a chair. The receiver's talk after the experimenters 'mm hm' receipt, then, may be termed a doubt-marked expansion sequence.

Doubt-marked expansion sequences routinely follow experimenters' 'mm hm' turns. In extract (8), an initial doubt-marked sequence is itself receipted by a minimal continuer, which in turn is met with further talk in which the receiver's circumspection about his imagery is even more strongly foregrounded.

**(8) [01–28]**

```
1    E:    and you said you felt you could see for mi:les (.)
2          across countryside,=
3    R:    =yea°f-s°, (0.3) .hh like I was flying across it
4          (0.5)
5    E:    (h) m↑hm
6    R:    ˙hh looking down over (0.5) .hhh hhh fields a- >I don't
7          know:< it was very odd hh yeah,
8    E:    °m°↑hm
9    R:    °.hhhh hhhh°
10         (0.3)
11   R:    (°mus:-°) >I'd-< ↑hh (.) .h ↑I'M NOT VERY GOOD
12         AT DESCRIBING IT it's a very weird >sort of<
13         va:gue (. ) .hh (1.2 ) >°it°< just felt like (>sort of
14         you<) so::: ( 0.3) .hh body's just: (1.2) taking off
```

Here there are three turns in which the receiver expands upon the imagery 'seeing miles across countryside'. In the first she establishes that this perspective was similar to that facilitated by flight (line 3). After the experimenter's first 'mm hm' expansion receipt (line 5), the receiver produces two turn components which establish a degree of uncertainty in her recollection and understanding of the imagery. She offers an 'I don't know' formulation (lines 6 and 7), and then explicitly refers to the strangeness of the image, 'it was very odd hh yeah' (line 7). There is another continuer (line 8) and, after a pronounced spate of breathing and a 0.3 second gap, the receiver unequivocally exhibits a basis for circumspection about her confidence in her recollection of the imagery: with a punched up intonational contour, and at a volume louder than preceding talk, she says '↑I'M NOT VERY GOOD AT DESCRIBING IT' (lines 11 and 12). This is then followed by further talk which identifies the strangeness of the experiences and refers to the lack of precision in her recollection 'it's a very weird >sort of< va:gue [image]'.

It appears, then, that receivers may hear minimal continuers as exhibiting the experimenter's understanding that the prior expansion is incomplete, and that there is, or should be, more to come. Moreover, from the design of their subsequent turns, it seems that receivers orient to the experimenters' 'mm hm' as making relevant a downgrading of the degree of expressed certainty; at least, they exhibit awareness of the contingencies which may effect clear recall of their earlier conscious imagery.

We can outline some theoretical and methodological implications which follow from these analytic observations. Demand characteristics are defined as 'the totality of cues and mutual expectations' relevant to an experimental setting (Orne and Whitehouse, 2000: 469). Although this definition includes interpersonal cues in experimental settings, subsequent research on the nature and effects of demand characteristics has not been concerned with interaction in the laboratory; not, at least, with the turn-by-turn trajectory of interaction as it is explored in conversation analysis. Yet this may be highly significant. Data from ganzfeld mentation reviews suggest that the receivers' understanding of the on-going interaction, and their inferences about the kinds of contributions which are expected, directly impact on their account of precisely those experiences the experiment is designed to investigate. What people say as experimental participants – their performance as subjects in a psychology laboratory – is intimately tied to the broader interactional infrastructure through which the experiment as a form of social encounter is conducted (Schegloff, 1991). And it is in this sense that a conversation analytic study of experimenter-participant interaction can contribute to our understanding of the social dynamics in psychology experiments more generally.

There is also a practical upshot, in that these kinds of analytic observations can be used to inform experimental design. For example, if researchers are concerned that the interactional nature of the review is systematically generating artefacts, then it would be easier to automate the entire review process: the mentation report could be audio recorded and then played back to the receiver, who would have the opportunity to stop the playback and record further impression or experiences onto another recording device. Alternatively, the analysis of communicative practices in the review could be used in the training of experimenters. And of course, the wider cumulative findings from the study of talk in institutional settings could be drawn upon to sensitize researchers to the ways in which everyday communicative practices may be adapted to meet formal institutional requirements. These observations are not limited to researchers in parapsychology, but are relevant also to all psychological experiments in which the experimenter talks to the research participant.

In the final section of this chapter we turn to a third area with which conversation analysts have developed a critical engagement: the linguistic study of phenomena such as grammar, prosody and intonation.

## Linguistics: grammar, prosody and social interaction

Although it is essentially a sociological endeavour, CA's focus on talk has always drawn its practitioners towards an interest in linguistics. At the same time, recent years have seen developments in areas of linguistics such as linguistic anthropology, pragmatics and functional grammar that have drawn many linguists away from traditional concerns with abstract syntactic structures towards a focus on naturally occurring language in use.

Linguistic phenomena of the type that many linguists tend to be interested in have long been central to the way that CA describes the organization of talk-in-interaction. As Schegloff (2007: 3–4) writes:

> The building blocks out of which turns are fashioned we call turn-constructional units, or TCUs. Grammar is one key organisational resource in building and recognising TCUs; for English and many other languages (so far we know of no exceptions), the basic shapes that TCUs take are sentences or clauses more generally, phrases, and lexical items. A second organisational resource shaping TCUs is grounded in the phonetic realisation of the talk, most familiarly, in intonational 'packaging'.

Grammar, phonetics, and intonation (or prosody) are all features of language that have figured centrally in the discipline of linguistics.

However, as Schegloff (2007: 4) goes on to note:

A third – and criterial – feature of a TCU is that it constitutes a recognis-
able action in context; that is, at that juncture of that episode of interaction, with those participants, in that place, etc.

It is here that we begin to find a key difference between the linguistic and
the conversation analytic interest in phenomena such as grammar or
prosody. This difference lies in what we have referred to as the *action orientation* of CA: its concern not just with the structural features of phenomena but with what those phenomena are being used to do by
participants in any given situated episode of talk-in-interaction.

This action orientation, which springs from CA's sociological background, has led it to adopt a very different approach to linguistic phenomena to that which prevailed in linguistics for most of the twentieth
century, and which still underpins a vast amount of linguistic research
today. This is the idea that language can only be properly described in
abstract, or decontextualized, terms. Such an idea is traceable back to
the work of Ferdinand de Saussure (1915); although its most influential
modern expression was in Noam Chomsky's (1965) argument that language should be understood in terms of two analytically distinct elements, linguistic *competence* and linguistic *performance*. For Chomsky,
competence is the abstract knowledge of grammatical structure that
humans acquire as they learn language, and that enables them to
produce meaningful sentences. This knowledge is unconscious: that is
to say, most ordinary speakers of a language do not know the technical
syntactic rules by which they put sentences together in meaningful ways.
However, these rules can be extracted and described by linguists who
study the properties of grammatical sentences. In order to engage in this
technical description, linguists need access to sentences that are perfectly grammatical. Chomsky argued that linguistic performance
(actual speech) only provides imperfect or contaminated examples of
grammatical sentences. Performance, in other words, is an essentially
degenerate realization of linguistic competence. The analytical logic of
this position therefore meant removing language from its actual contexts of use. The upshot was that linguists used *invented* sentences rather
than those taken from the everyday contexts of language use, because
the analyst could thereby ensure that the grammar and syntax to be
analysed would be free of the 'imperfections' that almost inevitably
occurred in natural speech.

By contrast, alongside other schools of thought which attempted to
foreground the social dimensions of language, such as sociolinguistics,
the ethnography of communication, and pragmatics, CA began from
the position that human language has to be seen as a form of social

practice and that meaning is inevitably bound to specific social contexts of use. But even in relation to these other socio-linguistic approaches, CA was distinctive on at least two important dimensions. First, in its emphasis on making recordings of talk in naturally occurring settings. Sacks, in his lectures on conversation, made a powerful argument against the prevailing reliance on intuition when it comes to the analysis of natural language use:

> One can invent new sentences and feel comfortable with them. One cannot invent new sequences of conversation and feel comfortable about them. You may be able to take 'a question and an answer', but if we have to extend it very far, then the issue of whether somebody would really say that, after, say, the fifth utterance, is one which we could not confidently argue. One doesn't have a strong intuition for sequencing in conversation. (Sacks, 1992, Vol. 2: 5)

Secondly, CA was distinctive in terms of its approach to the very analysis of such naturally occurring data. Sacks, Schegloff and Jefferson's (1974) early paper on turn-taking in conversation was the first study of language that really placed participants' own displayed understandings in interaction at the centre of analysis. Although the units of analysis, such as turn-constructional units, involved grammatically defined categories such as sentences, the aim was not to analyse these units abstractly but to focus on their uses in turn-taking that the participants themselves are observed to be orienting to.

As we have said, recent years have seen some attempts at a reconciliation between linguistics and conversation analysis. This has involved certain groups of linguists taking seriously CA's insistence that interaction is the natural home of language use and that therefore language should be studied via recordings of naturally occurring usage. It has similarly involved conversation analysts taking further and more serious account of linguists' claims that technical features of grammar, syntax and prosody play a more important role in the organization of talk than CA had previously acknowledged. The result has been that new approaches to grammar, prosody, and their relationship with interaction have begun to synthesize.

In terms of grammar, then, a range of scholars with backgrounds not just in CA but also in linguistic anthropology, pragmatics and functional grammar have argued that whereas linguistics has traditionally had a view of grammar as an autonomous system, 'grammar's integrity and efficiency are bound up with its place in larger schemes of human conduct, and with social interaction in particular' (Ochs, Schegloff and Thompson, 1996: 2–3). In other words, grammar and social interaction are bound up together and analysis should focus on the relationship between them, rather than separating grammar out as a system that exists independently of language-in-interaction.

For many linguists, such a position is counter-intuitive; but what is even more counter-intuitive in the developing relationship between CA and grammatical study is that contributors are starting to work with a variety of definitions of 'grammar' in the first place. These range from the traditional linguistic view of grammar as the set of rules for stringing words together in sentences, to far less conventional and more sociologically inclined ideas. So, for example, there have been comparative analyses of the linkages between sentence grammar and the construction of turns at talk, as in Fox, Hayashi and Jasperson's (1996) analysis of syntax and repair in American and Japanese conversation; or Lerner's (1996) study of how speakers use grammatical features to slot turns of their own into the 'turn-space' of a current speaker. These studies have clear links with earlier CA work on overlap and repair (see Chapter 2) which demonstrated, amongst other things, the importance of focusing on participants' orientations to grammatical units in language and how these do not necessarily map onto what linguistic theory might assume (for instance, the idea that 'repair' is not just related to correction of incorrect syntax, establishing truth and falsity, or other abstract notions).

A different conception of grammar is developed in work by Goodwin (1996) and Ochs, Gonzales and Jacoby (1996), among others. Goodwin (1996: 370) remarks that this conception of grammar is not restricted to 'sentential grammar' but also encompasses 'structures providing for the organization of the endogenous activity systems within which strips of talk are embedded'. Goodwin here is referring, among other things, to the use of gaze, gesture and overall bodily comportment which, he argues, are a part of the 'grammar' of overall social interaction. His complex video-based analysis of the organization of interaction in an airport control room shows the importance of physical orientations and interactional practices, rather than simply cognitive states, in underpinning the grammar of speakers' descriptions of ongoing events in the control room and the airport itself. In a similar vein, Ochs et al. (1996) analyse video recordings of research seminars given by scientists. Focusing on the relationship between the scientists' talk and the drawings they make on the blackboard, Ochs et al. show how grammatical phenomena such as 'person' (as in first person or third person descriptions) work as a means by which scientists attempt to 'take the role of' the complex physical phenomena they are trying to describe, thereby seeking to make their descriptions easier to follow.

A similar thrust is found in work which attempts to combine CA with the study of prosody and phonetics: 'auditory effects such as melody, dynamics, rhythm, tempo and pause' (Couper-Kuhlen and Selting, 1996: 11). Couper-Kuhlen and Selting (1996) note that much linguistic research on prosody is based on laboratory-generated and decontextualized speech data. It also involves what they describe as over-simplistic conceptual tools such as the 'tone unit': a category which is based on the analyst's intuitive hearing of a stretch of speech, which is then broken down into a series of such tone units. Clearly, for a CA-informed approach, the problem here is that it is not the participants' own observable orientations to prosodic tone units that drives analysis, but the linguist's intuitive hearing.

However, key to the engagement between CA and prosody is not just that phoneticians have paid little if any attention to the interactional functions of prosody in naturally occurring talk; though the work of Kelly and Local (1989; Local and Kelly, 1986; Local, 1996) is a notable exception here. Additionally, the argument is that conversation analysts have tended to ignore the role of prosodic phenomena in the interactional management of talk.

Studies have focused on how prosodic phenomena play a more significant role than hitherto acknowledged in the organization of turn-taking. Auer (1996), for example, argues that conversation analysts have largely grounded their analytic approach to turns, turn completion, speaker transition and competition for turn-space on syntactic phenomena. Recall, for instance, Schegloff's (2007) remark, quoted at the start of this section, about turn-construction units and their grammatical, lexical and phrasal elements. For Auer (1996; see also Wells and Peppe, 1996), syntax alone is insufficient in accounting for how participants themselves orient to the possible completion of turn-contruction units. Rather, in analysing how participants define turn boundaries and so manage turn transition, Auer shows the importance of bringing prosody into play. As we showed in Chapter 3, the transcription system that CA uses does utilize certain marks to indicate broad elements of prosody: for example, the comma is used to show a 'continuation' intonation, by which a current speaker can project another TCU to come in his or her turn. But Auer's point is that such features are only marked roughly, and are rarely systematically analysed in accounts of turn-taking. For him, a more detailed prosodic analysis is needed.

Another range of studies examine how conversational objects that appear superficially similar, such as the item 'Oh' or verbatim repeats of a prior turn, actually perform significantly different interactional functions according to prosodic features of their production (Local, 1996;

Selting, 1996). The method employed here has been developed over many years by Local and other researchers (see for example Kelly and Local, 1989). Utterances that are similar on lexical, syntactic and sequential grounds are collected and compared. Clusterings of observable prosodic features are then extracted that show how these similar utterances constitute different activity types. Once again, the key is to show that these prosodically framed activity types are themselves oriented to by participants.

As a simple example, we can briefly consider the phenomenon of verbatim repeats of a prior utterance as they occur in a collection of telephone calls to an airport flight inquiry service. In the course of another study (see Hutchby et al., 1997; Wooffitt et al., 1997) we searched through a database of 100 calls to this service for every example of a turn which consists entirely of a verbatim repetition of either the whole of the prior turn or some significant element of it. We will call these 'full or partial repetition' (FPR) turns. The 100 calls yielded 32 examples. The interesting thing about these is not just that they occur so regularly, but that different prosodic features indicate that the same type of turn is being used to do different types of action. And these differences are oriented to by recipients in the differential designs of their next turns.

In the majority of cases, the FPR turn is produced without any marked stress or emphasis and seems to be involved in the work of 'confirming information received'. For example:

**(9) [4:T1:SA:1317]**

| 1 | Agent: | Yes it landed at six fifty five. |
|---|---|---|
| 2→ | Caller: | Six fifty five |
| 3 | Agent: | Yeah. |
| 4 | Caller: | Thank goodness |

**(10) [38:T2:SA:1516]**

| 1 | Caller: | and uh- what time am I supposed to be at the |
|---|---|---|
| 2 | | airport to check in. |
| 3 | Agent: | Yes about two hours before de[parture |
| 4→ | Caller: | [Two hours. |
| 5 | Agent: | Y[es. |
| 6 | Caller: | [A:nd (.) which terminal is that. |

In both these cases, the caller produces a turn (arrowed) which repeats something the agent has just said. In both cases, the words that are repeated comprise a central element of the information the caller has called up to request: the arrival time of a flight (extract 9) and the check in time for a departure (extract 10). And in both cases, following the

FPR turn, the agent produces a third-turn acknowedgement of the information thereby confirmed.

In a smaller number of cases, agents themselves produced the FPR turn:

**(11) [55:T3:SB:568]**

| 1 | Agent: | It runs about every five minutes. |
|---|---|---|
| 2 | Caller: | Okay=what fr- fr- fr- from the same station? |
| 3→ | Agent: | From the same station ye[ah. |
| 4 | Caller: | [Okay, |

**(12) [38:T2:SA:1516]**

| 1 | Caller: | I wonder if you could tell me h the flight kay tee |
| 2 | | eight two oh four (0.2) is there any further |
| 3 | | information on that please. |
| 4→ | Agent: | Eight two oh four |
| 5 | | (3.3) |
| 6 | Agent: | That flight's still due to arrive at fourteen |
| 7 | | forty fi:ve |

Here, the repeats function slightly differently. In (11), the caller has asked about transport services between airport terminals and the agent has provided information about a bus shuttle. In line 2 the caller seeks to confirm whether the service always runs from 'the same station' and the agent's next turn uses an FPR to confirm that. This time, therefore, it is the caller who produces the third-turn acknowledgement (line 4). In (12), the agent repeats the flight number of the plane that the caller is requesting information about, prior to providing the requested arrival time. It is noticeable that, in this example, there is no third-turn acknowledgement from the caller. It is unclear why this should be the case; however, that is not the phenomenon we wish to focus on here.

Note how, in these examples, the FPR turn is produced with a fairly flat intonation. By contrast, in a small number of cases, we find FPR turns produced with markedly stressed intonation; and here, it seems, the stress itself (an aspect of the turn's prosody) renders the turn into a different kind of interactional object. Consider extracts (13) and (14).

**(13) [54:T3:SB:495]**

| 1 | Caller: | Uhm (.) I'm wondering how I'd find out a- about a |
| 2 | | flight list for Afghan airlines. |
| 3→ | Agent: | A *flight* list, |
| 4 | Caller: | Yeah I mean (y)ur(h)m is that information if I |
| 5 | | sort of .h give a na:me could I be told whether |
| 6 | | this individual's on the flight list. |

```
7     Agent:      No they'd need .ts you'd need the booking
8                 reference.
```

**(14) [35:T2:SA:1100]**
```
1     Caller:     I wonder if you can confirm for me
2                 British Airways to uhm Zurich is that terminal
3                 four
4           (2.3)
5     Agent:      If if the flight's going from Heathrow yes it is
6                 it's from terminal (.) er terminal one
7           (.)
8     Caller:     Te[rminal one
9→    Agent:         [To Zurich
10    Caller:     Ah- I (y) yeah I'm takin' to:: h-her:* Heathrow
11                now to go to Zurich >it'll be terminal one will
12                it=
13    Agent:      =Tu- terminal one
```

There are two significant differences in these extracts. The first is that an item in the caller's turn is not just repeated, as in the earlier examples; it is repeated and emphasized. The second point to notice is that what comes after the repeat turn is something quite different to the (optional) acknowledgement of the other extracts. It is a longer turn which, in (13), might be glossed as 'rephrasing' the initial request; and in (14), as 'providing additional background' for the original request.

It would seem, then, that the recipients of these particular FPR turns orient to the turn as requiring them to produce more talk in their next turn than the more common third-turn acknowledgement. For instance, consider that the case in extract (13) may have gone something like this:

**[Invented example]**
```
1     Caller:     Uhm (.) I'm wondering how I'd find out about a
2                 flight list for Afghan airlines.
3     Agent:      A flight list,
4     Caller:     Yeah
5     Agent:      One moment please . . . ((gets flight list))
```

However, in the actual example, the caller proceeds, after saying 'Yeah,' to provide further talk which rephrases and at the same time provides a more detailed version of the original request, the gist of which is, 'if I give someone's name, could you locate them on the flight list; is that information I could have?'. Clearly, given airline security regulations, the answer to such a question is 'No'. It is this that provides the grounds for the stressed repetition of 'A <u>flight</u> list' in line 3 of extract (13): the agent is not only seeking to confirm that she has heard the request correctly (as seems to be the case in extract 12, for instance); she is exhibiting an orientation to the request as an extraordinary or even questionable or suspicious one. And it is this orientation, conveyed via prosody alone, that the caller in turn orients to in offering further 'supporting' information.

Similarly, in (14), the caller's turn following the agent's stressed FPR, 'To <u>Zurich</u>,' provides fuller background for the original request. The gist here is that the caller is driving someone to catch a plane to Zurich, and needs to know which terminal to drop them off at. Here, the prosodically marked repeat emerges out of different circumstances than the problematic request found in extract (13). The agent appears to have provided, in lines 1–6, the information requested in the standard format (note the caller's confirmation using an FPR turn in line 8). However, the information that is provided ('terminal one') is different from that which the caller had guessed at in the course of his original request ('terminal four', line 2–3). This discrepancy is in fact traceable in the agent's slight self-repair in line 5–6, where she begins on 'yes it is it's from terminal', pauses, then completes the turn with 'terminal one'. Almost immediately after this, as the caller is producing the FPR confirmation, the agent starts up again to check that she has correctly heard the intended destination: 'To <u>Zurich</u>'. Hence, it seems that the stressed repeat here emerges from a perceived potential error in information-giving, something which would undermine the agent's professional competence and thus needs to be corrected before the caller, having confirmed the information, hangs up.

A common feature in each case is that the second version of the request, which follows the marked repeat of some central item in the original request, disambiguates that original request by providing a fuller version. The resource which participants are relying upon in order to reach this interpretation appears to be the actual intonational pattern of the marked repeat itself. In short, these last two examples fall into a pattern, which can be described thus:

1.  A turn which initiates an information request.
2.  A stressed repeat of a key item in 1.
3.  A fuller version of the action in 1.
4.  A response to the action in 1.

Of course, we recognize that these brief observations do not contain the level of technical detail about prosodic phenomena that tends to be described in most studies incorporating CA and prosody or phonetics (for example, the studies collected in Couper-Kuhlen and Selting, 1996). But our aim has been merely to provide an accessible illustration of the way in which prosodic phenomena can have observable interactional properties. Work along these lines shows how prosody itself cannot be understood in abstraction from interactional contexts. Similarly, it shows how analyses of talk-in-interaction can benefit substantially from a closer concern with prosodic features of utterance production. Here, as in all of the critical engagements that we have discussed in the present chapter, we see the interdisciplinary relevance of conversation analysis for a wide range of concerns in the social sciences, and get a sense of the significant analytical gains that can be made by means of careful and sophisticated cross-fertilization of concepts, methods and findings.

# References

Arminen, I. (2005) *Institutional Interaction*. London: Ashgate.

Atkinson, J. M. (1984a) *Our Masters' Voices: The Language and Body Language of Politics*. London: Methuen.

—— (1984b) Public speaking and audience response: some techniques for inviting applause. In Atkinson and Heritage (eds), (1984), 370–409.

Atkinson, J. M. and Drew, P. (1979) *Order in Court: The Organisation of Verbal Interaction in Judicial Settings*. London: Macmillan.

Atkinson, J. M. and Heritage, J. (eds) (1984) *Structures of Social Action: Studies in Conversation Analysis*. Cambridge: Cambridge University Press.

Auer, P. (1996) On the prosody and syntax of turn-continuations. In Couper-Kuhlen and Selting (eds), (1996).

Austin, J. L. (1962) *How to Do Things with Words*. Oxford: Oxford University Press.

Baker, C. (1982) Adolescent–adult talk as a practical interpretive problem. In G. Payne and E. Cuff (eds), *Doing Teaching: The Practical Management of Classrooms*. London: Batsford.

—— (1984) The search for adultness: membership work in adolescent–adult talk. *Human Studies*, 7: 301–23.

Beattie, G. (1983) *Talk: Analysis of Speech and Nonverbal Behaviour in Conversation*. Milton Keynes: Open University Press.

Becker, H. (1953) Becoming a marijuana user. *American Journal of Sociology*, 59: 41–58.

Bem, D. and Honorton, C. (1994) Does psi exist? Replicable evidence for an anomalous process of information transfer. *Psychological Bulletin*, 115: 4–18.

Berger, C. (1997) *Planning Strategic Interaction*. Hillsdale, NJ: Lawrence Erlbaum Associates.

Bergmann, J. R. (1992) Veiled morality: notes on discretion in psychiatry. In Drew and Heritage (eds) (1992), 137–62.

Billig, M. (1999) Whose terms? Whose ordinariness? Rhetoric and ideology in conversation analysis. *Discourse and Society*, 10: 543–58.

Black, M. (1965) *Philosophy in America*. London: Allen and Unwin.

Blount, B. and Sanchez, M. (eds) (1975) *Sociocultural Dimensions of Language Use*. New York: Academic Press.

Boden, D. (1994) *The Business of Talk*. Cambridge: Polity Press.

Boden, D. and Zimmerman, D. (eds) (1991) *Talk and Social Structure*. Cambridge: Polity Press.

Bourdieu, P. (1991) *Language and Symbolic Power*. Cambridge: Polity Press.

Brown, P. and Yule, G. (1982) *Discourse Analysis*. Cambridge: Cambridge University Press.

Button, G. (1990) Going up a blind alley: conflating conversation analysis and computational modelling. In Luff, Gilbert and Frohlich (eds) (1990).

—— (1992) Answers as interactional products: two sequential practices used in interviews. In Drew and Heritage (eds) (1992a).

—— (ed.) (1993) *Technology in Working Order*. London: Routledge.

Button, G. and Casey, N. (1984) Generating topic: the use of topic initial elicitors. In Atkinson and Heritage (eds) (1984).

Button, G. and Lee, J. R. E. (eds) (1987) *Talk and Social Organisation*. Clevedon: Multilingual Matters.

Button, G. and Sharrock, W. (1995) On simulacrums of conversation: towards a clarification of the relevance of conversation analysis for human–computer interaction. In Thomas (ed.) (1995).

Cawsey, A. (1990) A computational model of explanatory discourse. In Luff, Gilbert and Frohlich (eds) (1990).

Chomsky, N. (1965) *Aspects of the Theory of Syntax*. The Hague: Mouton.

Clark, H. and Haviland, S. (1977) Comprehension and the given-new contract. In R. O. Freedle (ed.), *Discourse Production and Comprehension*, Hillsdale, NJ: Lawrence Erlbaum Associates, 1–40.

Clayman, S. E. (1988) Displaying neutrality in television news interviews. *Social Problems*, 35: 474–92.

—— (1992) Footing in the achievement of neutrality: the case of news interview discourse. In Drew and Heritage (eds) (1992a).

Clayman, S. and Heritage, J. (2002) *The News Interview*. Cambridge: Cambridge University Press.

Coulter, J. (1982) Remarks on the conceptualization of social structure. *Philosophy of the Social Sciences*, 12: 33–46.

Couper-Kuhlen, E. and Selting, M. (eds) (1996) *Prosody in Conversation: Interactional Studies*. Cambridge: Cambridge University Press.

Cuff, E. and Payne, G. (1984) *Perspectives in Sociology*. London: Allen and Unwin.

Danby, S. and Baker, C. (1998) 'What's the problem?' Restoring social order in the preschool classroom. In Hutchby and Moran-Ellis (eds) (1998), 157–86.

Davidson, J. (1984) Subsequent versions of invitations, offers, requests, and proposals dealing with potential or actual rejection. In Atkinson and Heritage (eds) (1984), 102–28.

de Saussure, F. ([1915] 1984) *Course in General Linguistics*. London: Fontana.

Dickerson, P. (2006) Interview with Professor Charles Goodwin. Appliedca.co.uk, available at http://appliedca.co.uk/site/index.

Drew, P. (1984) Speakers' reportings in invitation sequences. In Atkinson and Heritage (eds) (1984), 129–51.

—— (1987) Po-faced receipts of teases. *Linguistics*, 25: 219–53.

—— (1990) Strategies in the contest between lawyer and witness in cross examination. In J. Levi and A. G. Walker (eds) *Language in the Judicial Process*. New York: Plenum, 39–64.

—— (1992a) Contested evidence in courtroom cross-examination: the case of a trial for rape. In Drew and Heritage (eds) (1992), 470–520.

—— (2005) Is confusion a state of mind? In H. te Molder and J. Potter (eds) *Discourse and Cognition: Perspectives and Arguments*, Cambridge: Cambridge University Press, 161–83.

Drew, P. and Heritage, J. (eds) (1992a) *Talk at Work: Interaction in Institutional Settings*. Cambridge: Cambridge University Press.

—— (1992b) Analyzing talk at work: an introduction. In Drew and Heritage (eds) (1992a), 3–65.

Drew, P. and Wootton, T. (eds) (1988) *Erving Goffman: Exploring the Interaction Order*. Cambridge: Polity Press.

Drummond, K. (1989) A backward glance at interruptions. *Western Journal of Speech Communication*, 53: 150–66.

Eder, D. (1991) Serious and playful disputes: variation in conflict talk among female adolescents. In A. Grimshaw (ed.), *Conflict Talk*. Cambridge: Cambridge University Press.

Edwards, D. (1995) Sacks and psychology: an essay review of Harvey Sacks' *Lectures on Conversation. Theory and Psychology*, 5: 579–96.
—— (1997) *Discourse and Cognition*. London: Sage.
Edwards, D. and Potter, J. (1992) *Discursive Psychology*. London: Sage.
—— (1995) Attribution. In R. Harré and P. Stearns (eds), *Discursive Psychology in Practice*, London: Sage, 87–119.
—— (2005) Discursive psychology, mental states and descriptions. In H. te Molder and J. Potter (eds) *Discourse and Cognition: Perspectives and Arguments*, Cambridge: Cambridge University Press, 241–59.
Ervin-Tripp, S. and Mitchell-Kernan, C. (eds) (1977) *Child Discourse*. New York: Academic Press.
Fairclough, N. (1995) *Media Discourse*. London: Edward Arnold.
Finkelstein, E. and Fuks, H. (1990) Conversation analysis and specification. In Luff, Gilbert and Frohlich (eds) (1990), 173–86.
Fox, B. A., Hayashi, M. and Jasperson, R. (1996) Resources and repair: a cross-linguistic study of syntax and repair. In Ochs, Schegloff and Thompson (eds) (1996), 185–237.
Frankel, R. (1984) From sentence to sequence: understanding the medical encounter through microinteractional analysis. *Discourse Processes*, 7: 135–70.
—— (1990) Talking in interviews: a dispreference for patient-initiated questions in physician–patient encounters. In Psathas (ed.) (1990), 231–62.
Frohlich, D. and Luff, P. (1990) Applying the technology of conversation to the technology for conversation. In Luff, Gilbert and Frohlich (eds) (1990), 187–220.
Garcia, A. (1991) Dispute resolution without disputing: how the interactional organization of mediation hearings minimizes argument. *American Sociological Review*, 56: 818–35.
Gardner, H. (1998) Social and cognitive competencies in learning: which is which? In Hutchby and Moran-Ellis (eds) (1998), 115–33.
Garfinkel, H. (1956) Conditions of successful degradation ceremonies. *American Journal of Sociology*, 61: 240–4.
—— (1963) A conception of, and experiments with, 'trust' as a condition of stable concerted actions. In O. J. Harvey (ed.), *Motivation and Social Interaction*, New York: Ronald Press, 187–238.
—— (1967) *Studies in Ethnomethodology*. Englewood Cliffs: Prentice-Hall.
Garfinkel, H. and Sacks, H. (1970) On formal structures of practical actions. In J. C. McKinney and E. A. Tiryakian (eds), *Theoretical Sociology*, New York: Appleton-Century-Crofts, 338–66.

Garvey, C. (1984) *Children's Talk*. Cambridge, MA: Harvard University Press.

Giddens, A. (1984) *The Constitution of Society: Outline of the Theory of Structuration*. Cambridge: Polity Press.

Gilligan, C. (1982) *In a Different Voice: Psychological Theory and Women's Development*. Cambridge, MA: Harvard University Press.

Givon, T. (ed.) (1979) *Syntax and Semantics, Volume 12: Discourse and Syntax*. New York: Academic Press.

Goffman, E. (1959) *The Presentation of Self in Everyday Life*. New York: Doubleday.

—— (1961) *Encounters*. New York: Bobbs-Merrill.

—— (1971) *Relations in Public*. New York: Basic Books.

—— (1981) *Forms of Talk*. Oxford: Blackwell.

—— (1983) The interaction order. *American Sociological Review*, 48: 1–17.

Goldberg, J. A. (1990) Interrupting the discourse on interruptions: an analysis in terms of relationally neutral, power- and rapport-oriented acts. *Journal of Pragmatics*, 14: 883–903.

Goodwin, C. (1981) *Conversational Organisation: Interaction between Speakers and Hearers*. New York: Academic Press.

—— (1984) Notes on story structure and the organisation of participation. In Atkinson and Heritage (eds) (1984), 225–46.

—— (1986) Between and within: alternative sequential treatments of continuers and assessments. *Human Studies*, 9: 205–17.

—— (1996) Transparent vision. In Ochs, Schegloff and Thompson (eds) (1996), 370–404.

—— (ed.) (2003a) *Conversation and Brain Damage*. Oxford: Oxford University Press.

—— (2003b) Conversational frameworks for the accomplishment of meaning in aphasia. In Goodwin (ed.) (2003a), 90–115.

Goodwin, M. H. (1990) *He-Said-She-Said: Talk as Social Organisation among Black Children*. Bloomington: Indiana University Press.

Graddol, D., Cheshire, J. and Swann, J. (1994) *Describing Language*. Milton Keynes: Open University Press.

Greatbatch, D. (1988) A turn-taking system for British news interviews. *Language in Society*, 17 (4): 401–30.

—— (1992) On the management of disagreement between news interviewees. In Drew and Heritage (eds) (1992a), 268–301.

Greatbatch, D. and Clark, T. (2005) *Management Speak: Why We Listen to What Management Gurus Tell Us*. London: Routledge.

Greenberg, J. (ed.) (1963) *Universals of Language*. Cambridge, MA: MIT Press.

Gumperz, J. and Hymes, D. (eds) (1972) *Directions in Sociolinguistics.* New York: Holt, Rinehart and Winston.

Harley, T. (2001) *The Psychology of Language* (2nd edn). Hove and New York: The Psychology Press.

Heath, C. (1992) The delivery and reception of diagnosis in the general practice consultation. In Drew and Heritage (eds) (1992a), 235–67.

Heath, C. and Luff, P. (eds) (2002) *Technology in Action.* Cambridge: Cambridge University Press.

Heeschen, C. and Schegloff, E. A. (1999) Agrammatism, adaption theory, conversation analysis: on the role of so-called telegraphic style in talk-in-interaction. *Aphasiology,* 13: 365–405.

—— (2003) Aphasic agrammatism as interactional artifact and achievement. In Goodwin (ed.) (2003a).

Heritage, J. (1984a) *Garfinkel and Ethnomethodology.* Cambridge: Polity Press.

—— (1984b) A change-of-state token and aspects of its sequential placement. In Atkinson and Heritage (eds) (1984), 299–345.

—— (1985) Analyzing news interviews: aspects of the production of talk for an overhearing audience. In T. van Dijk, (ed.), *Handbook of Discourse Analysis, Volume 3: Discourse and Dialogue,* London: Academic Press, 95–119.

—— (1989) Current developments in conversation analysis. In D. Roger and P. Bull (eds), *Conversation,* Clevedon: Multilingual Matters, 21–47.

Heritage, J. (2005) Cognition in discourse. In H. te Molder and J. Potter (eds), *Discourse and Cognition: Perspectives and Arguments,* Cambridge: Cambridge University Press, 184–202.

Heritage, J. and Greatbatch, D. (1986) Generating applause: a study of rhetoric and response at party political conferences. *American Journal of Sociology,* 19: 110–57.

—— (1991) On the institutional character of institutional talk: the case of news interviews. In Boden and Zimmerman (eds) (1991), 93–137.

Heritage, J. and Maynard, D. (eds) (2006) *Communication in Medical Care.* Cambridge: Cambridge University Press.

Heritage, J. and Sefi, S. (1992a) Dilemmas of advice: aspects of the delivery and reception of advice in interactions between health visitors and first time mothers. In Drew and Heritage (eds) (1992), 359–417.

Heritage, J. and Watson, D. R. (1979) Formulations as conversational objects. In Psathas (ed.) (1979), 123–62.

Hindmarsh, J. and Heath, C. (2000) Sharing the tools of the trade: the interactional constitution of workplace objects. *Journal of Contemporary Ethnography,* 29: 523–62.

Hirst, G. (1991) Does conversation analysis have a role in computational linguistics? *Computational Linguistics*, 17: 211–27.

Honorton, C., Berger, R. E., Varvoglis, M. P., Quant, M., Derr, P., Schecter, E. I. and Ferrari, D. C. (1990) Psi communicating in the ganzfeld: experiments with an automated testing system and a comparison with a meta-analysis of earlier studies. *Journal of Parapsychology*, 54: 99–139.

Hopper, R. (1989a) Conversation analysis and social psychology as descriptions of interpersonal communication. In D. Roger and P. Bull (eds), *Conversation*, Clevedon: Multilingual Matters, 48–65.

—— (1989b) Speech, for instance: the exemplar in studies of conversation. *Journal of Language and Social Psychology*, 7: 47–63.

—— (1992) *Telephone Conversation*. Bloomington: Indiana University Press.

Houtkoop-Steenstra, H. (1991) Opening sequences in Dutch telephone conversation. In Boden and Zimmerman (eds) (1991), 232–50.

—— (1997) Being friendly in survey interviews. *Journal of Pragmatics*, 28: 591–623.

—— (2000) *Interaction and the Standardized Survey Interview*. Cambridge: Cambridge University Press.

Hughes, E. (1970) *The Sociological Eye: Selected Papers*. New York: Aldine.

Hutchby, I. (1992a) The pursuit of controversy: routine scepticism in talk on talk radio. *Sociology*, 26: 673–94.

—— (1992b) Confrontation talk: aspects of 'interruption' in argument sequences on talk radio. *Text*, 12: 343–71.

—— (1996a) *Confrontation Talk: Arguments, Asymmetries and Power on Talk Radio*. Hillsdale, NJ: Lawrence Erlbaum Associates.

—— (1996b) Power in discourse: the case of arguments on talk radio. *Discourse and Society*, 7: 481–97.

—— (1997) Building alignments in public debate: a case study from British TV. *Text*, 17: 161–79.

—— (1999) Frame attunement and footing in the organisation of talk radio openings. *Journal of Sociolinguistics*, 3: 41–64.

—— (2001a) *Conversation and Technology: From the Telephone to the Internet*. Cambridge: Polity.

—— (2001b) The moral status of technology: being recorded, being heard, and the construction of children's concerns about family relationships. In Hutchby and Moran-Ellis (eds) (1998), 114–32.

—— (2002) Resisting the incitement to talk in child counselling: aspects of the utterance 'I don't know'. *Discourse Studies*, 4: 147–68.

—— (2005) Active listening: formulations and the elicitation of feelings-talk in child counselling. *Research on Language and Social Interaction*, 38: 303–29.

—— (2006) *Media Talk: Conversation Analysis and the Study of Broadcasting*. Maidenhead: Open University Press.

—— (2007) *The Discourse of Child Counselling*. Amsterdam: John Benjamins.

Hutchby, I., Fordham, A., Gilbert, N. and Wooffitt, R. (1997) Modelling talk in context: an exploration in the computational modelling of dialogue. *Papers in Sociology and Sociological Research*, 29. Department of Sociology, University of Surrey.

Hutchby, I. and Moran-Ellis, J. (eds) (1998) *Children and Social Competence: Arenas of Action*. London: Falmer Press.

Jayyusi, L. (1984) *Categorisation and the Moral Order*. London: Routledge.

Jefferson, G. (1972) Side sequences. In D. Sudnow (ed.), *Studies in Social Interaction*, New York: Free Press, 294–338.

—— (1973) A case of precision timing in ordinary conversation: overlapped tag-positioned address terms in closing sequences. *Semiotica*, 9: 47–96.

—— (1979) A technique for inviting laughter and its subsequent acceptance/declination. In G. Psathas (ed.), *Everyday Language*, Hillsdale NJ: Lawrence Erlbaum Associates, 79–96.

—— (1980) On 'trouble-premonitory' response to inquiry. *Sociological Inquiry*, 50: 153–85.

—— (1981) The abominable 'ne?': a working paper exploring the phenomenon of post-response pursuit of response. *Occasional Paper No. 6*. Department of Sociology, University of Manchester.

—— (1983) Notes on some orderlinesses of overlap onset. *Tilburg Papers in Language and Literature*, 28. Department of Linguistics, Tilburg University.

—— (1984) Notes on the systematic deployment of the acknowledgement tokens 'yeah' and 'hm mm'. *Papers in Linguistics*, 1, 7 197–206.

—— (1985) An exercise in the transcription and analysis of laughter. In T. van Dijk (ed.), *Handbook of Discourse Analysis, Volume 3: Discourse and Dialogue*, London: Academic Press, 25–34.

—— (1986) Notes on latency in overlap onset. *Human Studies*, 9: 153–83.

—— (1987) On exposed and embedded correction in conversation. In G. Button and J. R. E. Lee (eds), *Talk and Social Structure*, Clevedon: Multilingual Matters, 86–100.

—— (1989) Notes on a possible metric which provides for a 'standard maximum silence' of one second in conversation. In D. Roger and P. Bull (eds), *Conversation*, Clevedon: Multilingual Matters, 166–96.

—— (1990) List construction as a task and resource. In G. Psathas (ed.), *Interaction Competence*, Washington, DC: University Press of America, 63–92.

—— (2005) Glossary of transcript symbols with an introduction. In G. Lerner (ed.) *Conversation Analysis: Studies from the First Generation*, Amsterdam: John Benjamins, 13–31.

Jefferson, G., Sacks, H. and Schegloff, E. A. (1987) Notes on laughter in pursuit of intimacy. In G. Button and J. R. E. Lee (eds), *Talk and Social Structure*, Clevedon: Multilingual Matters, 152–205.

Kelly, J. and Local, J. (1989) On the use of general phonetic techniques in handling conversational material. In D. Roger and P. Bull (eds), *Conversation*, Clevedon: Multilingual Matters, 197–212.

Kendon, A. (1982) The organisation of behaviour in face-to-face inter-action: observations on the development of a methodology. In Scherer and Ekman (eds) (1982), 440–505.

—— (1990) *Conducting Interaction*. Cambridge: Cambridge University Press.

Knorr-Cetina, K. and Cicourel, A. V. (eds) (1981) *Advances in Social Theory and Methodology*. London: Routledge.

Labov, W. (1972) *Sociolinguistic Patterns*. Philadelphia: University of Pennsylvania Press.

Labov, W. and Waletsky, J. (1966) Narrative analysis: oral versions of personal experience. In J. Helm (ed.), *Essays on the Verbal and Visual Arts*, Seattle: University of Washington Press, 12–44.

Lamoreux, E. (1988–9) Rhetoric and conversation in service encounters. *Research on Language and Social Interaction*, 22: 93–114.

Lavin, D. and Maynard, D. W. (2002) Standardization vs rapport: how interviewers handle the laughter of respondents during telephone surveys. In Maynard, Houtkoop-Steenstra, Schaffer and van der Zouwen (eds) (2002), 335–64.

Lakoff, R. (1975) *Language and Women's Place*. New York: Harper.

Lerner, G. (1996) On the 'semi-permeable' character of grammatical units in conversation: conditional entry into the turn space of another speaker. In Ochs, Schegloff and Thompson (eds) (1996), 238–76.

Lesser, R. and Perkins, L. (1999) *Cognitive Neuropsychology and Conversation Analysis in Aphasia: An Introductory Casebook*. London: Whurr.

Levinson, S. (1983) *Pragmatics*. Cambridge: Cambridge University Press.

—— (1992) Activity types and language. In Drew and Heritage (eds) (1992a), 66–100.

Lindsay, J. and Wilkinson, R. (1999) Repair sequences in aphasic talk: a comparison of aphasic-speech therapy and aphasic-spouse conversations. *Aphasiology*, 13: 305–25.

Lindstrom, A. (1994) Identification and recognition in Swedish telephone conversation openings. *Language in Society*, 23: 231–52.

Local, J. (1996) Conversational phonetics: some aspects of news receipts in everyday talk. In Couper-Kuhlen and Selting (eds) (1996), 177–230.

Local, J. and Kelly, J. (1986) Projection and silences: notes on phonetic and conversational structure. *Human Studies*, 9: 185–204.

Luff, P., Gilbert, N. and Frohlich, D. (eds) (1990) *Computers and Conversation*. London: Academic Press.

Luff, P. and Heath, C. (2002) Broadcast talk: initiating calls through a computer-mediated technology. *Research on Language and Social Interaction*, 35: 337–66.

Lynch, M. and Bogen, D. (1994) Harvey Sacks' primitive science. *Theory, Culture and Society*, 11: 65–104.

McHoul, A. (1978) The organisation of turns at formal talk in the classroom. *Language in Society*, 19: 183–213.

Marlaire, C. L. and Maynard, D. W. (1990) Standardised testing as an interactional phenomenon. *Sociology of Education*, 63: 83–101.

Maynard, D. W. (1985). How children start arguments. *Language in Society*, 14: 1–30.

—— (1986) The development of argumentative skills among children. In A. Adler and P. Adler (eds), *Sociological Studies of Child Development, Volume 1*, Greenwich, CT: JAI Press.

—— (2005) Social actions, gestalt coherence and designations of disability: lessons from and about autism. *Social Problems*, 52: 499–524.

Maynard, D. W., Houtkoop-Steenstra, H., Schaeffer, N. C. and van der Zouwen, J. (eds) (2002) *Standardization and Tacit Knowledge: Interaction and Practice in the Survey Interview*. New York: Wiley.

Maynard. D. W. and Schaeffer, N. C. (1997) Keeping the gate: declinations of the request to participate in a telephone survey interview. *Sociological Methods and Research*, 26: 334–79.

—— (2002) Standardization and its discontents. In Maynard, Houtkoop-Steenstra, Schaeffer and van der Zouwen (eds) (2002), New York: Wiley, 3–46.

Mead, G. H. (1934) *Mind, Self and Society*. Chicago: University of Chicago Press.

Mishler, E. (1984) *The Discourse of Medicine: Dialectics of Medical Interviews*. Norwood, NJ: Ablex.

Moerman, M. (1972) Accomplishing ethnicity. In Turner (ed.) (1972), 54–68.

—— (1977) The preference for self-correction in a Thai conversational corpus. *Language*, 53: 207–29.

—— (1988) *Talking Culture: Ethnography and Conversation Analysis.* Philadelphia: University of Pennsylvania Press.

Montgomery, M. (1986) Language and power: a critical review of 'Studies in the Theory of Ideology' by John B. Thompson. *Media, Culture and Society*, 8: 41–64.

Moore, R. J. and Maynard, D. W (2002) Achieving understanding in the standardized survey interview: repair sequences. In Maynard, Houtkoop-Steenstra, Schaffer and van der Zouwen (eds) (2002), 281–312.

Myers, G. (1994) *Words in Ads*. London: Edward Arnold.

—— (1998) Displaying opinions: topics and disagreements in focus groups. *Language in Society*, 27: 85–111.

Norman, M. and Thomas, P. (1990) The very idea: informing HCI design from conversation analysis. In Luff, Gilbert and Frohlich (eds) (1990), 51–66.

Ochs, E., (1979) Transcription as theory. In Ochs and Schieffelin (eds) (1979), 43–72.

—— (1988) *Culture and Language Development.* Cambridge: Cambridge University Press.

Ochs, E. Gonzales, P. and Jacoby, S. (1996) 'When I come down, I'm in the domain state': grammar and graphic representation in the interpretive activity of physicists. In Ochs, Schegloff and Thompson (eds) (1996), 328–69.

Ochs, E. and Schieffelin, B. (eds) (1979) *Developmental Pragmatics.* New York: Academic Press.

—— (1983) *Acquiring Conversational Competence*. London: Routledge.

Ochs, E., Schegloff, E. A. and Thompson, S. (eds) (1996) *Interaction and Grammar*. Cambridge: Cambridge University Press.

Orne, M. T. (1962) On the social psychology of the psychological experiment: with particular reference to demand characteristics and their implications. *American Psychologist*, 17: 776–83.

Orne, M. T. and Whitehouse, W. G. (2000) Demand characteristics. In A. E. Kazdin (ed.), *Encyclopedia of Psychology*, Washington, DC: American Psychological Association and Oxford University Press, 469–70.

Park, R. (1952) *Human Communities: The City and Human Ecology.* New York: Free Press.

Parret, H. and Verschueren, J. (eds) (1992) *(On) Searle on Conversation.* Amsterdam: John Benjamins.

Parsons, T. (1937) *The Structure of Social Action*. New York: McGraw-Hill.

Peräkylä, A. (1995) *AIDS Counselling: Institutional Interaction and Clinical Practice*. Cambridge: Cambridge University Press.

Perkins, M. and Howard, S. (eds) (1995) *Case Studies in Clinical Linguistics.* London: Whurr.

Pinch, T. J. and Clark, C. (1986) The hard sell: 'patter merchanting' and the strategic (re)production and local management of economic reasoning in the sales routines of market pitchers. *Sociology*, 20: 169–91.

Pomerantz, A. (1978) Compliment responses: notes on the cooperation of multiple constraints. In Schenkein (ed.) (1978), 79–112.

—— (1980) Telling my side: 'limited access' as a 'fishing' device. *Sociological Inquiry*, 50: 186–98.

—— (1984a) Agreeing and disagreeing with assessments: some features of preferred/dispreferred turn-shapes. In Atkinson and Heritage (eds) (1984), 79–112.

—— (1984b) Giving a source or basis: the practice in conversation of telling 'how I know'. *Journal of Pragmatics*, 8: 607–25.

—— (1986) Extreme case formulations. *Human Studies*, 9: 219–30.

—— (1988/9) Constructing skepticism: four devices for engendering the audience's skepticism. *Research on Language and Social Interaction*, 22: 293–313.

—— (2005) Using participants' video-stimulated comments to complement analyses of interactional practices. In H. te Molder and J. Potter (eds), *Discourse and Cognition: Perspectives and Arguments*, Cambridge: Cambridge University Press, 93–113.

Potter, J. (1996) *Representing Reality: Discourse, Rhetoric and Social Construction.* London: Sage.

—— (1997) Discourse analysis as a way of analysing naturally occurring talk. In D. Silverman (ed.), *Qualitative Analysis: Issues of Theory and Method*, London: Sage, 144–60.

—— (1998) Cognition as context (whose cognition?). *Research on Language and Social Interaction*, 31: 29–44.

—— (2000) Post-cognitive psychology. *Theory and Psychology*, 10: 31–7.

—— (2006) Cognition and conversation. *Discourse Studies*, 8: 131–40.

Potter, J. and Wetherell, M. (1987) *Discourse and Social Psychology.* London: Sage.

Psathas, G. (ed.) (1979) *Everyday Language: Studies in Ethnomethodology.* Hillsdale, NJ: Lawrence Erlbaum Associates.

—— (ed.) (1990) *Interaction Competence.* Washington, DC: University Press of America.

Psathas, G. and Anderson, T. (1990) The 'practices' of transcription in conversation analysis. *Semiotica*, 78: 75–99.

Puchta, C. and Potter, J. (2004) *Focus Group Practice.* London: Sage.

Roger, D., Bull, P. and Smith, S. (1988) The development of a comprehensive system for classifying interruptions. *Journal of Language
and Social Psychology*, 7: 27–34.

Sacks, H. (1963) Sociological description. *Berkeley Journal of
Sociology*, 8: 1–16.

—— (1972a) An initial investigation of the usability of conversational
data for doing sociology. In Sudnow (ed.) (1972), 31–74.

—— (1972b) Notes on police assessment of moral character. In
Sudnow (ed.) (1972), 280–93.

—— (1972c) On the analysability of stories by children. In J. Gumperz
and D. Hymes (eds) (1972), 325–45.

—— (1975) Everyone has to lie. In Blount and Sanchez (eds) (1975),
57–80.

—— (1979) Hotrodder: a revolutionary category. In Psathas (ed.)
(1979), 7–14.

—— (1984a) Notes on methodology. In Atkinson and Heritage (eds)
(1984), 21–7.

—— (1984b) On doing 'being ordinary'. In Atkinson and Heritage
(eds) (1984), 413–29.

—— (1987) On the preferences for agreement and contiguity in
sequences in conversation. In Button and Lee (eds) (1987), 54–69.

—— (1992) *Lectures on Conversation, Volume 1 and Volume 2*. Oxford:
Blackwell.

Sacks, H. and Schegloff, E. A. (1979) Two preferences in the organisation of reference to persons in conversation and their interaction. In
Psathas (ed.) (1979), 15–21.

Sacks, H., Schegloff, E. A. and Jefferson, G. (1974) A simplest systematics for the organisation of turn-taking for conversation.
*Language*, 50: 696–735.

Sapir, E. (1921) *Language: An Introduction to the Study of Speech*. New
York: Harcourt Brace and World.

Schaeffer, N. C. and Maynard, D. W. (2005) From paradigm to proto-
type and back again: interactive aspects of 'cognitive processing' in
standardized survey interviews. In H. te Molder and J. Potter (eds)
*Discourse and Cognition: Perspectives and Arguments*, Cambridge:
Cambridge University Press, 114–33.

Schegloff, E. A. (1968) Sequencing in conversational openings.
*American Anthropologist*, 70: 1075–95.

—— (1972) Notes on a conversational practice: formulating place. In
Sudnow (ed.) (1972), 75–119.

—— (1979a) The relevance of repair to syntax-for-conversation. In
Givon (ed.) (1979), 261–88.

—— (1979b) Identification and recognition in telephone conversation openings. In Psathas (ed.) (1979), 23–78.

—— (1980) Preliminaries to preliminaries: 'can I ask you a question?'. *Sociological Inquiry*, 50: 104–52.

—— (1982) Discourse as an interactional achievement: some uses of 'uh huh' and other things that come between sentences. In Tannen (ed.) (1982), 71–93.

—— (1984) On some gestures' relation to talk. In Atkinson and Heritage (eds) (1984), 266–96.

—— (1986) The routine as achievement. *Human Studies*, 9: 111–52.

—— (1987a) Recycled turn-beginnings. In Button and Lee (eds) (1987), 70–85.

—— (1987b) Analysing single episodes of interaction: an exercise in conversation analysis. *Social Psychology Quarterly*, 50: 101–14.

—— (1988a) Presequences and indirection: applying speech act theory to ordinary conversation. *Journal of Pragmatics*, 12: 55–62.

—— (1988b) Goffman and the analysis of conversation. In Drew and Wootton (eds) (1988), 89–135.

—— (1988c) On an actual virtual servo-mechanism for guessing bad news: a single case conjecture. *Social Problems*, 32: 442–57.

—— (1991). Reflections on talk and social structure. In Boden and Zimmerman (eds) (1991), 44–70.

—— (1992a) Introduction. In Sacks (1992), ix–lxii.

—— (1992b) To Searle on conversation. In Parret and Verschueren (eds) (1992), 113–28.

—— (1992c) Repair after next turn: the last structurally provided defense of intersubjectivity in conversation. *American Journal of Sociology*, 97: 1295–345.

—— (1997) Whose text? Whose context?. *Discourse and Society*, 8: 165–87.

—— (1998) Reply to Wetherell. *Discourse & Society*, 9: 413–16.

—— (1999a) 'Schegloff's texts' as 'Billig's data': a critical reply. *Discourse and Society*, 10: 558–72.

—— (1999b) Discourse, pragmatics, conversation, analysis. *Discourse Studies*, 1: 405–35.

—— (2000) Overlapping talk and the organisation of turn-taking for conversation. *Language in Society*, 29: 1–63.

—— (2002) Survey interviews as talk-in-interaction. In Maynard, Houtkoop-Steenstra, Schaffer and van der Zouwen (eds) (2002), 151–7.

—— (2007) *Sequence Organisation in Interaction*. Cambridge: Cambridge University Press.

Schegloff, E. A., Koshik, I., Jacoby, S. and Olsher, D. (2002) Conversation analysis and applied linguistics. *Annual Review of Applied Linguistics*, 22: 3–31.

Schegloff, E. A. and Sacks, H. (1973) Opening up closings. *Semiotica*, 7: 289–327.

Schegloff, E. A., Jefferson, G. and Sacks, H. (1977) The preference for self-correction in the organisation of repair in conversation. *Language*, 53: 361–82.

Schenkein, J. (1978) Sketch of the analytic mentality for the study of conversational interaction. In J. Shenkein (ed.) *Studies in the Organisation of Conversational Interaction*. New York: Academic Press (1982), 57–78

Scherer, K. R. and Ekman, P. (eds) (1982) *Handbook of Methods in Nonverbal Behaviour Research*. Cambridge: Cambridge University Press.

Schieffelin, B. (1990) *The Give and Take of Everyday Life*. Cambridge: Cambridge University Press.

Searle, J. (1965) What is a speech act? In Black (ed.) (1965), 221–39.

—— (1969) *Speech Acts*. Cambridge: Cambridge University Press.

Selting, M. (1996) Prosody as an activity-type distinctive cue in conversation: the case of so-called 'astonished' questions in repair initiation. In Couper-Kuhlen and Selting (eds) (1996), 231–70.

Sheldon, A. (1992a) Conflict talk: sociolinguistic challenges to self-assertion and how young girls meet them. *Merrill-Palmer Quarterly*, 38: 95–117.

—— (1992b) Preschool girls' discourse competence: managing conflict. In K. Hall, M. Bucholtz and B. Moonwomon (eds), *Locating Power*. Berkeley CA: University of California, Berkeley Linguistic Society.

—— (1996) You can be the baby brother but you aren't born yet: preschool girls' negotiation for power and access in pretend play. *Research on Language and Social Interaction*, 29: 57–80.

Silverman, D. (1987) *Communication and Medical Practice*. London: Sage.

—— (1996) *Discourses of Counselling*. London: Sage.

—— (1998) *Harvey Sacks: Social Science and Conversation Analysis*. London: Sage.

Silverman, D., Baker, C. and Keogh, J. (1998) The case of the silent child: advice-giving and advice-reception in the parent–teacher interview. In Hutchby and Moran-Ellis (eds) (1998), 220–40.

Sinclair, J. and Coulthard, M. (1975) *Towards an Analysis of Discourse*. Oxford: Oxford University Press.

Suchman, L. (1987) *Plans and Situated Actions*. Cambridge: Cambridge University Press.

—— (1996) Constituting shared workspaces. In Y. Engeström and D. Middleton (eds), *Cognition and Communication at Work*, Cambridge: Cambridge University Press, 35–60.

Suchman, L. and Jordan, B. (1990) Interactional troubles in face-to-face survey interviews. *Journal of the American Statistical Association*, 85: 232–41.

Sudnow, D. (ed.) (1972) *Studies in Social Interaction*. New York: Free Press.

Tannen, D. (ed.) (1982) *Analysing Discourse: Text and Talk*. Washington, DC: Georgetown University Press.

ten Have, P. and Psathas, G. (eds) (1995) *Situated Order: Studies in the Social Organisation of Talk and Embodied Activities*. Washington, DC: University Press of America.

Terasaki, A. (2005) Pre-announcement sequences in conversation. In G. Lerner (ed.), *Conversation Analysis: Studies from the First Generation*, Amsterdam: John Benjamins, 171–224.

Thomas, P. (ed.) (1995) *The Social and Interactional Dimensions of Human–Computer Interfaces*. Cambridge: Cambridge University Press.

Thompson, J. B. (1984) *Studies in the Theory of Ideology*. Cambridge: Polity Press.

Thornborrow, J. (1998) Children's participation in the discourse of children's television. In Hutchby and Moran-Ellis (eds) (1998), 134–53.

Turner, R. (ed.) (1972) *Ethnomethodology*. Harmondsworth: Penguin.

Watson, R. and Weinberg, T. (1982) Interviews and the interactional construction of accounts of homosexual identity. *Sociological Analysis*, 11: 56–78.

Weinreich, U. (1963) On the semantic structure of language. In Greenberg (ed.) (1963), 142–216.

Wells, B. and Peppe, S. (1996) Ending up in Ulster: prosody and turn-taking in English dialects. In Couper-Kuhlen and Selting (eds) (1996), 101–30.

Wetherell, M. (1998) Positioning and interpretative repertoires: conversation analysis and post-structuralism in dialogue. *Discourse and Society*, 9: 387–412.

Wetherell, M. and Potter, J. (1992) *Mapping the Language of Racism*. Hemel Hempstead: Harvester Wheatsheaf.

Whalen, M. and Zimmerman, D. (1990) Describing trouble: practical epistemology in citizen calls to the police. *Language in Society*, 19: 465–92.

Whyte, W. F. (1943) *Street Corner Society*. Chicago: University of Chicago Press.

Widdicombe, S. and Wooffitt, R. (1995) *The Language of Youth Subcultures: Social Identity in Action*. Hemel Hempstead: Harvester.

Wieder, D. L. (1974) *Language and Social Reality*. The Hague: Mouton.

Wilkinson, R. (1995) Aphasia: conversation analysis of a non-fluent aphasic person. In Perkins and Howard (eds) (1995), 271–92.

Wilkinson, R. (1999a) Introduction. *Aphasiology*, 13: 251–58.

—— (1999b) Sequentiality as a problem and resource for intersubjectivity in aphasic conversation: analysis and implications for therapy. *Aphasiology*, 13: 327–43.

Wilkinson, R., Bryan, K., Lock, S., Bayley, K., Maxim, J., Bruce, C., Edmundson, A. and Moir, D. (1998) Therapy using conversation analysis: helping couples adapt to aphasia in conversation. *International Journal of Language and Communication Disorders*, 33: 144–8.

Wilkinson, S. (2006) Analysing interaction in focus groups. In P. Drew, G. Raymond and D. Weinberg (eds), *Talk and Interaction in Social Research Methods*, London: Sage, 50–62.

Wooffitt, R. (1992) *Telling Tales of the Unexpected: Accounts of Paranormal Experiences*. Hemel Hempstead: Harvester.

—— (2003) Conversation analysis and parapsychology: experimenter–subject interaction in ganzfeld experiments. *Journal of Parapsychology*, 67: 299–324.

—— (2005) *Conversation Analysis and Discourse Analysis: A Comparative and Critical Introduction*. London: Sage.

—— (2007) Interaction and laboratory experience: observations from parapsychological data. *British Journal of Social Psychology*, 46(3): 477–501

Wooffitt, R., and Allistone, S. (2005) Towards a discursive parapsychology: language and the laboratory study of anomalous communication. *Theory and Psychology*, 15: 325–55.

Wooffitt R., Fraser, N., Gilbert, G. N. and McGlashan, S. (1997) *Humans, Computers and Wizards: Analysing Human-(Simulated)-Computer Interaction*. London: Routledge.

Wooffitt, R. and Widdicombe, S. (2006) Interaction in interviews. In P. Drew, G. Raymond and D. Weinberg (eds), *Talk and Interaction in Social Research Methods*, London: Sage, 28–49.

Wootton, A. J. (1997) *Interaction and the Development of Mind*. Cambridge: Cambridge University Press.

# Index

A conversation analytic examination of the 'raw data', however, indicated that these issues were not of interest simply to academic researchers, but were real concerns for the respondents themselves in the course of the interviews. Furthermore, these issues were not relevant in some absent or second-hand sense, in that they had to be recovered from the interview data via a complex series of methodological transformations: they had a very live and immediate relevance to the respondents in the unfolding exchanges with the interviewer. Analysis revealed that the interviewees' tacit reasoning about their self-categorization and group membership was embodied in the design of their contributions to the interview.

The application of a conversation analytic approach, then, not only illuminated features of the social organization of the interview as a form of talk-in-interaction, but also revealed some aspects of the interactional management of category ascription, resistance and affiliation. On the basis of this, Widdicombe and Wooffitt were able to make some critical points regarding the assumptions underlying Social Identity Theory and the purchase it affords in understanding processes of group affiliation and self-categorization. This is evidence that, at least in some cases, it is possible that a CA approach can make a contribution to the substantive concerns of a study for which a set of semi-structured interviews had originally been collected.

## The focused, open ended or unstructured interview

We turn now to the third kind of interview commonly used in gathering social science data. Due to the informal, open-ended character of the interview, it is common to find that interviewees here engage in long, uninterrupted stretches of talk. During these accounts, stories, anecdotes, explanations and so on the interviewer may be entirely silent, or may contribute no more than an occasional 'mm hm' or 'yeah'. Given the emphasis in CA on turn-taking and sequence organization, such data may therefore seem to be problematic. Indeed it is sometimes claimed that monologue in general constitutes a methodological problem for the conversation analytic approach (Montgomery, 1986). However, we have already seen, in Chapter 5, that CA is able to contribute distinctively to the analysis of narrative and storytelling, activities that are frequently characterized as monologic. In this section we show how a CA approach can equally reveal distinctively interesting features of the monologic descriptions produced by respondents in unstructured interviews.